GRAPHIC ENGINEERING GEOMETRY

John R. Bedford M. Coll. H.

Formerly Head of Technical Subjects, Steyning Grammar School, Sussex
Author of *A Basic Course of Practical Metalwork* and *Metalcraft Theory and Practice*

JOHN MURRAY   FIFTY ALBEMARLE STREET   LONDON

PREFACE

This book is intended for students of engineering drawing, not only those who are preparing for examinations, but also for the practising draughtsman who wishes to expand his facility in handling the many geometrical problems inherent in design work.

Considerable effort has been given to simplifying the material by presenting it as a series of worked examples, each set in its logical sequence of development, from the first examination level to more advanced work. Text has been kept to the minimum and pictorial illustrations have been used where it was felt that they would aid understanding. Given points and lines are labelled with block capitals to differentiate them from points and lines derived through the constructions, these latter being labelled with lower case versions of their originals. Important intersections and terminal points in constructions are marked with a dot. Although this is not good drawing practice, it is done in this case to assist in following the logical sequence of construction.

It is necessary in many constructions to evenly divide circles as in conics and loci and the development of cylinders. The choice of twelve sectors is purely arbitrary. Fewer than twelve will produce a less accurate curve. A larger number of divisions will produce a more accurate curve but will take correspondingly more time to draw.

Increasing use is being made of third angle projection in engineering drawings and many students find that this system aids both making and interpreting drawings. Third angle projection can also be applied to descriptive geometry. Nevertheless, where it is found helpful to prepare a pictorial sketch as a preliminary aid to the understanding of a problem and its constructions, then first angle projection will follow more naturally than third angle. Hence both first and third angle working are included in the chapter on lines and planes.

All drawings are dimensioned in millimetres and are drawn in third angle projection unless otherwise stated.

CONTENTS

PROJECTION OF LINES AND PLANES

Most solid objects are made up of surfaces bounded by lines which terminate in corners. These corners can be considered as points in space. To gain a thorough understanding of the principles of projection it is necessary to be able to determine the true positions of these points and lines in space relative to the various projection planes. This is achieved by means of properly projected views.

The commonest method of drawing solid objects is termed **orthographic projection.** This involves drawing on flat planes various projections or views of the object taken from different viewpoints. Objects are usually represented by elevation views drawn on the **vertical plane** (*VP*) and, at right angles to this, by plan views drawn on the **horizontal plane** (*HP*). The intersection of these two planes is termed the ground line, or the *xy* line as in fig. 1.

Point *P* in fig. 2 is set at given distances from the *VP* and the *HP*. The projections of this point p_1 and p_2 are given by the projection lines Pp_1 and Pp_2 which are drawn from *P* parallel to *HP* and *VP* respectively. Fig. 3 shows the *HP* turned through 90° about *xy* to form a continuous plane with the *VP*, thus giving an orthographic drawing of *P*. This turning of a plane about the *xy* line is called **rabatting**.

Space may be divided into four quadrants or dihedral angles by extending the *VP* and *HP* as shown in fig. 4. (A dihedral angle is the angle at the intersection of two plane surfaces.) It is conventional to number these: first, second, third and fourth angles in the order shown. A point *P* is shown at a given distance from both the *VP* and the *HP* in each of the four angles or quadrants. It is possible to produce orthographic drawings detailing the position of this point in all four quadrants, but in practice only the first and third quadrants are used, the derived drawings being called **first** and **third angle projections** respectively.

By convention the whole extent of the *HP* is turned through 90° as in fig. 3 and objects in the third quadrant are depicted as if seen *through transparent planes* from the first angle viewpoint.

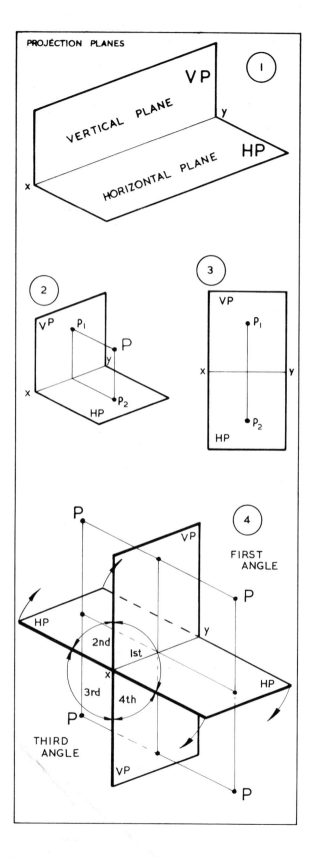

TRUE LENGTHS OF LINES

Fig. 5 shows a pictorial sketch of an oblique line AB set in the first quadrant. The projection of points A and B into the VP and HP respectively gives points a, b, a_1, b_1. Joining ab produces the elevation in the VP and joining a_1b_1 produces the plan in the HP as shown.

Fig. 6. If the HP is rabatted through 90° it will give orthographic projections of AB. It should be noted that neither of these views gives the true length of AB. This is obtained by rabatting the line about either its elevation or its plan. The pictorial sketch shows the line rabatted about its elevation to give the true length.

Fig. 7 shows the rabatted orthographic projections necessary to find the true length using the method illustrated pictorially in fig. 6.
Method. Draw a line from a in the elevation perpendicular to the elevation, and of a length equal to the perpendicular from the xy line to a_1 in the plan. Similarly, draw a perpendicular from b the same length as xy to b_1. Join the outer ends of these two lines to obtain the true length. Alternatively, the same method may be used in the plan, with line 3 in the elevation transferred to a perpendicular from b_1 and line 4 perpendicular to a_1. Joining the outer ends of these two lines will similarly give the true length of AB.

An alternative method for finding the true length of oblique lines is given on pages 79 and 80 in the section dealing with developments and interpenetrations.

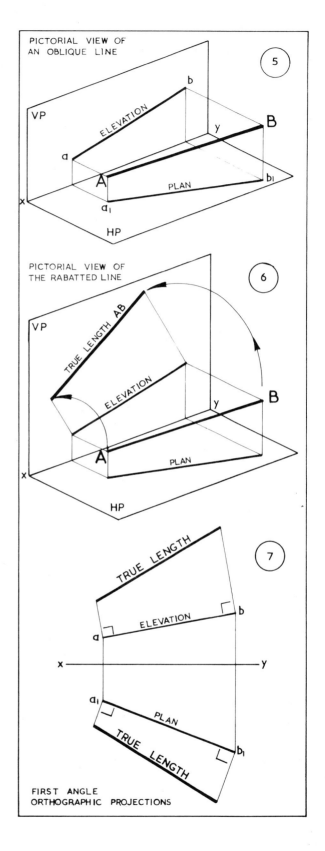

PICTORIAL VIEW OF AN OBLIQUE LINE (5)

PICTORIAL VIEW OF THE RABATTED LINE (6)

(7)

FIRST ANGLE ORTHOGRAPHIC PROJECTIONS

INCLINATION ᴀɴᴅ TRACES ᴏғ ᴀ LINE

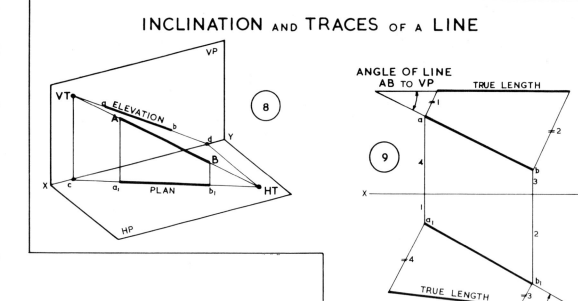

8

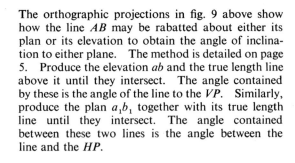

9

ANGLE OF LINE AB TO VP — TRUE LENGTH

TRUE LENGTH — ANGLE OF LINE AB TO HP

Fig. 8 above is a pictorial sketch of an oblique line *AB* set in space. The elevation, plan and the line itself have all been produced to converge at points *HT* and *VT*, and also to cut the *xy* line in *c* and *d*. It will readily be seen that angle *A VT a* is the angle or inclination of *AB* to the *VP*. Similarly, angle *B HT b₁* is the inclination of *AB* to the *HP*.

The traces of a line are the points in which the line, or the line produced, penetrates the *VP* or the *HP*. The point of intersection on the *VP* is called the **vertical trace** (*VT*) and that on the *HP* the **horizontal trace** (*HT*). Fig. 8 clearly illustrates this. It should be noted that the orthographic elevation and plan produced intersects the given line *AB* produced in its traces.

The orthographic projections in fig. 9 above show how the line *AB* may be rabatted about either its plan or its elevation to obtain the angle of inclination to either plane. The method is detailed on page 5. Produce the elevation *ab* and the true length line above it until they intersect. The angle contained by these is the angle of the line to the *VP*. Similarly, produce the plan *a₁b₁* together with its true length line until they intersect. The angle contained between these two lines is the angle between the line and the *HP*.

To determine the traces of line *AB*

Method. Fig. 10 shows the orthographic projections necessary to establish the traces of the line. Produce the elevation and the plan to cut the *xy* line in *c* and *d* respectively. From *c* erect a perpendicular to cut the elevation *ab* produced in the *VT*. Similarly, from intersection *d* erect a perpendicular to cut the plan produced in the *HT*. The *HT* and *VT* are the traces of the line *AB*.

In orthographic projections the *VT* of a line is usually located in the *VP* above the *xy* line and the *HT* below it. In figs. 11 to 14 opposite the line is so positioned that both traces appear above or below the *xy* line.

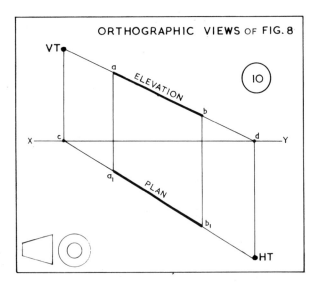

ORTHOGRAPHIC VIEWS ᴏғ FIG. 8

10

POINT TRACES OF LINES

SEE BOTTOM OF PAGE 6

FIRST ANGLE PROJECTION

PICTORIAL VIEW

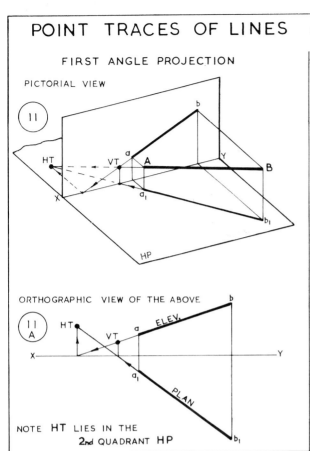

11

ORTHOGRAPHIC VIEW OF THE ABOVE

11
A

ELEV.

PLAN

NOTE HT LIES IN THE
2nd QUADRANT HP

THIRD ANGLE PROJECTION

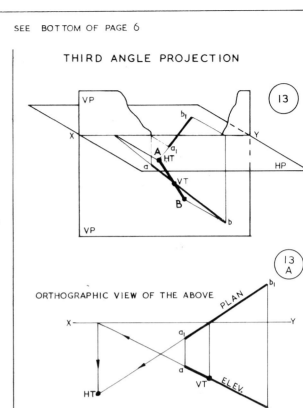

13

ORTHOGRAPHIC VIEW OF THE ABOVE

13
A

PLAN

ELEV.

NOTE HT LIES IN THE 1st QUADRANT HP
VT LIES IN THE 4th QUADRANT VP

PICTORIAL VIEW

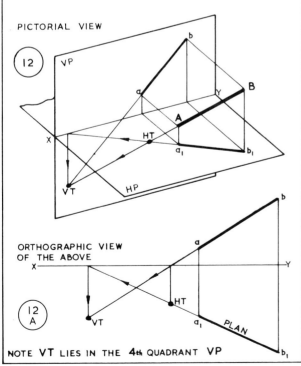

12

ORTHOGRAPHIC VIEW
OF THE ABOVE

PLAN

12
A

NOTE VT LIES IN THE 4th QUADRANT VP

PICTORIAL VIEW

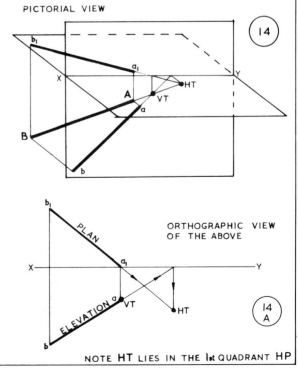

14

ORTHOGRAPHIC VIEW
OF THE ABOVE

PLAN

ELEVATION

14
A

NOTE HT LIES IN THE 1st QUADRANT HP

PROJECTION OF PLANES

In addition to the two main planes of projection already considered (*VP* and *HP*) other types of planes can be used in the manipulation of problems in descriptive geometry. These other planes are conveniently represented by the intersection lines where they meet the main projection planes. These intersection lines are called the **traces** of the planes. The intersection on the main vertical projection plane (*VP*) is called the **vertical trace** (*VT*). Similarly, the line of intersection in the main horizontal projection plane (*HP*) is called the **horizontal trace** (*HT*).

It is customary to classify planes in the following groups:

Vertical planes, as shown pictorially in fig. 15, and in the orthographic projections of their respective traces in fig. 15a.

The **auxiliary horizontal plane.** This is parallel to the main horizontal plane and has one trace only as shown in figs. 16 and 16a.

The **inclined plane** as shown in fig. 17. This plane is always perpendicular to the *VP*. Its orthographic traces are given in fig. 17a.

Oblique planes as shown in fig. 18. These are always inclined to both planes of projection and therefore neither trace is perpendicular to the *xy* line and neither trace gives the true inclination of the oblique plane to the planes of projection.

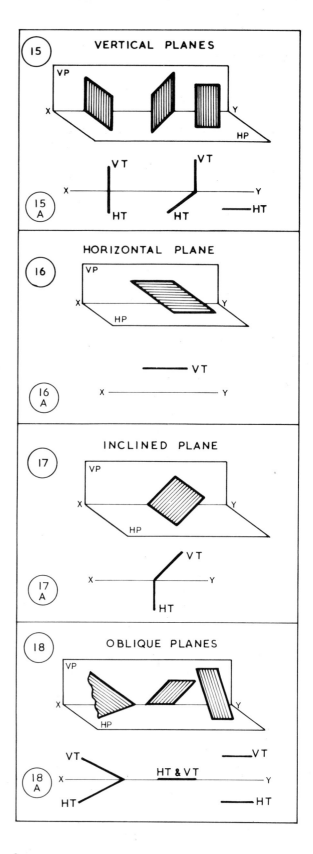

8

All the problems on lines in space considered in figs. 5 to 14 could also be treated as lines in auxiliary planes. Fig. 8, for instance, could be a line on a perpendicular plane as in fig. 19. The solution would be similar.

It is often easier to visualize a possible solution to a problem if preliminary sketches are made treating the line as being part of an auxiliary plane, as in fig. 19. Indeed, it cannot be too strongly stressed that pictorial sketches such as figs. 11, 12, 13, 14, 19 and 20 offer the quickest method of visualizing, and thus solving, this type of problem.

TRACES OF AN OBLIQUE LINE SET ON A VERTICAL PLANE

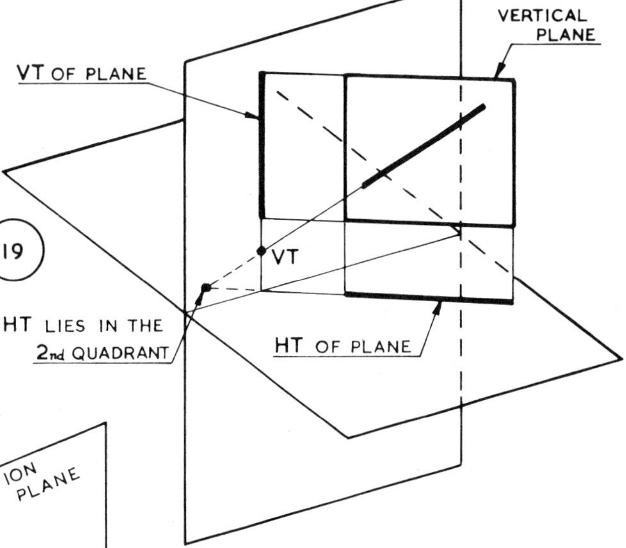

VERTICAL PLANE

VT OF PLANE

(19)

VT

HT LIES IN THE 2nd QUADRANT

HT OF PLANE

TRACES OF AN OBLIQUE LINE SET ON AN OBLIQUE PLANE

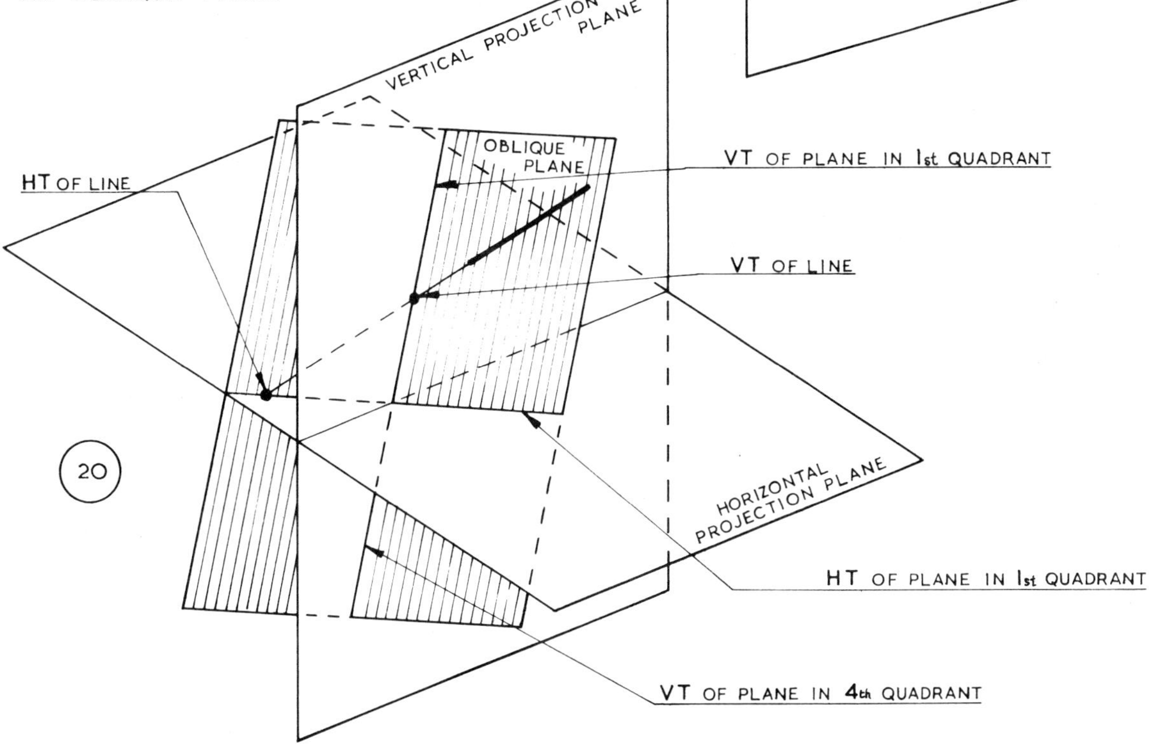

VERTICAL PROJECTION PLANE

OBLIQUE PLANE

HT OF LINE

VT OF PLANE IN 1st QUADRANT

VT OF LINE

(20)

HORIZONTAL PROJECTION PLANE

HT OF PLANE IN 1st QUADRANT

VT OF PLANE IN 4th QUADRANT

FIRST ANGLE
PROJECTION OF PLANE TRACES

VT
ELEVATION
X————————————Y
PLAN
HT

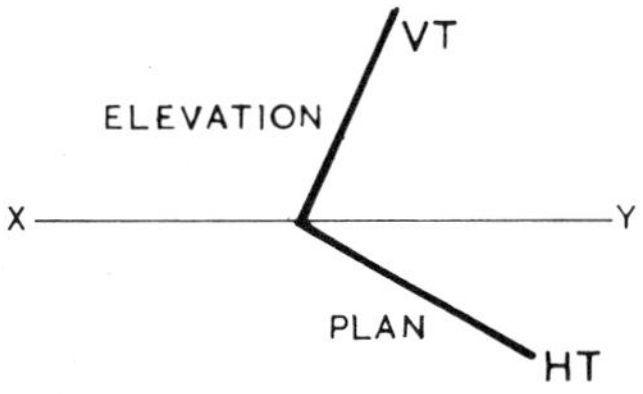

(21)

THIRD ANGLE PROJECTION OF PLANE TRACES

HT
PLAN
X————————————Y
ELEVATION
VT

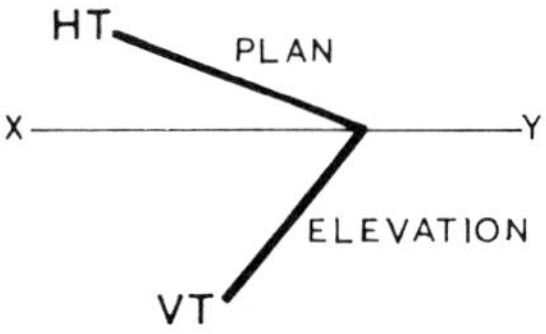

If a cone of equal inclination is placed against an oblique plane as in fig. 22, the inclination between the oblique and horizontal planes must equal the base angle of the cone. Therefore, a centreline section through the cone taken perpendicular to the oblique plane will produce a triangle of equal inclination. This triangle is shown inset in the cone.

To determine the inclination of a plane to the *HP* given its traces (first angle projection)

Method (fig. 23). Draw a perpendicular from any convenient point in *HT* at *ab*. With *ab* as radius and *b* as centre, draw an arc to cut *xy* in *d*. This is a sector of the base plan of the cone. Draw a perpendicular from *b* to cut the vertical trace in *c*. Join *cd* to give the true inclination of the oblique plane to the *HP*.

Fig. 24 shows an alternative method based on the projection of the triangle section to an auxiliary *xy* line (first angle projection).

Method. Draw a perpendicular from any convenient point in *HT* at *ab*, and from it erect the perpendicular *b* to *c*. Draw an auxiliary *xy* line parallel to *ab* giving x_1y_1. Project *HT* to x_1y_1 giving T_1. Project a line from *b* parallel to *HT* to cut x_1y_1 in b_1 and continue the line to form a perpendicular to x_1y_1. Cut this perpendicular at c_1 to a height equal to *bc* in the elevation.
(*Note*: Projections of a point are always perpendicular to the *xy* line and of equal heights above the *xy* line in all elevations.)
Draw the new VT_1 through T_1 and c_1. This is an edge-on view of the oblique plane, thus converting it to an inclined plane. θ is the true inclination between the *HP* and the oblique plane.

Fig. 25 shows the same method used to find the true inclination of the oblique plane to the *VP* (first angle projection).

To determine the *HT* of a plane when its *VT* is at 45° to *xy* and its inclination to *HP* is 60°

Method (fig. 26). Draw the *VT* at 45° to the *xy* line. From a convenient point on the *VT* drop a perpendicular *ab* (the centreline of the cone in fig. 22). From *a* draw a line at 60° to *c* in the *xy* line. Using *b* as centre and *bc* as radius, draw a base plan of the cone. Through the intersection of the *VT* and the *xy* line draw a line tangential to the cone to give the required *HT*.
(*Note*: This is the reverse procedure to fig. 23.)

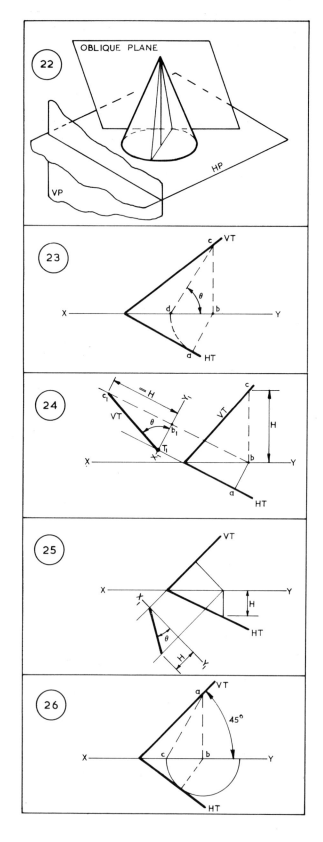

To determine the common line of intersection of two oblique planes

The pictorial sketch (fig. 27) clearly shows that the line of intersection AB runs from the intersection of the two vertical traces to the intersection of the horizontal traces.

Fig. 28 gives the completed first angle orthographic projection of the intersection line AB, the elevation being line ab and the plan a_1b_1.

To determine the dihedral angle of two oblique planes

(*Note:* The dihedral angle is measured in a plane perpendicular to the intersecting line.)

The pictorial sketch (fig. 29) shows a triangular plane cde which is perpendicular to the intersection line AB.

Method (fig. 30). In the first angle projections it will readily be seen from the first auxiliary elevation that triangle cde is in fact perpendicular to AB. Draw an auxiliary line parallel to a_1b_1 and on this project a new elevation a_2b_2 of the line a_1b_1. Dimension H is transferred from the elevation. (θ is the true inclination of the line AB to the HP.) Project ce from the direction of the arrow X to x_1y_1 and from this point erect a perpendicular to line a_2b_2. This auxiliary elevation gives a true length view of AB together with an edge-on view of the triangular plane cde, thus ensuring they are perpendicular to each other. Looking from the direction of arrow Y, project a second auxiliary view, this being an end-on view of a_2b_2. Rabat the plan dimensions as shown to give θ_2, the required dihedral angle.

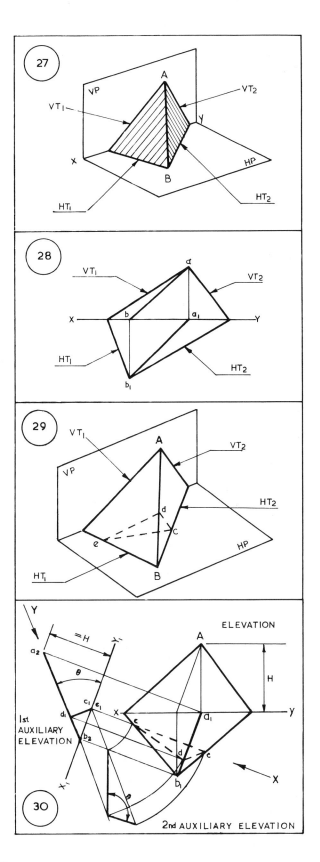

11

To determine the shortest distance between a point and an oblique plane

The shortest distance will of course be a perpendicular line from P to the plane. The pictorial sketch (fig. 31) shows point P and the plane.

Method (fig. 32). Draw the elevation and plan of the traces of both the plane and the point. Draw an edge-on auxiliary elevation T_1 of the plane looking in the direction of the arrow X (as detailed in fig. 24). Project p_1 from the plan to p_2 in the auxiliary elevation and transfer the height H from the elevation to the auxiliary elevation giving p_2. From p_2 draw a perpendicular to the auxiliary elevation. This line gives the shortest distance from the point to the plane. The intersection of this perpendicular line with T_1 may be projected back to cut the perpendicular from p_1 in the plan to give the plan of the point of intersection HT_2. This can then be projected into the elevation and the height transferred from the auxiliary elevation to give the trace of the intersection VT_2.

To determine the point of intersection between a line and an oblique plane

The perspective sketch (fig. 33) shows the line intersecting the plane.

Method (fig. 34). Draw an elevation and plan of the line and the traces of the plane. Project an auxiliary elevation, giving an edge-on view of the plane (as in figs. 24 and 32). Project the ends of the line from the plan to the new elevation, ab to a_1b_1. Height a_1 to x_1y_1 is similar to A to xy, and b_1 to x_1y_1 similar to B to xy. The two lines in the auxiliary elevation cross at the point of intersection in p_1. Project this point back to the plan, and from there to the elevation to give the points where the line intersects the elevation and plan of the plane VT_1 and HT_1 respectively.

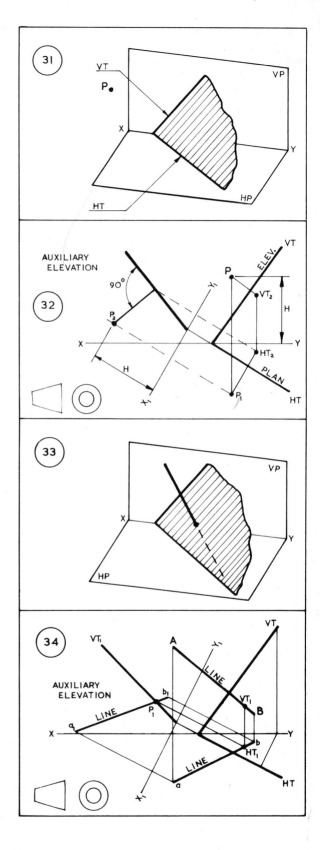

To determine the shortest line between two skew lines

Skew lines are lines which neither intersect nor are parallel. The shortest line that can be drawn between them is their common perpendicular.

The first step is to construct a view that shows the true length of one of the lines and then from this project a view showing this line as an end-on point. This is done by constructing a plane passing through one of the lines and parallel to the other.

Method (fig. 35). Draw the elevation of the lines ab and cd and the plan $a_1b_1c_1d_1$. Draw an auxiliary xy line x_1y_1 parallel to a_1b_1. Construct an auxiliary elevation of the two lines by projection from the plan. The heights of the new elevation lines a_2b_2 and c_2d_2 above x_1y_1 are similar to the heights of the lines ab and cd above xy as at *2,3,4,5*. The line a_2b_2 is now shown in its true length. Draw a second auxiliary xy line x_2y_2 perpendicular to the true length line and project a new elevation looking in the direction of the arrow *V*. This reduces the line a_2b_2 to an end-on dot. Project c_2d_2 to c_3d_3. The heights of this line and the dot above x_2y_2 are transferred from x_1y_1 to a_1b_1 and x_1y_1 to c_1d_1. A perpendicular from the dot to c_3d_3 gives the shortest line.

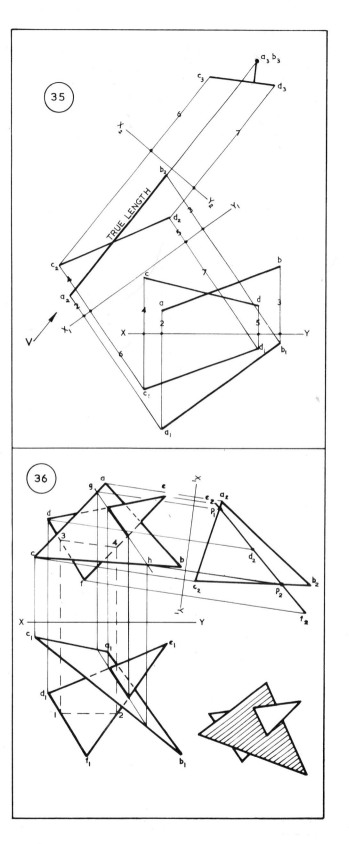

To determine the intersection line between two oblique planes

The solution which is easiest to visualize is to construct a new view showing one or other of the planes as an edge, i.e. a straight line as in figs. 32 and 34.

Method (fig. 36). Draw the given elevation and plan, and letter the corners of the planes. Draw a horizontal section *1,2*, (shown as broken line) across the plane $d_1e_1f_1$. Draw vertical projectors from this to *3* and *4* in the plan *def*. The inclination of this line *3* to *4* gives the direction of projection for the auxiliary elevation. Draw x_1y_1 at right angles to the line *3* to *4*. Project points d,e,f to d_2,e_2,f_2 respectively. Distances of points d_2,e_2,f_2 to x_1y_1 are identical to the distances of points d_1, e_1, f_1 below xy. This gives an edge-on view of plane *def*. Repeat the construction with plane *abc* to give $a_2b_2c_2$ in the auxiliary view. Mark in the intersecting points P_1 and P_2 on plane $a_2b_2c_2$. Project these back to the plane *abc*, P_1 cutting line *ac* at *g* and P_2 cutting line *cb* at *h*. The line joining *g* and *h* will give the intersection line where it crosses plane *def*. Project the intersection line from the plan to the elevation.

Given the traces of an oblique plane (fig. 37), to draw the projections on this plane of a square lamina having a diagonal perpendicular to the horizontal trace
VT to *xy* 40°; *HT* to *xy* 60°.

Method (fig. 38). Draw the given traces of the plane. Project an auxiliary elevation as detailed in figs. 24 and 32. Draw the true shape of the square on the plan (this is shown in broken outline and is drawn as if lying flat on the *HP*). Project its corners to x_1y_1. Rabat these three points to the auxiliary vertical trace VT_1 and from this line project the points directly back to give the oblique plane plan. Project the corners from the plan to the elevation making the heights a_2, b_2, c_2, from the *xy* line equal to a_1, b_1, c_1 from x_1y_1.

(*Note:* A similar construction may be used to draw a circle in the oblique plane, treating the circle as a series of points. After all the points have been projected to VT_1 and rabatted back they are joined by a fair curve to form an ellipse.)

To convert a square plan to a pyramid and a circular plan to a cone it is only necessary to draw the appropriate elevation on the auxiliary VT_1 and then project the apex back to the plan (see figs. 31 and 32) and from there to the elevation, finally joining the apex to the base in both views.

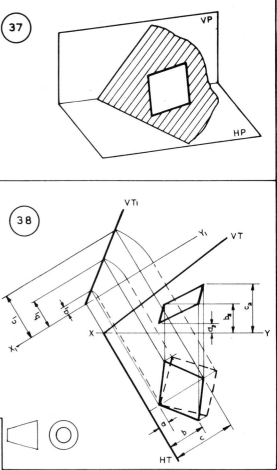

Given the traces of an oblique plane and the plan view of a triangular lamina, to determine the elevation and the true shape of the lamina

Method (fig. 39). Draw the plan and elevation of the traces and the plan of the triangular lamina. Draw an auxiliary *xy* line at x_1y_1 and on this erect an edge-on elevation of the plane (as detailed in fig. 24). Project the corners of the triangular plan to the elevation and also to cut the auxiliary trace VT_1. Transfer the perpendicular heights of these points *a,b,c* to the elevation projection lines. Join the three points to obtain the elevation of the triangle. The true shape is found by 'laying over' the auxiliary elevation in the reverse order to fig. 36. The true shape is shown in broken outline.

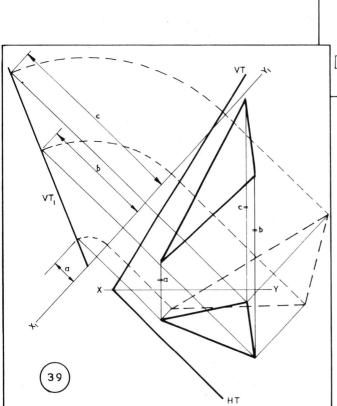

14

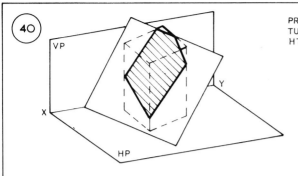

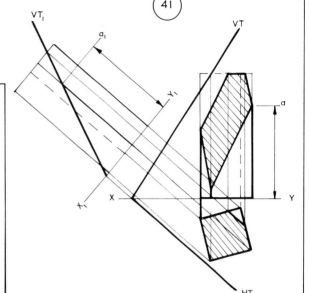

SECTIONS

To determine the sectional elevation and plan of a right square prism cut by an oblique plane

Fig. 40 gives a pictorial view of the plane intersecting the prism.

Method (fig. 41). Draw an edge-on view of the oblique plane as detailed in fig. 24. Draw an auxiliary elevation on x_1y_1 projected from the plan. Project back the VT_1 cutting points to give a sectional plan. Project the cutting points in the plan vertically to the elevation. Transfer the heights of the cutting points above the x_1y_1 line to the elevation as x_1y_1 to a_1 equals xy to a. Complete the sections as shown.

To determine the sectional elevation and plan of a hexagonal pyramid cut by an oblique plane

Method (fig. 42). Draw an edge-on view of the oblique plane as shown in figs. 24 and 32. Draw an auxiliary elevation of the pyramid set on x_1y_1 and projected from the plan. Take each point in turn where the VT_1 cuts the edges of the pyramid and project back these intersection points to the plan to cut the corresponding edge lines. Project these latter intersecting points to the elevation to cut the corresponding edge lines. (*Note:* The accuracy of the drawing may then be tested by comparing the perpendicular heights of the xy line to the corners of the cut face in the elevation with the corresponding height x_1y_1 to VT_1; xy to a_4 should equal x_1y_1 to a_2.)

HEXAGONAL PYRAMID,
90mm A/F IN THE BASE,
100mm HIGH

To determine the sectional elevation and plan of a right cone cut by an oblique plane

Method (fig. 43). Draw an edge-on view of the oblique plane on the auxiliary x_1y_1 line as detailed in fig. 24. Project an auxiliary elevation of the cone from the plan to the new x_1y_1 line. Divide that portion of the auxiliary elevation which is cut by the plane trace VT_1 into a convenient number of horizontal slices as at a, b, c, d. Divide the elevation similarly and show these slices as circles in the plan view. One slice only is shown in complete projection: c_1c_1 to c_2 cut by the line from c_3 on cc. All the other slices have been omitted to give a clear drawing. Project the other cutting points from VT_1 back to cut the plan circles as in c_3, thus giving the completed sectional plan. Project these plan cutting points to the elevation and complete as shown.

To determine the sectional elevation, plan and true shape of the cut face of a cylinder intersected by an oblique plane

Method (fig. 44). All three outlines are obviously ellipses and these can be obtained by cutting an auxiliary end elevation into a number of horizontal slices as at ab, projecting the points where these slices cut the circumference across to the VT and from there vertically to the xy line and from there parallel to the HT to give the plan as a_1b_1. Widths in the ellipse are transferred from the auxiliary end view, e.g. ab equals a_1b_1. The true shape of the cut face is obtained from an auxiliary elevation laid over from the VT as shown. Here again, widths of ordinates are transferred from the first auxiliary elevation as ab equals a_2b_2.
(*Note:* The cut face cross-hatching has been omitted for the sake of clarity.)

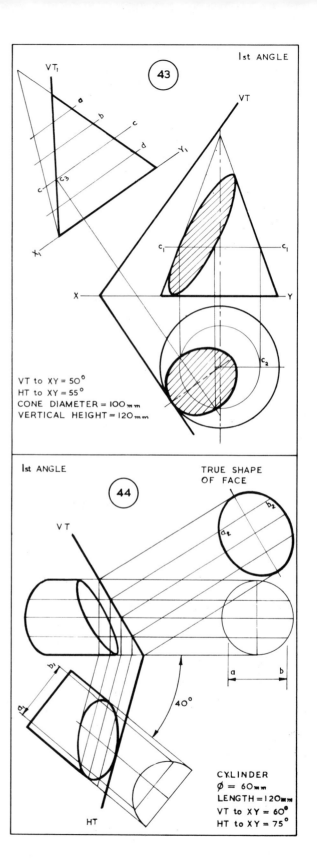

43

1st ANGLE

VT to XY = 50°
HT to XY = 55°
CONE DIAMETER = 100 mm
VERTICAL HEIGHT = 120 mm

44

1st ANGLE

TRUE SHAPE OF FACE

40°

CYLINDER
⌀ = 60 mm
LENGTH = 120 mm
VT to XY = 60°
HT to XY = 75°

Sections of an annular toroid

A toroid is a solid of revolution generated by moving a sphere round a circular path.

To draw a vertically sectioned toroid

Method (fig. 45). Because the given section plane is vertical the easiest solution is to use radial sections. Draw an elevation and plan of the ring and insert a centreline in the elevation. Draw a circle in the plan equal in diameter to the cross section. Draw a line from the centre of the toroid through the centre of the circle *Oa*. Draw a chord *cc* on this circle at the point *b* where line *Oa* intersects the section plane. This chord *cc* is the true width of the section at this particular point. Draw a projection line from this point to cut the elevation in b_1 and step off distances *bc* at b_1c_1. Repeat this construction at a number of convenient points to obtain other points on the curve of section. Join all these points in a fair curve as shown.

To draw a sectioned plan of a toroid cut by a section plane which is perpendicular to *VP* and set at 30° to *HP*

Method (fig. 46). Because the section plane is inclined it will be necessary to take horizontal slice sections. Divide the elevation into a convenient number of slices by means of horizontal ordinates, one of which is lettered *aa*. At the points where these cut the skin of the toroid draw projectors cutting the plan centreline as in *bb*. Draw in the plan circles of these cutting planes. Draw a projection line from the point where ordinate *aa* cuts the section plane in *c* to cut the plan circles in *dd*, two points in the sectioned face of the toroid. Repeat this construction to gain a suitable number of points along the curve of section. Join all these points in a free curve to complete the drawing.

To draw a sectioned plan of a semi-circular cable guide cut by a section plane angled similarly to that in fig. 46

Method (fig. 47). Follow the method detailed above starting with the section along the outer skin of the toroid. When this is complete take a series of section planes across the central hole and treat similarly.

(*Note*: The section planes in figs. 46 and 47 have been lettered identically to facilitate comparison.)

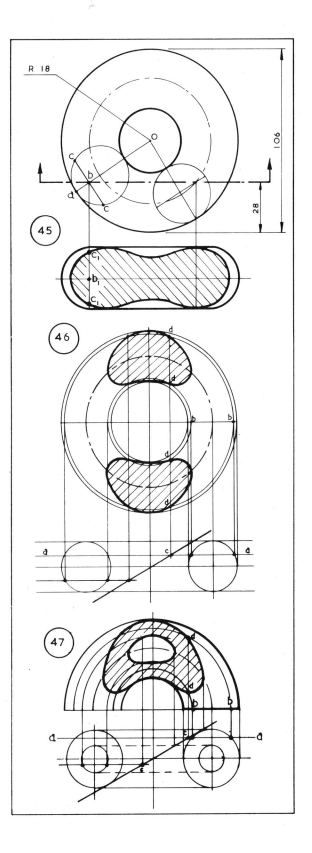

17

SOLIDS IN CONTACT

The surface of a curved solid in contact with a plane has a normal at the point of contact. Similarly, two curved surfaces in contact have each a common normal passing through the point of contact. If a sphere is in contact with a plane or a solid, the centre of the sphere will be of radius distance from the point of contact, and the line from the contact point to the sphere centre will be normal to the plane or the surface of the solid. Similarly if two spheres touch one another, the centres of the spheres and the point of contact all lie on a straight line.

To determine the traces of a plane, given the plan of a sphere and the point P at which it touches the tangent plane

Method (fig. 48). Draw the plan and elevation of the sphere. Determine P_1 by taking a vertical section in the plan at AA. Join O_1P_1 and draw an auxiliary plan on x_1y_1 parallel to O_1P_1. Project P_1 to the circumference of the circle at P_2. Draw the tangent plane through P_2. Draw a projector from P_2 through P_1 to xy. Parallel to this and from the intersection of the auxiliary tangent plane in x_1y_1 draw VT, the vertical trace of the required tangent plane. Draw a horizontal line from P_1 to cut VT in P_3. From this point drop a perpendicular to the xy line and from there to cut P in the plan. Draw HT parallel to this latter line.

To draw projections of two spheres, given the plan of one sphere and the point P at which it touches the second sphere

Method (fig. 49). Draw the elevation and plan of the given sphere. Mark in P and transfer it to P_1 in the elevation by taking a vertical section through the plan. Project P_1 to the circumference and draw the second sphere at O_2. Project the second sphere to the plan and swing its centre round until it cuts the normal through P thus establishing the position of the second sphere. Draw this in plan and project to the elevation.

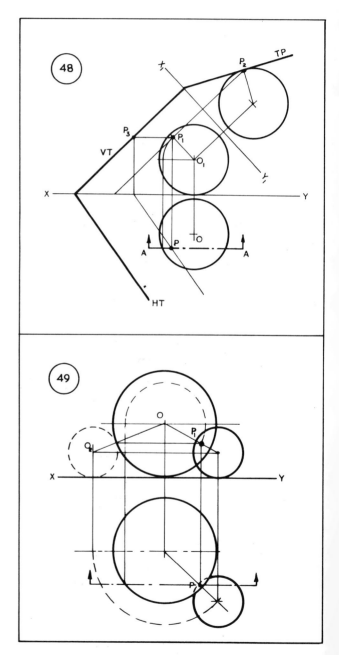

SPHERES IN CONTACT

To draw the plan and elevation of four touching spheres of equal diameter supporting a fifth sphere of smaller diameter

Method (fig. 50). The only problem here is to establish the height of the centre of the fifth sphere above the *xy* line. Draw the plan of the four spheres. Superimpose the fifth sphere centrally above the other four. Draw a centre-line *AB* through two large and the one smaller sphere at the angle shown. Draw an auxiliary elevation on x_1y_1 parallel to the *AB* centreline. This gives the height of the fifth sphere above *xy*. Project the elevation of two spheres and add the fifth by transferring the centre height from the auxiliary elevation (first angle projection).

To draw the plan and elevation of three spheres of differing diameters in mutual contact on *HP* and to indicate the points of contact

Method (fig. 51). Draw an elevation of the spheres with their centres parallel to *VP* as shown. This establishes the horizontal distances between their centrelines. Project the plan of two of the spheres and rabat the centre of the third from both sides of the plan. The third sphere lies at the intersecting point of these rabatted centres. Points of contact lie along the common normals of each pair of spheres as shown at H_1 and H_2 above the *xy* line (first angle projection).

To draw the plan and elevation of a sphere touching a cone at a given point

Method (fig. 52). Draw the plan view and mark in *P* at the specified point of contact. Draw the cone generator and normal to the sphere at *P* to *ON*. Draw an auxiliary elevation of the cone on x_1y_1 parallel to *ON*. Project *P* to P_1 on the cone and draw the sphere normal to this point. Project P_1C_1 to the normal *ON* and return vertical projectors on which P_2 and C_2 can be stepped off at the same height above *xy* as P_1C_1 above x_1y_1. Draw the sphere in elevation and project *P* to give P_2 (first angle projection).

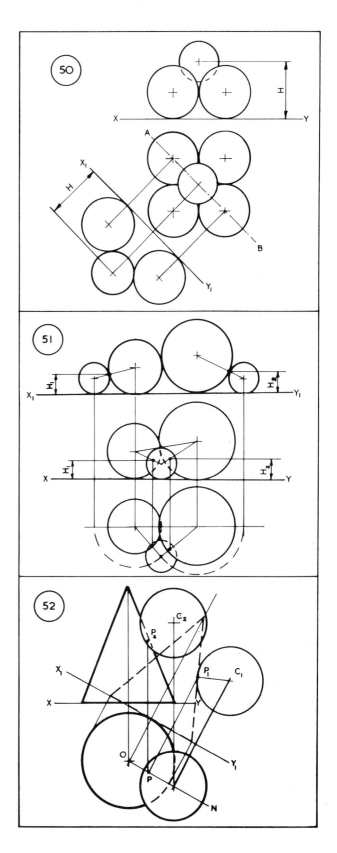

EXERCISES
DETERMINE THE TRUE LENGTH, THE INCLINATION TO HP AND VP, AND MARK IN THE TRACES OF THE LINES. SHOW ALL CONSTRUCTION LINES.

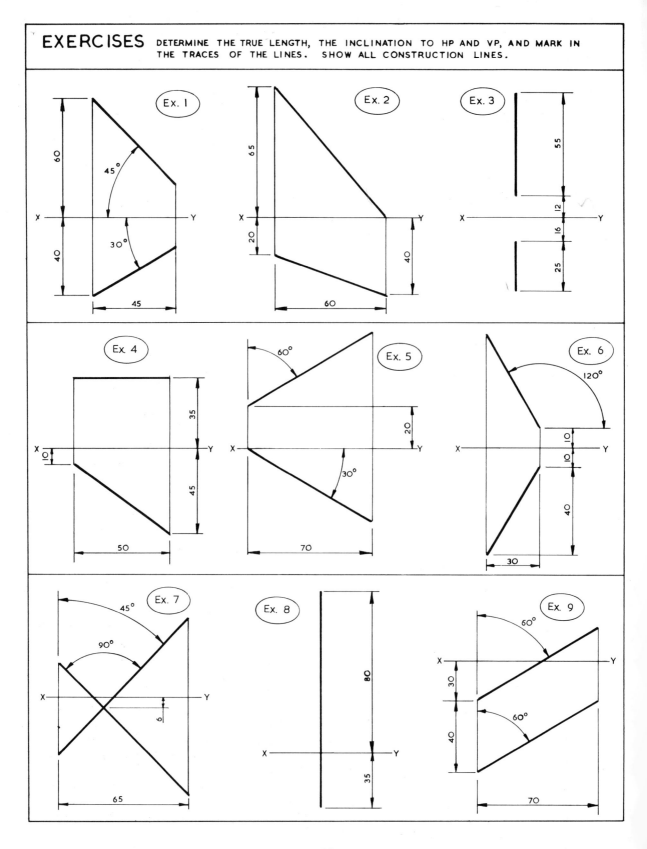

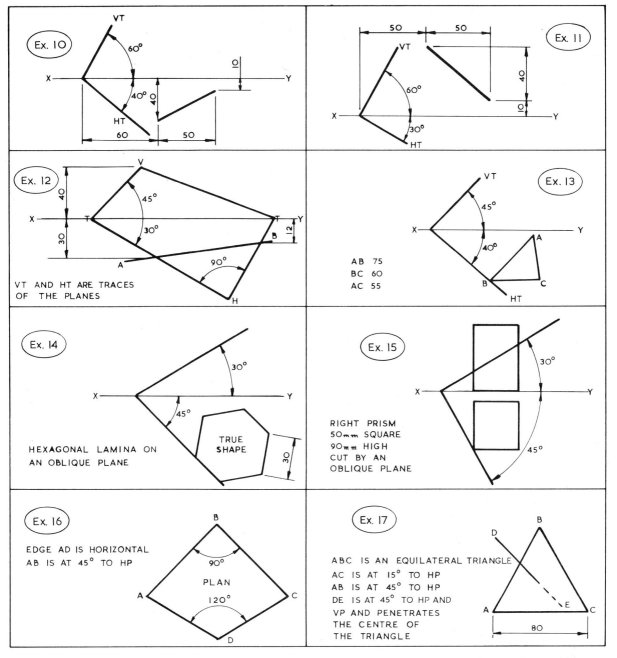

EXERCISES

(Nos. 10 to 15 are in first angle projection)

10 Draw the elevation and give the true length of the line and the inclination of the plane to the horizontal.

11 Draw the plan and find the true length of the line and the inclination of the plane to the horizontal.

12 Given the traces of two oblique planes, find the true angle between them and the points of intersection of line *AB* and the planes.

13 Draw the elevation and true shape of the triangle.

14 Draw the elevation and plan of the hexagonal lamina situated in the oblique plane.

15 Draw the sectional elevation, end elevation and plan of the prism and the true shape of the section face.

16 Draw the elevation and true shape of the lamina.

17 Draw the elevation and plan of the triangle and the line.

PROJECTION OF SOLIDS

AXONOMETRIC PROJECTIONS

Strictly used, the term **axonometric projection** covers all types of drawings that incorporate the three principal surfaces in one view with the object being projected from a point at infinity so that its parallel edges are shown as parallel lines in the drawing. This system of drawing is a great aid to visualization and can be readily understood by people who are untrained in the reading of formal workshop drawings. It includes all the following projections:
Isometric, in which all three axes are inclined at 120° to each other. This is easily constructed with the 30° set square.
Dimetric, where two axes present equal angles to to the vertical plane. The so-called **architectural axonometric** is a special case of this where two axes use any two complementary angles, usually 45°/45° or 30°/60°. This has the advantage of containing a true plan from which verticals are drawn to produce a pictorial view. It gives the impression of being drawn from a high viewpoint, and is particularly suitable for showing details of the exterior and interior of a building in the one view.
Trimetric, which is a general term covering projections that present each plane at a different angle to the plane of projection.
Oblique, in which one of the principal faces is parallel to the vertical plane, and the projectors are all inclined at 45° to this face.

Fig. 55 shows a simple solid drawn in orthographic and isometric projections. In both cases the lines are of similar lengths. Consideration shows that the solid appears larger in the isometric view. Therefore, where visual proportions are more important than actual measurements, the lengths of lines in the isometric drawing are adjusted to an isometric scale to compensate for the apparent disproportion.

Fig. 56 shows a square lamina drawn in isometric projection. The broken lines show its true plan, a square. The line *AB* therefore represents the true length of the line *AC*. These two lines and the proportions between them form the basis for the isometric scale.

The 45° true length line *AB* is divided to match the dimensions used in the drawing. Perpendiculars are dropped from these calibration points to the 30° isometric line *AC*. The divisions along *AC* are marked in a similar manner to those on *AB* and are now to isometric scale and can be used to set out the isometric drawing. The actual scale reduction is 0.8165.

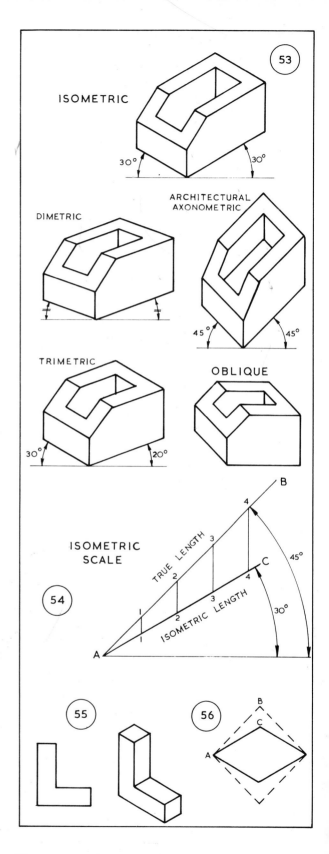

ISOMETRIC PROJECTIONS

Note that in fig. 57 all the edges are parallel to one or other of the axes of projection. When this occurs in an isometric drawing all the lines are of true length. Fig. 58 contains four lines which are not parallel to the axes and careful checking will prove that none of them is of true length. This is always the case with lines that are not parallel to the axis of projection.

All isometric projections, especially those containing curved lines, are easier to draw if they are considered to be enclosed within one or more rectangular cages as shown below.

Method (figs. 59-65). Draw a suitable number of orthographic projections or profiles (fig. 59). Surround the profile or projection with a rectangular 'cage' (fig. 60). Draw an isometric rectangle to the same dimensions as the cage (fig. 61). Draw a suitable number of ordinates from the edge of the cage to salient points in the elevation. Where a curve is included this is divided into convenient slices (fig. 62). Draw the same number of ordinates at exactly the same spacing across the isometric cage thus transferring salient points, or points along the curve, from the orthographic to the isometric drawing (fig. 63). Link all these transferred points to produce the isometric outline (fig. 64). Add the thickness by using a series of ordinates taken at 30° to the outline which has already been drawn, as *aa* in fig. 65. This completes the isometric projection.

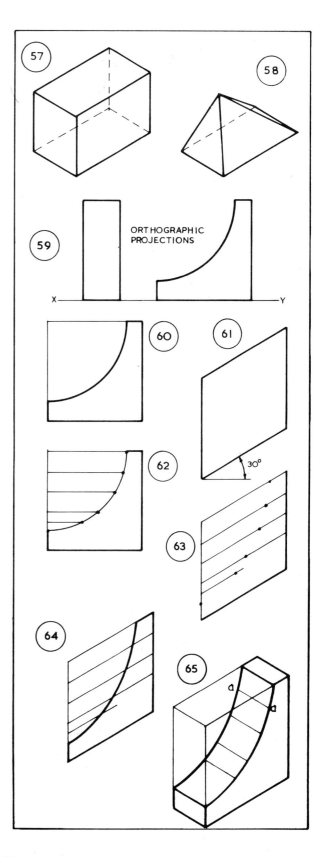

23

EXAMPLES IN ISOMETRIC PROJECTION

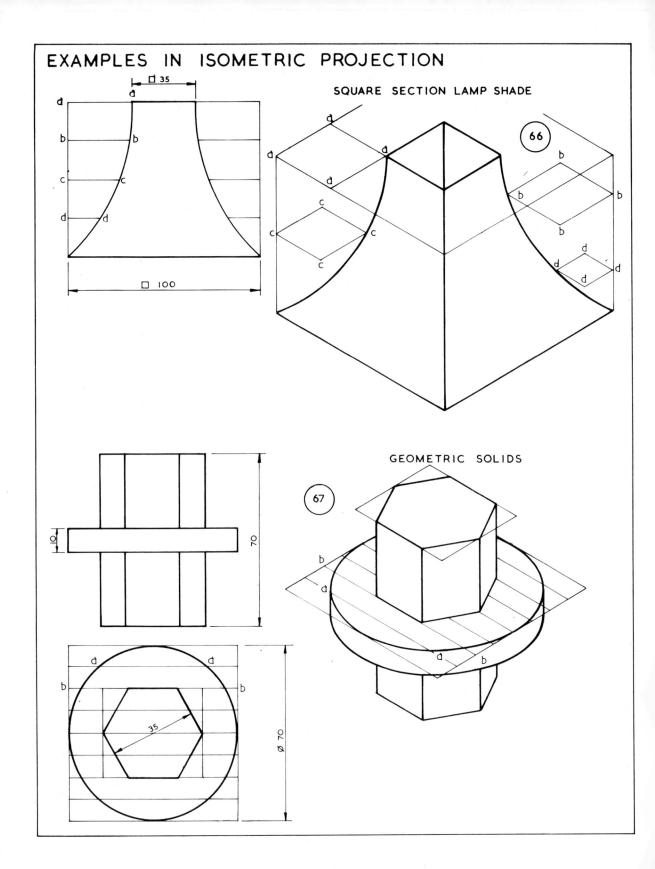

SQUARE SECTION LAMP SHADE

66

GEOMETRIC SOLIDS

67

24

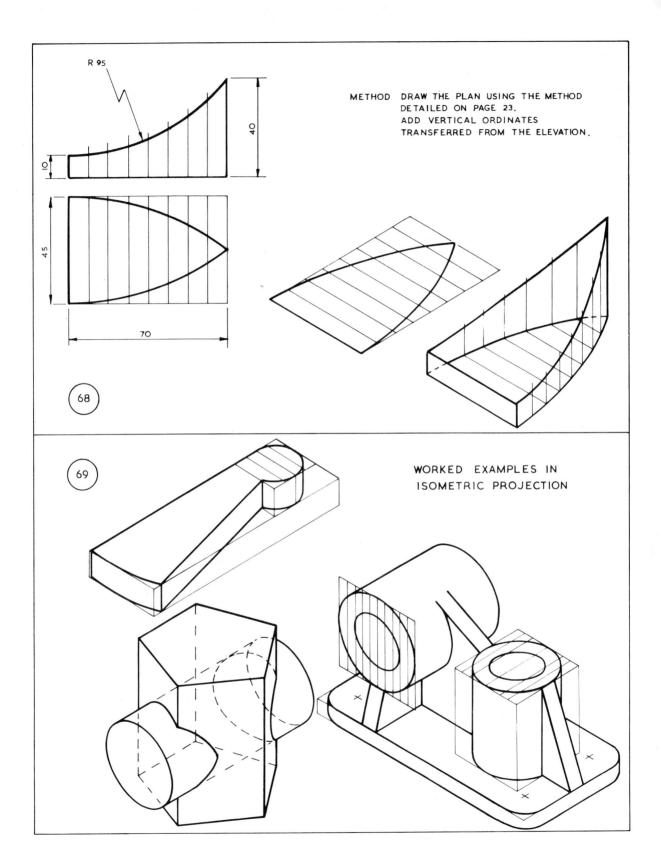

R 95

METHOD   DRAW THE PLAN USING THE METHOD
DETAILED ON PAGE 23.
ADD VERTICAL ORDINATES
TRANSFERRED FROM THE ELEVATION.

40

10

45

70

68

69

WORKED EXAMPLES IN
ISOMETRIC PROJECTION

OBLIQUE PROJECTIONS

This system of pictorial projection is exceptionally useful when drawing an object which contains a large amount of detail on one face, especially when it includes circles or arcs of circles.

Method (figs. 70-74).   The face which contains most detail is first drawn on a plane parallel to the *VP* (fig. 70).   This view corresponds to the elevation view in orthographic projection.   The sides of the object are then added at 45° to the *VP* (fig. 71). This is called **cavalier oblique** projection.   In this all lines which are contained in the front face, or are perpendicular to it, are shown in their true lengths.   Cavalier projection often exaggerates the appearance of depth, back to front (figs. 72 and 73). Choice of viewpoint may minimize this (fig. 75), but the accepted method is to reduce the oblique lines to one half their true length (fig. 74).   This is called **cabinet oblique** projection.

It will readily be seen from the examples that the principal value of this system is that it enables circles to be drawn by compass instead of as an ellipse plotted from ordinates as in isometric projections.

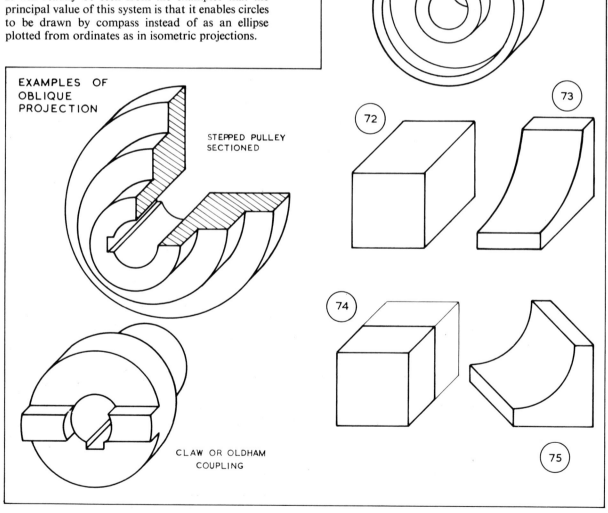

EXAMPLES OF OBLIQUE PROJECTION

STEPPED PULLEY SECTIONED

CLAW OR OLDHAM COUPLING

EXERCISES   DRAW EACH FIGURE IN ISOMETRIC AND OBLIQUE PROJECTION

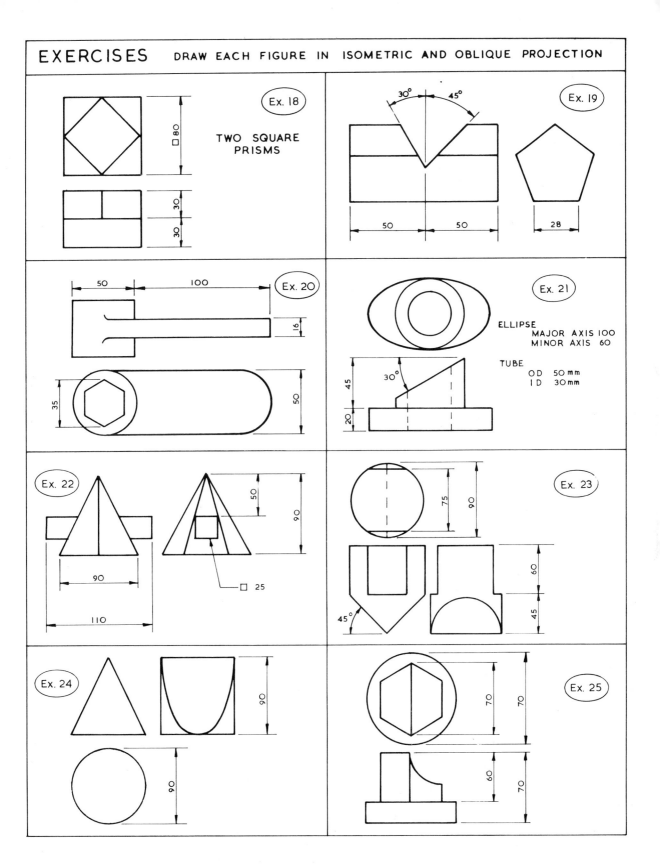

Ex. 18

TWO SQUARE PRISMS

□ 80

30 30

Ex. 19

30° 45°

50 50

28

Ex. 20

50 100

16

35

50

Ex. 21

ELLIPSE
   MAJOR AXIS 100
   MINOR AXIS 60

TUBE
   OD 50 mm
   ID 30 mm

45

20

30°

Ex. 22

50

90

□ 25

90

110

Ex. 23

75

90

60

45

45°

Ex. 24

90

90

Ex. 25

70 70

60 70

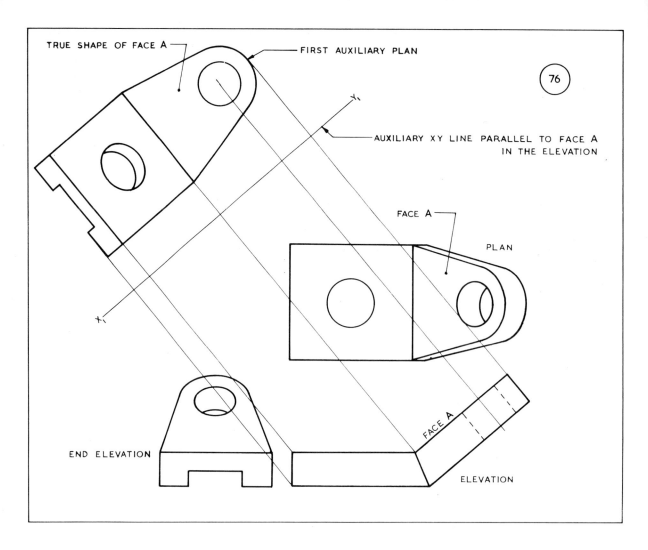

TRUE SHAPE OF FACE A

FIRST AUXILIARY PLAN

76

AUXILIARY XY LINE PARALLEL TO FACE A IN THE ELEVATION

FACE A

PLAN

FACE A

END ELEVATION

ELEVATION

AUXILIARY PROJECTIONS

Common practice amongst the manufacturing nations of the world has established orthographic projections, first or third angle, as the standard method of depicting items of engineering. Most of these items can be adequately described by the three views: elevation, plan, and end elevation. Additional projections are used to meet special needs. Cross-sectional drawings show hidden details in the interior or on the rear face of the item; where angled or sloping faces need to be detailed a system of auxiliary projections is used. These are projected from the normal views contained in the *HP* and the *VP* to auxiliary planes set at predetermined angles. These angles are usually so arranged as to give an auxiliary *xy* line parallel

with the angled face thus producing a true shape of the face.

This method of drawing auxiliary projections can also be extended to produce a pictorial view. To do this a normal elevation and plan are drawn on the coordinate horizontal and vertical planes. These views are then used to produce a 'first auxiliary elevation' situated on a new auxiliary *xy* line (x_1y_1) which can be set to any desired angle. This view is then in turn projected to a second auxiliary *xy* line (x_2y_2) to give the 'second auxiliary plan'. This latter will then appear as a form of perspective drawing. Alternatively, the drawings can be taken in the reverse order — elevation to first auxiliary plan, then to second auxiliary elevation — when this too will appear as a form of perspective drawing.

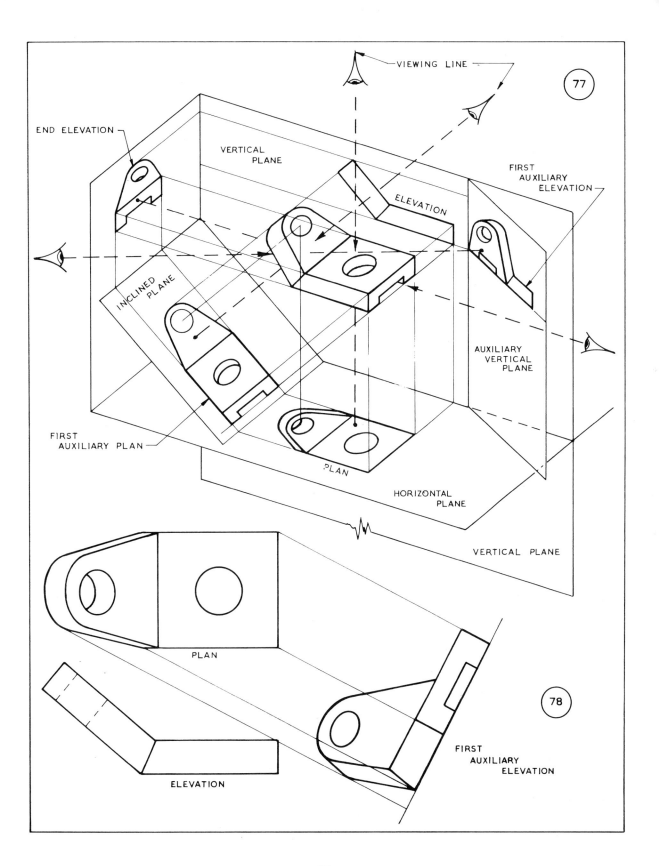

VIEWING LINE

(77)

END ELEVATION

VERTICAL PLANE

FIRST AUXILIARY ELEVATION

ELEVATION

INCLINED PLANE

AUXILIARY VERTICAL PLANE

FIRST AUXILIARY PLAN

PLAN

HORIZONTAL PLANE

VERTICAL PLANE

PLAN

(78)

FIRST AUXILIARY ELEVATION

ELEVATION

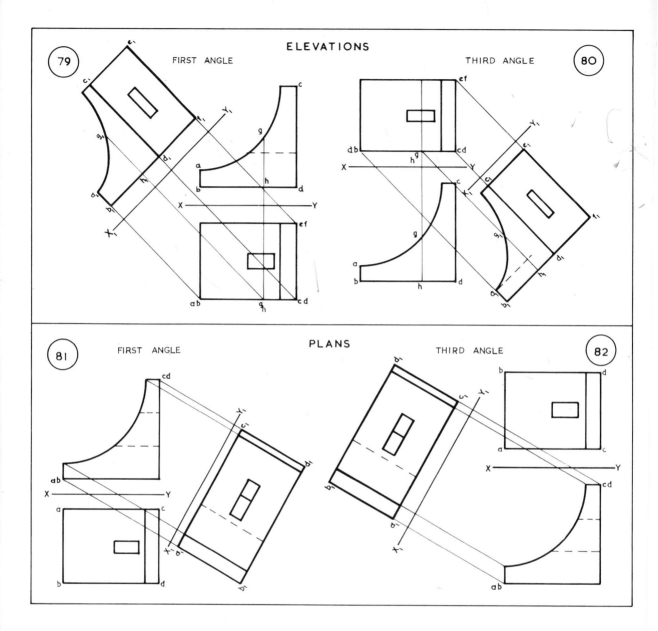

ELEVATIONS

79 FIRST ANGLE

80 THIRD ANGLE

PLANS

81 FIRST ANGLE

82 THIRD ANGLE

First auxiliary views (first and third angle projections)

In each of the four cases shown above the standard elevation and plan are first drawn from a common xy line. Points (at corners) are then projected from one of these views to give lines in the required auxiliary view, as shown from point a to give line ab, and so on.

Three important points to note:

(1) Projection lines must cross the relevant xy line at right angles. ·

(2) Plans can only be projected from elevations and vice versa.

(3) The distance of any given point from the xy line in the standard views is similar to the distance of the same point to the auxiliary xy line in the auxiliary views.

Method. Draw the conventional elevation and plan. Draw the auxiliary datum line x_1y_1 at the required angle. Project points a, c, e at right angles to x_1y_1. Using dividers transfer heights ab, ef, cd from the elevation to the appropriate projectors in the auxiliary elevation at a_1b_1, c_1d_1, e_1f_1. Draw any convenient number of ordinates across the arc in the elevation. Project these ordinates across to the plan and from there to the auxiliary elevation. Transfer the heights of these ordinates as with gh to g_1h_1. Draw a fair curve through the points so obtained. This completes the first auxiliary projection.

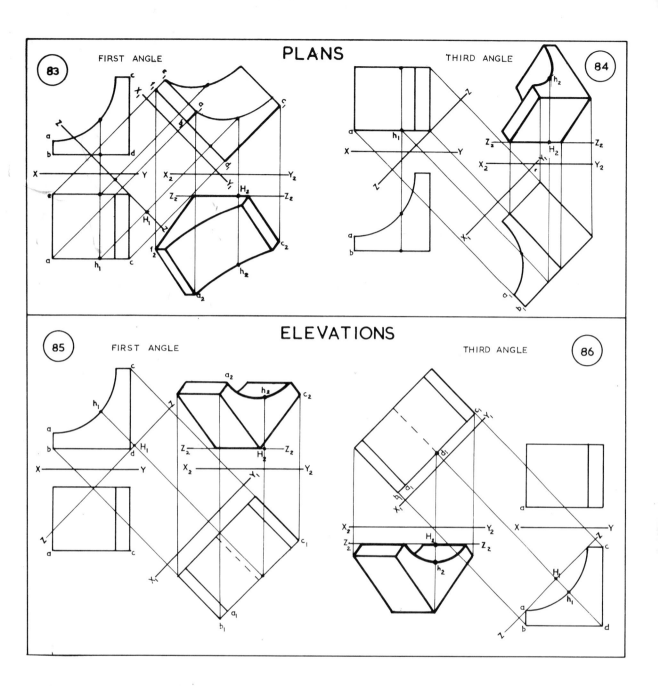

PLANS

83 FIRST ANGLE

84 THIRD ANGLE

ELEVATIONS

85 FIRST ANGLE

86 THIRD ANGLE

Second auxiliary views (first and third angle projections)

Second auxiliary plans are projected from first auxiliary elevations and vice versa as shown above. An important point to note is that the x_1y_1 line is often moved outward from the standard views to give more convenient spacing for the auxiliary views within the available space. When this is done a 'shadow' x_1y_1 line (marked zz above) is drawn touching the view which is to be projected. This 'extra' xy line makes it easier to transfer heights of points from the standard views to the second auxiliary views as at H and h.

Method. Draw the conventional elevation and plan and from these project the first auxiliary elevation. Draw projectors from points in this view to cross the x_2y_2 line at right angles. Transfer the heights of points such as H_1 and h_1 above the shadow x_1y_1 line (marked zz) to the appropriate projectors H_2 and h_2 above the z_2z_2 line. Note that all the dimensions necessary to produce the second auxiliary plan are taken from the original plan and the first auxiliary elevation, the original elevation being ignored.

31

PERSPECTIVE DRAWINGS

Normally the eye produces one image of any one object, the image including height, width and length. This is called a perspective view. A geometric method of reproducing this perspective view is given in fig. 89 opposite. Fig. 87 below shows pictorially the arrangement needed to produce this view. The object is situated on the *HP*. A point of sight, or station point, is chosen. This corresponds to the position of the observer's eye and should be about central to the object. Interposed between this station point and the object is a vertical transparent picture plane. On this will be marked points where it intersects visual rays from the eye to salient points on the object. These points, when joined together, will produce the complete perspective view. The picture plane intersects the horizontal plane in the base line. An orthographic projection of the station point to the picture plane will give the centre of vision. A vertical line drawn from this centre to the *HP* will give the true length line, along which all true heights are transferred from the elevation of the object. A horizontal line drawn through the centre contains the vanishing points VP_1 and VP_2. These are points at which all the 'horizontal' lines in the object converge. The vanishing points are determined by drawing lines parallel to the base edges of the object from *SP* to the picture plane. Having established the position of the object, the picture plane, the observer and the vanishing points, it is then necessary to check the field of vision. Fig. 88 shows this set out in plan form. The field of vision is a cone of space of about 30° included

angle in which the whole of the object can be accommodated.

If the object extends beyond the limits of the cone then the *SP* must be moved further away from the picture plane or the image will be excessively foreshortened. The axis of the cone of vision passes through *SP* and is approximately perpendicular to the picture plane. This sight line intersects the picture plane in the centre of vision.

Method (fig. 89). Draw a true plan of the object. Establish the position of the observer (*SP*), the picture plane, the vanishing points and the true length line as detailed above. Transfer all true heights from the elevation to the true length line. Join each of these points to both of the vanishing points as follows: take point *A* in the plan and draw a ray from *A* to *SP* stopping short at the picture plane in a_1; drop a vertical from a_1; draw a ray from o_1 (bottom of the true length line, i.e. the front bottom corner of the enclosing rectangle) to VP_1; repeat with the top of the true length line (i.e. the total height of the elevation); these two rays will intersect the vertical from a_1 in a_2 and a_3 establishing the edge corresponding to *A* in the plan; repeat with corners *B, C, D, E, F, G* to establish the outline of the object in a perspective view. To insert the circle draw rays from *E* and *F* and suitable intermediate points as before. Step off the heights of these points from the elevation to the true length line. Draw rays from these vertical height points to VP_2 to intersect the verticals dropped from the rays *E* and *F* to *SP*. Draw a free curve through all the intersecting points to complete the circle in projection.

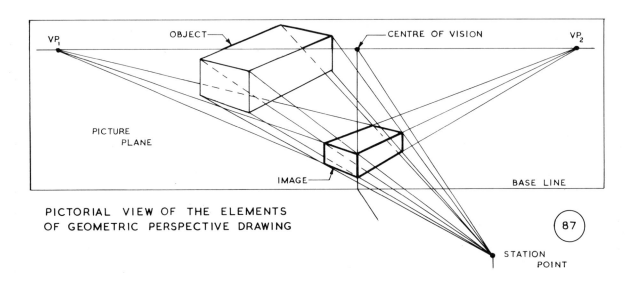

PICTORIAL VIEW OF THE ELEMENTS
OF GEOMETRIC PERSPECTIVE DRAWING

87

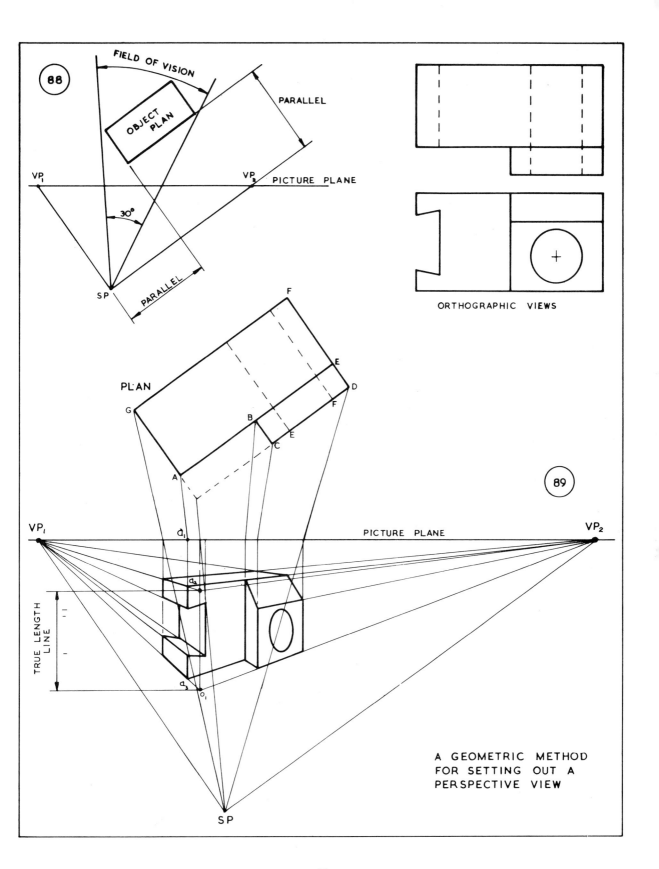

FIELD OF VISION

88

OBJECT PLAN

PARALLEL

VP₁   VP₃   PICTURE PLANE

30°

SP   PARALLEL

ORTHOGRAPHIC VIEWS

PLAN

F
E
D
G
B
C
F
E
A

89

VP₁   d₁   PICTURE PLANE   VP₂

TRUE LENGTH LINE

a₃
o₁

SP

A GEOMETRIC METHOD
FOR SETTING OUT A
PERSPECTIVE VIEW

EXERCISES

Draw a standard elevation and plan of each object and then project a first auxiliary plan on x_1y_1 and a second auxiliary elevation on x_2y_2.

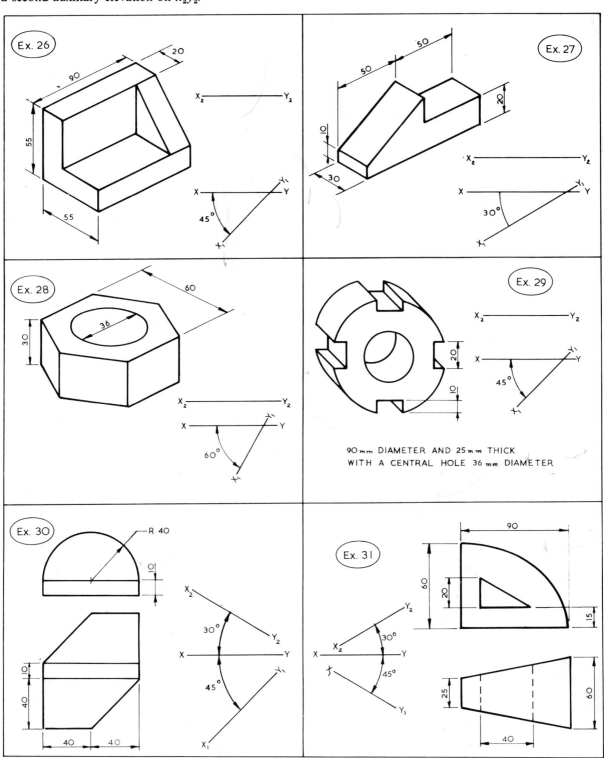

Ex. 26

Ex. 27

Ex. 28

Ex. 29

90 mm DIAMETER AND 25 mm THICK
WITH A CENTRAL HOLE 36 mm DIAMETER

Ex. 30

Ex. 31

EXERCISES

Draw a standard elevation and plan of each object and then project a first auxiliary elevation on x_1y_1 and a second auxiliary plan on x_2y_2.

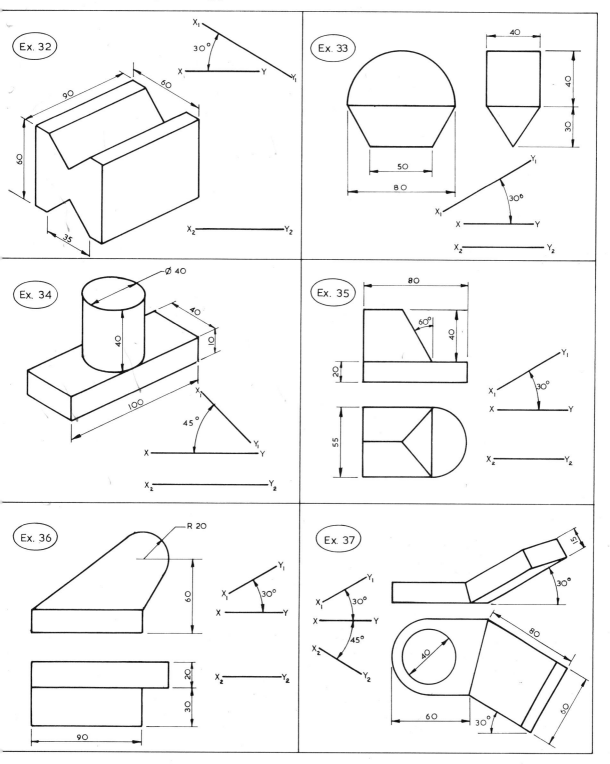

LOCI, CONICS, SPECIAL CURVES

The locus of a point is the path traced by that point when moving under given conditions. For example, if point *A* moves so that it is always equidistant from point *B* it will trace out a circle, or if a circle rolls along a straight line a point on its circumference will trace out a cycloidal curve. Many curves can be included under the heading loci; the ellipse, parabola, hyperbola, hypocycloid, etc.

The study of loci is especially important in machine design where it is often necessary to determine the space needed for a linkage, or the envelope of a mechanism for the provision of effective guards. The usual method for drawing the locus of a particular point in a mechanism is to construct outline or skeleton drawings of the mechanism in a number of positions, plotting the point in each position and then drawing a smooth curve (the locus) through the points so obtained.

Fig. 90. *AO* is a crank arm which revolves about *O*. This drives a piston *B* horizontally by means of connecting rod *AB*.

To trace the locus of point *P* on this rod for one complete revolution of crank *OA*

Method. Draw link *AB* in several positions as *A* turns through one revolution. Plot the position of *P* in each of these positions. Draw a smooth curve through all these points to obtain the locus as shown.

Fig. 91 shows a four-bar chain. *OA* is fixed, *OB* revolves about *O*, *AC* swings about *A* and *BC* extends to *D*.

To trace the locus of point *D*

Method. Set out the link mechanism in at least eight different positions around the periphery of the circle (greater accuracy results from twelve positions). Plot the position of *D* in all these positions. Draw a smooth curve through the points thus obtained.

Note how the outline shape of the locus has been changed by the addition of the extra bar. This locus has an oscillating movement common in automatic packaging machinery.

Fig. 92. Crank *OA* revolves about *O* and actuates a rod *AB* which is constrained to slide through a fixed trunnion at *C*.

To determine the locus for the end of the rod at *B*

Method. This is similar to both the above and consists of dividing the circle into eight or twelve parts and plotting the position of the mechanism from each of these division points, finally drawing a smooth curve through the derived locus points.

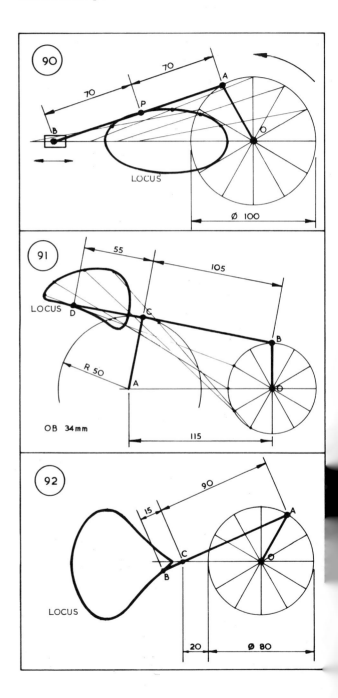

LINKAGES

The early engineering designers had to find some means of guiding a beam engine pump rod along a straight line although the beam end moved through a circular arc. One of these straight line linkages was devised by James Watt. In its simplest form it consists of two equal links *OA* and *OB* connected by a third link *AB*. When the two links *OA* and *OB* oscillate, moving the link *AB* through all possible positions, the locus of *P* will follow a straight line for a part of the movement.

To trace the locus of point *P*

Method (fig. 93). Mark off the points *A*, *P*, *B* along the straight edge of a strip of paper and move this through all positions keeping the points *A* and *B* on their respective arcs. Dot the position of *P* at intervals of about 5 mm. Joining all these interval points with a fair curve will produce the locus.

Fig. 94 shows the skeleton drawing of a simple quick return motion suitable for driving a shaping machine ram. The crank pin *A* revolves with the flywheel about the centre *O*. This pin slides along a slot in the radius arm O_1B causing it to oscillate. This in turn drives the ram through the connecting rod *BR*.

To determine the crank angle during the return and forward strokes and reduce this to a ratio of $1:x$

Method. Using a suitable scale, say 1:3, draw the skeleton outline at both extremes of the movement making O_1B tangential to the crank pin circle at *A*. Draw normals from the two tangent points. Measure and state the top arc (driving) and the bottom arc (return):

    Bottom arc $= 138°$
    Top arc $= 222°$
    Ratio $= 138:222 = 1:1.6$

Fig. 95 shows a Whitworth quick return motion. The slotted link *AB* is driven by the crank arm *OA*. *BR* connects the link *AB* to the ram. The crank rotates at a uniform angular velocity.

To draw the linkage half size and find the length of the stroke and the ratio of the forward to the return time as $1:x$

Method. Draw the linkage with *RBA* in a straight line (fig. 95a). This gives the forward position. Draw the linkage with *RAB* in a straight line (fig. 95b). This gives the terminal return position. Measure the distance *R* to *R* in the two drawings to obtain the length of stroke. Measure the two arcs and reduce to the simplest ratio as in fig. 94 above.

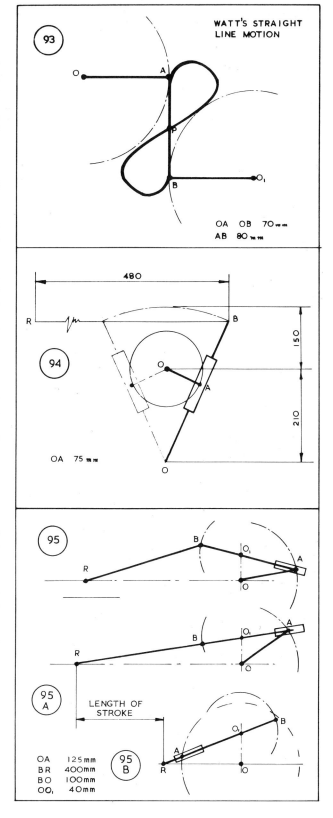

93 WATT'S STRAIGHT LINE MOTION

OA OB 70 mm
AB 80 mm

94 OA 75 mm

480

150

210

95

95 A LENGTH OF STROKE

95 B

OA 125 mm
BR 400 mm
BO 100 mm
OO_1 40 mm

CONIC SECTIONS

The section face formed where a plane intersects a right circular cone is called a conic section. Depending upon the relationship between the plane and the slant surface of the cone, the outline may be a circle, an ellipse, a parabola or a hyperbola. The section is a circle when the cutting plane is perpendicular to the axis, an ellipse when the plane is inclined to the axis and cuts all the generators (fig. 96), a parabola when the plane is parallel to a slant side of the cone (fig. 97) and a hyperbola when the plane will cut two similar cones placed apex to apex (fig. 98). All these special curves may be treated as both loci and plane sections.

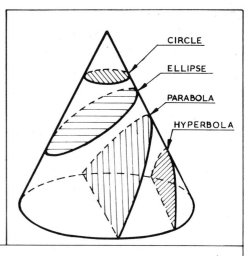

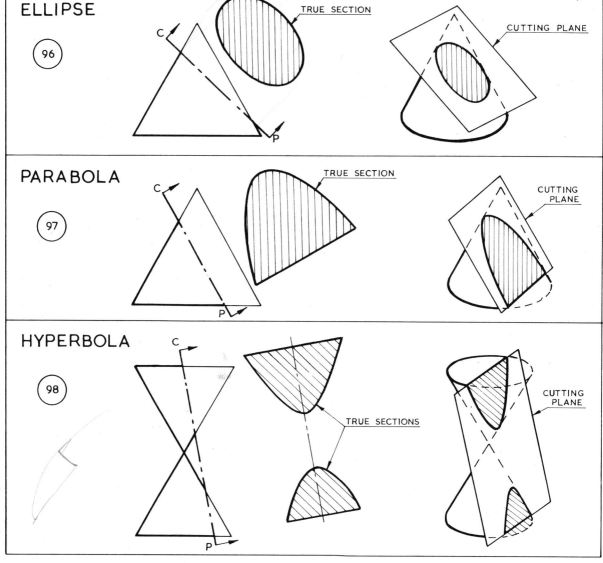

38

ELLIPSE

An ellipse is the section formed when a plane cuts a cone obliquely across both slant sides. Note that in fig. 99 the ellipse contains two foci and has two directrices as shown at F_1F_2 and D_1D_2 respectively. If a sphere is inserted in the cone to touch the cutting plane and slant sides as shown, then the point of contact F_1 between the plane and the sphere is one of the foci of the ellipse. The second focus is similarly located at the point where the plane is touched by a second contained sphere at F_2. Lines drawn to the plane through the tangent points where the focal spheres touch the slant sides of the cone will give the two directrices.

In all conics a line drawn from the focus to any point in the curve bears a fixed ratio to the perpendicular from that point to the directrix. This ratio is called the eccentricity of the conic, and in an ellipse it is always less than unity as B/A. Fig. 100 shows the method for obtaining the normal and tangent at a given point in the curve. Join the point to the two foci and bisect the included angle.

Figs. 101 and 102 display different ellipse constructions, the drawings being self-explanatory.

Fig. 103. Conjugate diameters are each parallel to the tangent drawn at the extremity of the other. Thus the tangents produced will give the circumscribing rectangle.

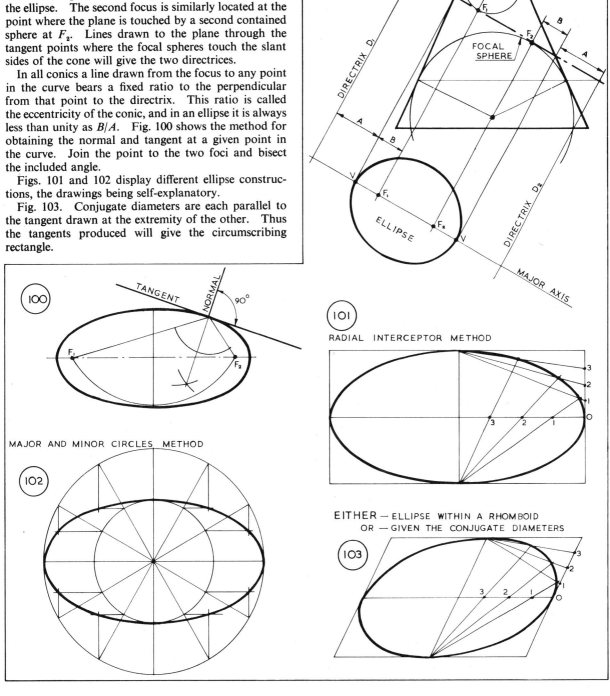

CENTRE OF CURVATURE, EVOLUTE

Fig. 104 shows a circular arc, centre O, drawn through three points A, B, C on a given conic curve. If the three points are moved along the curve towards each other, then the limiting position of O as the three points converge in, say, B is called the centre of curvature at the point B in the conic curve. A number of different points on the curve given similar treatment will produce a number of different centres of curvature. These can then be linked by a fair curve, the locus of the centres. The resultant figure is called the evolute of that particular conic.

To find the centre of curvature at point P

Method (fig. 105). Draw a line from P through the focus. Draw the normal through point P (see fig. 100). From the point where the normal crosses the major axis draw a perpendicular to cut the line from P through the focus in X. Draw a perpendicular from X to cut the normal in C. This is the centre of curvature for point P.

To draw the evolute for a given ellipse

Method (fig. 106). The evolute contains four similar lobes, one to each quarter of the ellipse as shown. Consideration shows that the full construction is only required for one lobe of the evolute, the remaining three lobes then being produced from vertical and horizontal ordinates. Plot the centre of curvature of a suitable number of points along one quarter of the ellipse. Join all the centres of curvature by a fair curve. This gives one quarter of the evolute. Transfer this curve by the use of ordinates to the other three quarters of the ellipse.

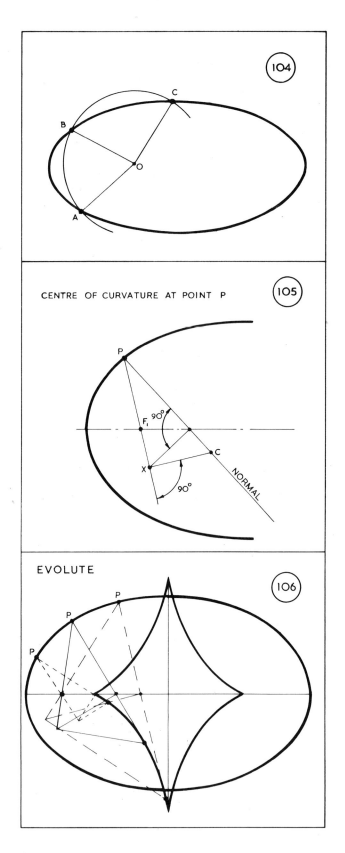

CENTRE OF CURVATURE AT POINT P

EVOLUTE

PARABOLA

Fig. 107. A parabola is the section formed when a plane cuts a cone parallel to a slant side. It has one focus and one directrix. The focus derives from the point where the focal sphere is tangential to the plane. A line drawn through the two points where the sphere is tangential to the sides of the cone and produced to cut the plane will give the directrix as shown. The ratio of eccentricity is always unity, i.e. the distance from the focus to the vertex always equals the perpendicular distance from the vertex to the directrix. Parabolic reflectors are much used in lamps and heaters where, if the filament is placed on the focus, a parallel beam of heat or light is reflected. The trajectory of missiles, e.g. thrown stones, takes the form of a parabola.

Fig. 108 gives the radial intersector method of drawing a parabola and is self-explanatory.

To draw the normal and tangent at point *P*

Method (fig. 109*a*). Draw a line from the focus to pass through point *P*. Draw a line through *P* parallel to the axis. The bisector of the included angle is the normal. A perpendicular to the normal at *P* gives the tangent.

To draw the evolute

Method (fig. 109*b*). The loci of the centres of curvature are drawn in a similar manner to that of the ellipse on page 40. Draw normals from suitable points *1*, *2*, etc. Join these points to the focus. Erect perpendiculars to cut the focal chord from the point where each normal crosses the axis. From these cutting points erect perpendiculars back to the normal. These second points are centres of curvature. Join them in a fair curve to obtain the evolute.

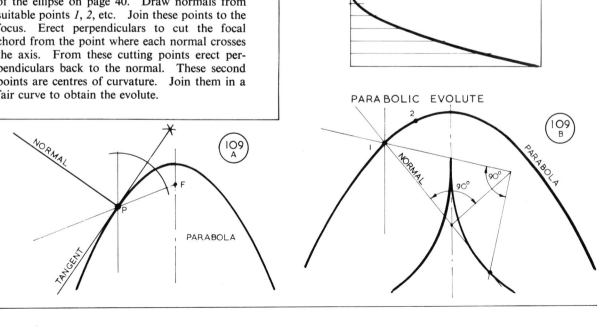

HYPERBOLA

Fig. 110. A hyperbola is the section formed when a plane cuts both nappes of a double cone to one side of the axis. Each part of the hyperbola contains a focus projected from the tangent point, focal sphere to section plane. Each part also has its directrix projected from the intersection of the horizontal line from the tangential points sphere and cone sides. The asymptotes are projections of the outer generators of the cone and approach the hyperbolic curves indefinitely without ever meeting them. The ratio of eccentricity is always greater than unity.

To draw a hyperbola, given the foci and the transverse axis

Method (fig. 111). Mark in any convenient points a, b, c on the axis. With centre F_2 and radius Va describe an arc. With centre F_1 and radius V_1a draw a second arc cutting the first one in A_1. The same radii and procedure will give points on the other three arms of the hyperbola. The same procedure using points b and c will give eight other points through which may be drawn fair curves to establish the hyperbola.

To draw a tangent and normal from point P

Method (fig. 111). Draw lines from the given point on the curve to the two focal points. The tangent is the bisector of the included angle. The normal is perpendicular to the tangent at point P.

To draw a rectangular hyperbola through point P

Method (fig. 112). Draw the asymptotes OA and OB. Add parallel lines passing through P. Draw suitable radials from O and construct parallelograms at the cutting points as shown to obtain points along the curve of the hyperbola.

To draw the evolute of a given hyperbola

Method (fig. 113). The evolute loci are drawn by taking a number of centres of curvature from a series of suitable points along the conic curve as with the ellipse on page 40 and the parabola on page 41.

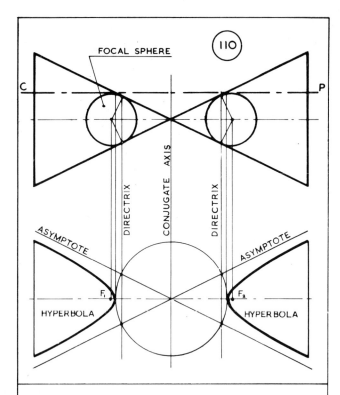

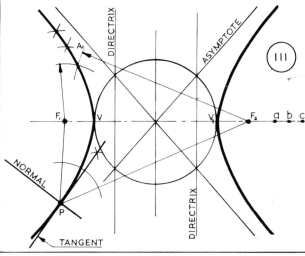

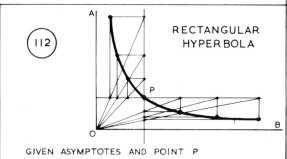

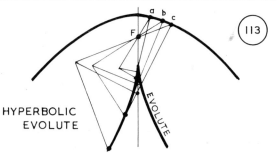

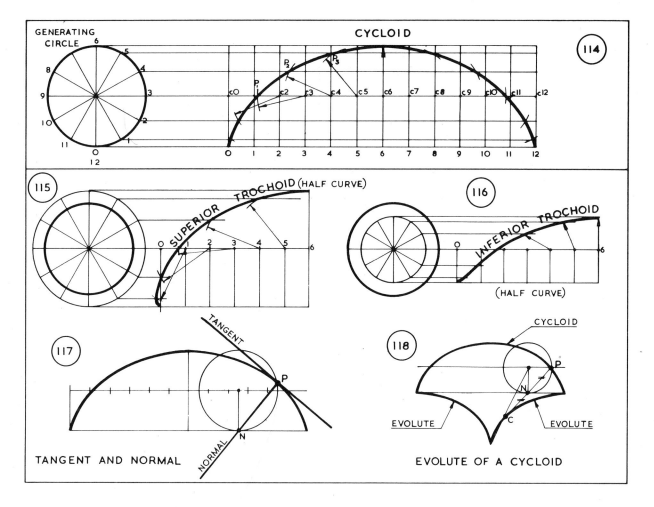

CYCLOID

A cycloid is the locus traced by a point on the circumference of a circle when that circle rolls along a straight line.

Method (fig. 114). Divide the rolling circle into twelve equal parts. Draw the straight base line of length equal to the circumference of the circle. Divide the line into twelve equal parts and erect perpendiculars from each division. Project the circle division points horizontally to cut across the perpendiculars. Using the radius of the circle and the centres c_1, c_2, c_3, etc., describe arcs to cut the horizontals in *1, 2, 3*, etc. The points of intersection P_1, P_2, P_3, etc. all lie on the cycloidal curve.

To draw a tangent from a given point *P*

Method (fig. 117). Draw the rolling circle to pass through *P*. Drop a vertical from the centre of the circle to cut the base line in *N*, the point of contact between the circle and the base line. The normal passes from *P* through this point. The tangent is perpendicular to the normal at point *P*.

To draw the evolute

Method (fig. 118). Produce the normal to *C* making *CN* equal to *NP*. Thus *C* is the centre of curvature of point *P*. Take a number of such points on the curve and establish their centres of curvature. A fair curve drawn through these will give the evolute. Consideration will show that the evolute is itself of cycloidal form.

Superior trochoid (fig. 115).
This is the name given to the locus of a point which lies outside the generating circle.

Inferior trochoid (fig. 116).
This is the name given to the locus of a point which lies inside the generating circle. In both cases the construction layout is similar to that of the cycloid, only the tracing radii are different.

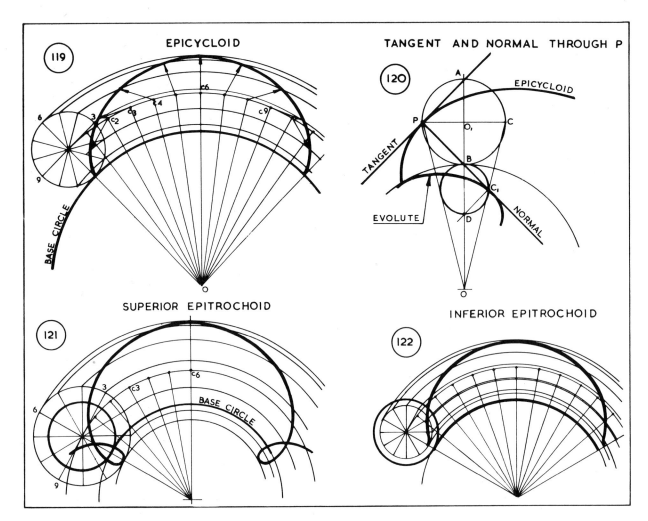

EPICYCLOID

TANGENT AND NORMAL THROUGH P

SUPERIOR EPITROCHOID

INFERIOR EPITROCHOID

EPICYCLOID

An epicycloid is the locus traced by a point on the circumference of a circle which rolls round the outside of a fixed base circle. All such loci, developed by one curve rolling upon another curve, are called roulettes.

Method (fig. 119). Draw the generating circle and divide it into twelve equal parts. Draw an arc of the base circle and step off twelve divisions equal in length to the arcs of the generating circle divisions. Draw radials through these points from O, the centre of the base circle. Describe concentric arcs from centre O through points *1, 2, 3, 4*, etc. in the generating circle. Using the radius of this circle and centres c_1, c_2, c_3, c_4, etc., strike arcs across the base circle concentric arcs in *1, 2, 3, 4*, etc. A fair curve drawn through all twelve points will give the epicycloid.

To draw a tangent, normal and centre of curvature at point P

Method (fig. 120). Draw the rolling circle through P. Join its centre to the base circle centre, O_1 to O. Produce this line to cut the rolling circle at A. Then AP is the tangent at P and a line drawn from P through the point of contact of the rolling circle with the base arc at B is the normal. Draw a diameter from P through O_1 to C on the rolling circle and add a line from C to the base arc centre O. This line cuts the normal in C_1, the centre of curvature of point P.

To draw the evolute

Method (fig. 120). Draw a perpendicular from the normal at C_1 to D. The arc of radius OD is the base circle and DB is the generating circle of an epicycloid which will coincide with the evolute, i.e. the evolute of an epicycloid is itself an epicycloid.

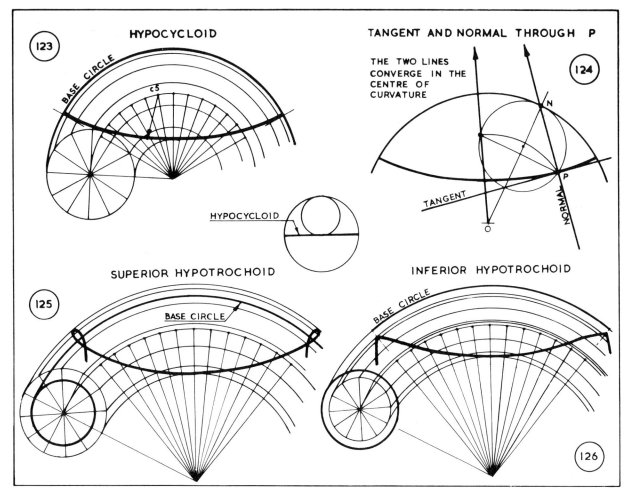

Superior epitrochoid (fig. 121).
This is the name given to the locus of a point which lies outside the generating circle.

Inferior epitrochoid (fig. 122).
This is the name given to the locus of a point which lies inside the generating circle. In both cases the construction layout is similar to that of the epicycloid, only the tracing radii are different.

HYPOCYCLOID

A hypocycloid is the locus traced by a point on the circumference of a circle which rolls round the interior of a fixed base circle.

Method (fig. 123). The construction is similar in every detail to that of the epicycloid given on page 44, except that the generating circle rolls round the interior of the base circle. A special case is shown in the centre of the page. When

the radius of the generating circle is half that of the base circle the hypocycloid takes the form of a straight line which coincides with the diameter of the base circle.

To draw a tangent, normal, evolute and centre of curvature for a given hypocycloid

Method (fig. 124). Given the tangent point *P*, proceed as detailed on pages 43 and 44. Draw the generating circle. Draw a line through *P* and the point of contact between the circle and the base arc. This line is the normal. The tangent is perpendicular to it at point *P*. The construction shown is self-explanatory. The evolute is the locus of a number of centres of curvature and is itself a hypocycloid.

Trochoids (figs. 125, 126). The inferior hypotrochoid is the locus of a point within the circumference of the generating circle and the superior hypotrochoid is the locus of a point outside the circumference of the generating circle which rolls round the inside of the base circle.

INVOLUTES AND SPIRALS

If a straight line is rolled round a circle the locus of any point on the line is an **involute** of the circle. Similarly, if a taut thread is unwound from the surface of a cylinder, the end will describe an involute of the circular section of that cylinder.

To draw an involute on a circle

Method (fig. 127). Divide the generating circle into twelve equal parts and draw tangents from the division points. Step successive lengths along the tangents equal to 1/12, 2/12, 3/12, 4/12, etc. of the circumference and join these points with a free curve. The normal from point P is tangential to the base circle and the tangent at P is perpendicular to the normal.

The evolute is the original circle. A point to note is that the tangent to the evolute is also the normal to the involute.

A **spiral** is a locus traced by a point which winds about a pole from which it continually recedes. An **Archimedean spiral** is characterized by equal movement towards or away from the pole during equal angular movement about the pole. Thus it is a spiral of arithmetic progression.

To draw an Archimedean spiral

Method (fig. 128). Given the pole and the limiting vectors A and B, set these out on a straight line. Divide the distance AB into twelve equal parts and draw twelve equidistant radii. With centre O and radii $O1$, $O2$, $O3$, etc., draw arcs cutting successive radii in 1, 2, 3, etc. Draw a fair curve through the twelve cutting points to develop the spiral.

To draw a tangent and normal at point P

Method (fig. 128). Join P to O. Set off ON perpendicular to PO and of length equal to constant C in the formula below. Draw the normal from N to P. The tangent is perpendicular to the normal at P.

$$C = \frac{r - a}{\theta}$$ where r is the radius to O
a is the initial radius vector
θ is the vectorial angle in radians

Logarithmic spiral (fig. 129). The radii of this spiral increase by a constant ratio, thus forming a spiral of geometric progression.

To draw a logarithmic spiral given an initial radius vector of 12 mm and a ratio of 3:2 at 45°

Method (fig. 129). Draw lines O_1A and O_1B at 45°. Set off O_1P_0 on O_1A at 12 mm distance. Divide this into two equal parts. Mark off three parts of similar length O_1 to P_1 along O_1B. Join P_0 to P_1 with a straight line. With centre at point O_1 strike an arc from P_1 to give point 1. From this draw a line parallel to P_0P_1 to give P_2. Continue for all eight radius vectors. Draw the pole O and the radiating vectors. Step off along these the successive lengths O_1P_1, O_1P_2, O_1P_3, O_1P_4, etc. Trace a fair curve through all these points to obtain the spiral.

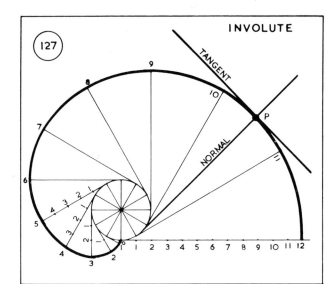

INVOLUTE

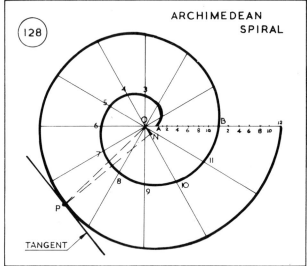

ARCHIMEDEAN SPIRAL

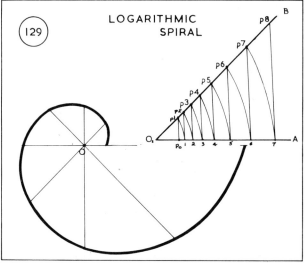

LOGARITHMIC SPIRAL

SPECIAL CURVES

In addition to the curves set out on the preceding pages, there are many more mathematical curves of great interest. A few are shown here.

The cardiod

Method (fig. 130).   Draw the base circle.   Mark in the fixed point *P*.   Divide the base circle into a convenient number of equal divisions starting from *P*.   Using each division as centre and the division point to *P* as radius, draw a number of circles. Produce the cardiod by enclosing the circles in an envelope as shown.   The cardiod is an epicycloid of special proportions.

The limaçon

Method (fig. 131).   Draw a base circle and mark in point *P* at a given distance outside the circle.   Divide the circle into a suitable number of even parts. Using these division points as centres, draw a series of circles each cutting through point *P*.   The envelope is a limaçon.   This is an epitrochoid of special proportions.

The astroid

Method (fig. 132).   Draw two rectangular axes *OX* and *OY*.   Draw a line *AB* in many positions across the arms of the axes.   The envelope is an astroid. This is a series of hypocycloids.   It has been called a cubocycloid.

The nephroid

Method (fig. 133).   Draw a base circle and its vertical diameter.   Divide the circumference evenly and using these division points as centres draw circles to touch the diameter.   The envelope is a nephroid.   This can also be drawn as a double epicycloid of special proportions.

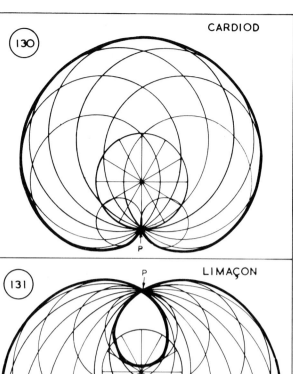

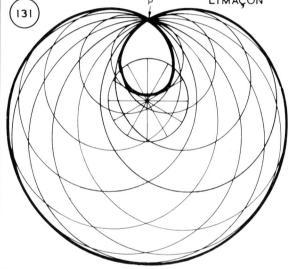

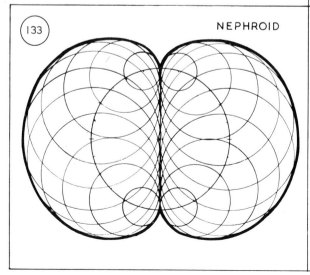

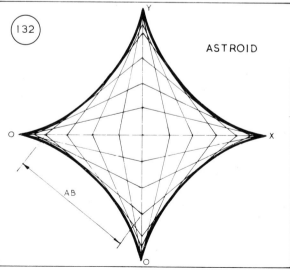

EXERCISES

38 Trace the locus of the circle centre as it rolls round the semi-ellipse from *A* to *B*. Draw the normal, tangent and point of curvature from the point where the locus crosses the minor axis produced.

39 *OD* is a fixed link in the four bar chain. *ABC* is a rigid bar pin jointed in *A* and *B*. Draw the locus of *C* while *OA* turns through one complete revolution. Invert and draw the mechanism so that it permits point *C* to trace a circle.

40 A right circular cone of 100 mm vertical height and 80 mm base diameter is set with its axis at 45° to *HP*. Draw a plan showing the cone cut by the horizontal plane passing through the base edge at *X*.

41a Draw the elevation and plan of the cone. Show the true shape of the parabolic section *AB* and insert on this the focus and directrix.

41b Draw the elevation and plan of the cone showing the hyperbolic section *CD*. Include the true shape of the section, the focus and the directrix.

42 *OA* is a crank arm turning about *O*. Rod *CB* is pin jointed to the crank at *A* and is constrained to move through a trunnion set at point *E*. Trace the loci of points *C* and *B* as the crank arm turns through one revolution.

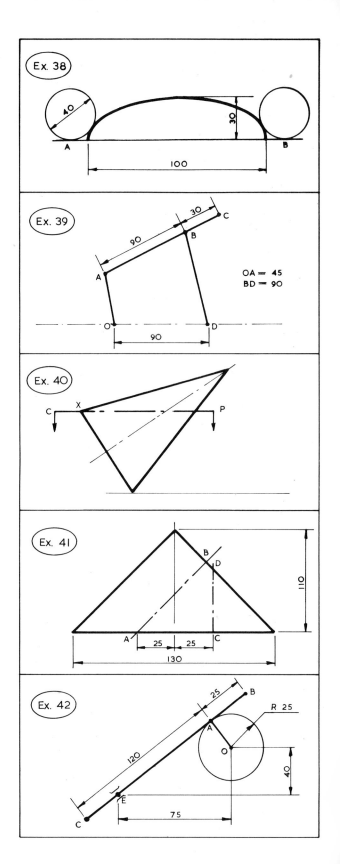

EXERCISES

43 Draw an ellipse (major axis 100 mm; minor axis 75 mm). Insert the foci and directrices and state the eccentricity of the conic.

44 Draw a parabola having its focus 40 mm from the directrix. Draw the tangent, normal and centre of curvature for a point on the curve at 75 mm perpendicular distance from the directrix.

45 Draw both sections of a hyperbola having an eccentricity of 30/20 and focus set at 45 mm from a directrix.

46 Draw a hyperbola having a vertex 20 mm from the directrix and 35 mm from the focus. Draw in the tangent at a point 40 mm from the focus.

47 Construct a cycloid having a rolling circle of 70 mm diameter. Draw the tangent, normal and centre of curvature at a point on the curve 40 mm from the base line.

48 A generating circle of 60 mm diameter rolls round the outside of a 150 mm diameter base circle. A straight line carrying two points passes through the centre of the generating circle. Point *A* is 20 mm and point B is 40 mm from the centre of the generating circle. Draw the loci of *A* and *B* through one complete revolution of the generating circle. Name the derived curves.

49 Repeat the requirements of question 48 but with the generating circle rolling round the inside of the 150 mm diameter base circle. Name the resultant curves.

50 Draw an epicycloid traced by a point on the circumference of a circle of 40 mm diameter rolling along a base circle of 100 mm radius.

On the same base circle draw a hypocycloid traced by a 40 mm diameter generating circle.

51 Draw the involute of a base circle of 70 mm diameter.

52 Draw two convolutions of an Archimedean spiral of minimum radius 20 mm and maximum radius 92 mm.

53 Draw one convolution of a logarithmic spiral having a ratio of 5:6 between radius vectors enclosing 30°, the shortest vector being 20 mm.

54 A straight line carrying two points passes through the centre of a generating circle. Point *A* is 25 mm and point *B* is 45 mm from the centre of the circle. Draw and name the curves traced by the two points as the generating circle, of 30 mm radius, rolls one complete revolution along a straight line.

55 A circle makes four complete revolutions when rolling round the outside of a 180 mm diameter circle. Draw the locus of a point on the circle as it makes one revolution. Name the resultant curve. Draw the tangent, normal and centre of curvature at the mid-point of the curve.

56 A 50 mm diameter disc rolls round the inside of a 250 mm diameter rim. Draw one lobe of the locus of a point *P* which is 15 mm from the centre of the disc. Name the locus.

57 Draw a rectangular hyperbola within a 150 mm square given that a point *P* on the curve is situated at 30 mm from one asymptote and 60 mm from the other.

58 Draw an ellipse within a parallelogram *ABCD* where *AB* = *CD* = 120 mm and *BC* = *AD* = 80 mm and angle *ABC* = 60°. Draw the normal and tangent from the mid-point on the curve between *A* and *B*.

GEARS

Fig. 134. If two cylinders are situated as shown and have some degree of pressure between them so as to maintain contact, then any rotating movement in one cylinder will be transmitted to the other by friction along the line of contact.

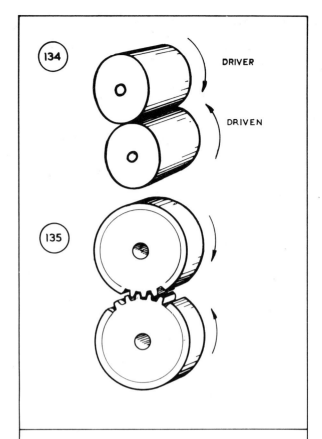

Fig. 135. It is obvious that the slightest loading applied to the driven cylinder will cause it to slip. To overcome this slipping, matching teeth are cut in both cylinders transforming them into a pair of meshing gear wheels.
(*Note:* If the driving cylinder is rotating clockwise then the driven cylinder will rotate anticlockwise, and vice versa.)

For reasons of economy in production (e.g. fewer cutting tools are needed, and these are of simpler shape) modern gear teeth are almost exclusively cut to an involute form.

The involute is a curve which is generated by rolling a straight line round a circle, where the end of the line will trace an involute. All involute gears, whatever the diameter, will run together providing they have the same pressure angle and diametral pitch.

To draw an involute

Method (fig. 136). Draw the base circle. Divide it into twelve equal sectors and number the lines. Draw tangents from each of the twelve cutting points around the circumference. Step off on each successive tangent the length of its corresponding base circle arc, i.e. on tangent *1* mark off a distance equal to the length *0* to *1* round the circumference; on tangent *2* mark off a distance equal to the length of the arc from *0* to *2*, and so on taking the tangents in due order. Join by a fair curve all the points so obtained to produce the involute (see also page 46).

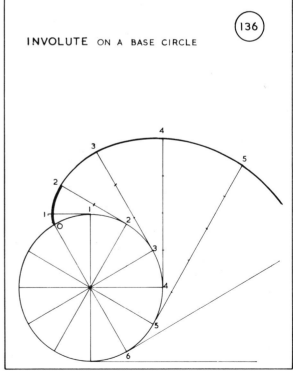

INVOLUTE ON A BASE CIRCLE

INVOLUTE GEAR TERMINOLOGY

The **pitch circle** (fig. 137) can be likened to the circumference of the original cylinder (fig. 134). It is the effective line along which the load is transmitted. Note that the teeth are cut partly inside and partly outside the pitch circle.

The **pitch point** (*P*) lies on the pitch circle and is the point of contact common to two gear wheels which are in mesh (running together).

The **line of action** passes through the pitch point and is tangential to the base circle, usually at the angle of $20°$ (very occasionally at $14\frac{1}{2}°$).

The **base circle** is concentric with the pitch circle and is tangential to the line of action. It forms the base for the construction of the involute.

The **addendum** is the height of the tooth outside the pitch circle (added to the pitch circle).

The **dedendum** is the depth of the tooth which lies below the pitch circle (deducted from the pitch circle).

The **outside diameter** (*OD*) is the diameter of the circle containing the tips of the teeth (this is the same as the addendum circle).

The **root diameter** is the diameter of the circle containing the roots or bottoms of the tooth spaces (this is the same as the dedendum circle).

The **clearance** is the space between the tip of a tooth and the corresponding root of the two meshing teeth on the other wheel. It is the difference between the addendum and the dedendum.

Circular pitch is the distance, measured round the pitch circle, between the centres of adjacent teeth.

Diametral pitch is the ratio of the number of teeth in the wheel divided by the diameter of the pitch circle in inches.

British module is the pitch diameter in inches divided by the number of teeth in the wheel.

Metric module is the pitch diameter in millimetres divided by the number of teeth in the wheel.

(*Note:* It is common practice to specify gears by either diametral pitch or by module.)

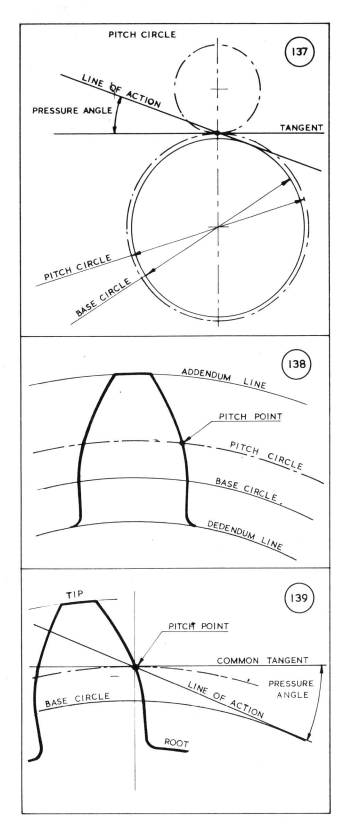

SPUR GEAR TERMS

PARTS	METRIC		IMPERIAL	
TEETH (No OF TEETH)	T	$\dfrac{PCD}{m}$	T	$PCD \times DP$
PITCH CIRCLE DIAMETER	PCD	$T \times m$	PCD or D	$\dfrac{T}{DP}$
DIAMETRAL PITCH		MODULE EQUIVALENT IS $\dfrac{25.4}{DP}$	DP	$\dfrac{T}{PCD}$
MODULE	m	$\dfrac{PCD}{T}$	m	$\dfrac{1}{DP}$
ADDENDUM	A	m	A	$\dfrac{1}{DP}$
DEDENDUM	D	1.157 m	d	$A + c$
CLEARANCE	c	0.157 m	c	$\dfrac{P}{20}$
CIRCULAR PITCH	p	$\dfrac{PCD \times \pi}{T}$	p	$\dfrac{\pi}{DP}$

Workshop drawings of gear wheels usually show the front elevation together with a cross-sectioned end elevation. It should be noted that the teeth flanks are never cross-hatched in the section drawing. The elevation includes the addendum, dedendum, and pitch circles.

Metric gear specifications usually give the number of teeth, the module and the pressure angle. British gear specifications usually give number of teeth, diametral pitch, and pressure angle.

The pitch circle is always drawn in thin long chain line because it is a centre line. It is common practice to show two teeth of one wheel meshing with three teeth of the other wheel, the remainder of both wheels being left in blank outline only. Other relevant tooth data should be given in tabular form.

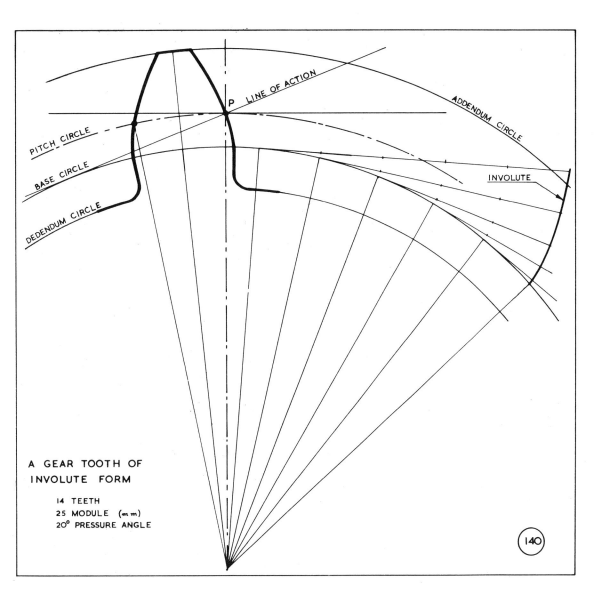

PITCH CIRCLE

BASE CIRCLE

DEDENDUM CIRCLE

P LINE OF ACTION

ADDENDUM CIRCLE

INVOLUTE

A GEAR TOOTH OF
INVOLUTE FORM

14 TEETH
25 MODULE (mm)
20° PRESSURE ANGLE

(140)

To draw a gear tooth of involute form

Method (fig. 140). Draw the vertical centreline (this would of course pass through the centres of both meshing gears). Draw a horizontal centreline. The intersection of both these lines forms the pitch point. Through this point draw the line of action (20° from horizontal). Calculate the pitch circle diameter (350 mm) and draw an arc of the pitch circle to pass through the pitch point. Draw the base circle tangential to the line of action. Calculate the addendum (25 mm). Add this to the radius of the pitch circle and draw an arc of the addendum circle. Calculate the dedendum (29 mm). Subtract this from the radius of the pitch circle and draw an arc of the dedendum circle.

Set out and draw an involute on the base circle as shown to the right of the drawing above. Copy this gear profile on to tracing paper including a section of the base circle to aid correct alignment of the tracing. Set the tracing with the gear profile passing through the pitch point and running from the base circle to the addendum circle. That part of the tooth flank which lies inside the base circle is a radius line. The corner between the tooth flank and the dedendum circle should be rounded off to a radius of 0.1 of the pitch. From the pitch point step off along the pitch circle an arc equal in length to half the circular pitch. Turn the tracing over and draw the other half of the tooth profile. Draw the flank along the radius line and round off the root corner as before. Line in the tip of the tooth along the addendum circle to complete the drawing.

INVOLUTE SPUR GEARS
INCH TERMINOLOGY

TWO TEETH ON THE PINION
MESHING WITH THREE
TEETH ON THE WHEEL

FOR METHOD OF DRAWING
SEE PAGE 53

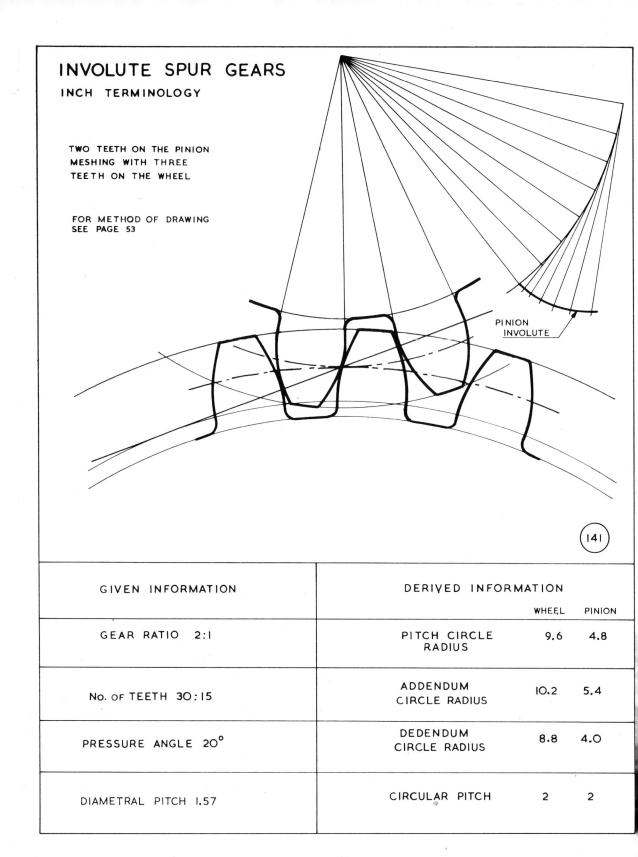

PINION
INVOLUTE

141

GIVEN INFORMATION	DERIVED INFORMATION	WHEEL	PINION
GEAR RATIO 2:1	PITCH CIRCLE RADIUS	9.6	4.8
No. OF TEETH 30:15	ADDENDUM CIRCLE RADIUS	10.2	5.4
PRESSURE ANGLE 20°	DEDENDUM CIRCLE RADIUS	8.8	4.0
DIAMETRAL PITCH 1.57	CIRCULAR PITCH	2	2

INVOLUTE SPUR GEARS
METRIC TERMINOLOGY

FOR METHOD OF DRAWING
SEE PAGE 53

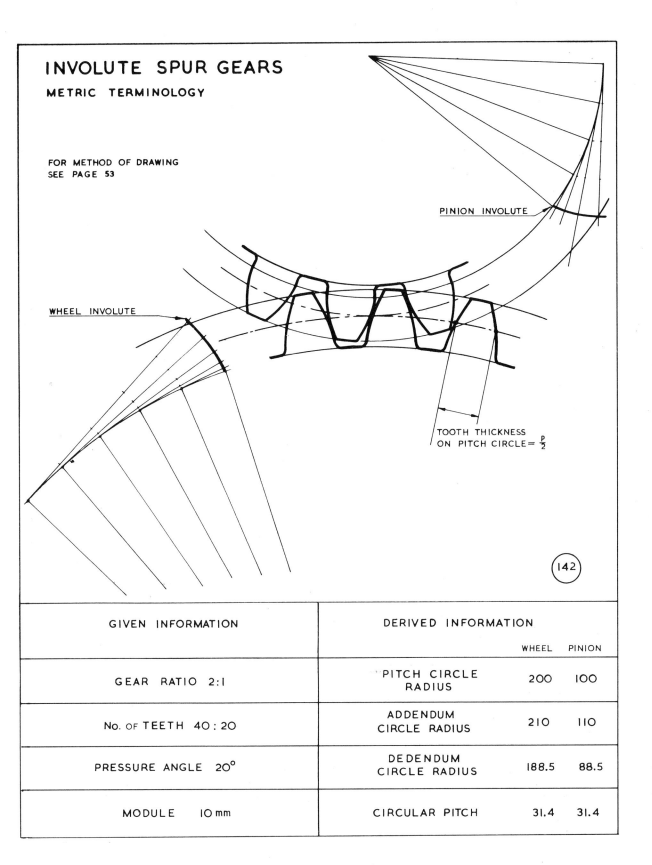

PINION INVOLUTE

WHEEL INVOLUTE

TOOTH THICKNESS
ON PITCH CIRCLE = $\frac{P}{2}$

(142)

GIVEN INFORMATION	DERIVED INFORMATION	WHEEL	PINION
GEAR RATIO 2:1	PITCH CIRCLE RADIUS	200	100
No. OF TEETH 40 : 20	ADDENDUM CIRCLE RADIUS	210	110
PRESSURE ANGLE 20°	DEDENDUM CIRCLE RADIUS	188.5	88.5
MODULE 10 mm	CIRCULAR PITCH	31.4	31.4

BEVEL GEARS

These are gears with sloping faces and are designed to transmit motion between shafts whose axes intersect. For simplification we can consider these gears as two cones held together under some pressure so that one will drive the other through surface friction (fig. 143). These cones can then become the pitch cones of the gears and the cone bases the pitch circles.

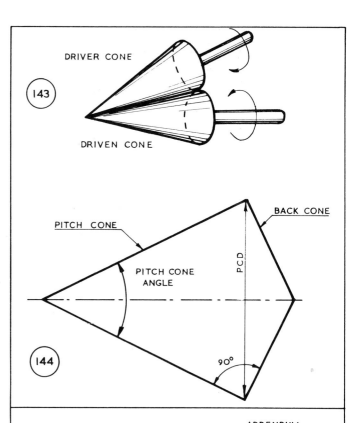

To draw a centreline cross-section of a bevel gear (*T* 24, *m* 5 mm, pitch cone angle 50°)

Method (figs. 144 and 145). Draw the centreline of the gear with the pitch circle diameter (120 mm) at right angles, and about these two draw the pitch cone. Draw the back cone making the generators of both cones form right angles (fig. 144). (*Note:* The true shape tooth profile lies on this back cone. This is because the addendum and the dedendum are always measured at the outer or larger end of the teeth.) Calculate the addendum (5 mm) and the dedendum (5.8 mm) and mark these off on the back cone, adding the addendum to the outside of the pitch cone and drawing the dedendum inside the cone. Draw lines from these points to the cone apex to give the tooth outline (fig. 145). Draw in the remainder of the gear outline and cross-hatch the section plane taking care not to section the teeth. (*Note:* In practice the face width is usually a quarter to a third of the slant height of the cone.)

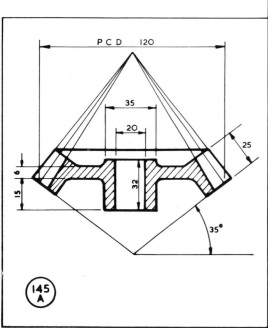

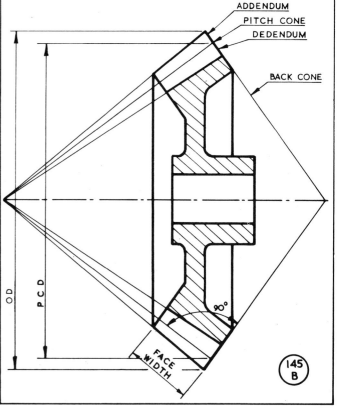

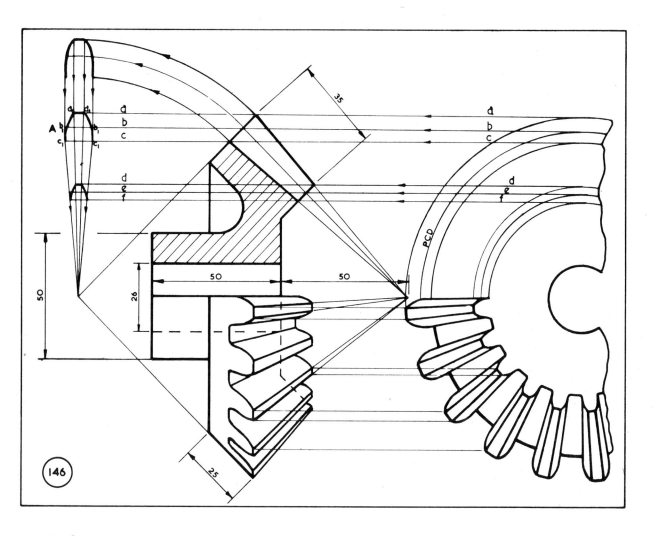

(146)

To draw a bevel wheel (end elevation in half section)

Given data

Given data	*Derived data*
T 20; m 6.5 mm	PCD 130 mm
Pressure angle 20°	A 6.5 mm; D 7.5 mm
Pitch cone angle 90°	CP 20.4 mm

Method (fig. 146). Start by drawing the sectional end elevation as detailed in fig. 144. Using the apex of the back cone, swing over the addendum, dedendum, and pitch circles as if drawing a development of the cone surface. Draw in the pressure angle and its tangential base circle. From this latter produce the involute tooth form. Draw horizontal projectors from the end elevation *abc* and drop vertical projectors from the true shape involute to produce the foreshort-ened view of the tooth profile at *A*. Repeat with the inner edge of the tooth *def*. Draw in projectors and from these the addendum, dedendum, and pitch circles. Step off alternate teeth and tooth spaces round the pitch circle making each of them equal to half *CP*. Transfer the widths of the tooth *A* (with dividers) from the lines a_1a_1, b_1b_1, c_1c_1 to the elevation and draw in the tooth profiles. Repeat similarly with the smaller ends of the teeth.

(*Note:* A bevel gear tooth has the same sectional profile, but on a diminishing scale from the outer to the inner edge.)

Line in the tips and the roots of the teeth. Project back the main points on the teeth profiles from the elevation to the end elevation as shown to complete the drawing.

Mitre bevel gear wheels

Identical bevel wheels for shafts which intersect each other at right angles are known as mitre bevel gears (fig. 147).

The involute rack

When a base circle is enlarged to infinite diameter its involute becomes a straight line. Therefore as the base of a rack is itself a straight line it follows that the sides of the teeth must also form straight lines.

Method (fig. 148). Set out the pitch line, the addendum and dedendum lines. Mark off along the pitch line distances equal to half the circular pitch of the mating gear. Using a pressure angle of 20°, draw the teeth flanks passing through the marked-off points. Round off the root corners.

Worm gearing

Worm gearing takes the form of a large coarse thread screw turning a spur gear wheel. This gives a large reduction in velocity and an increase in mechanical advantage. Worms may be single or multi-threaded and the axial section of the tooth is similar to that of the tooth in the involute rack (fig. 148). The mating worm wheel tooth section is of involute spur gear form.

The reduction ratio is given by setting the number of teeth in the wheel against the number of starts in the worm, e.g. a single start worm driving a 42 tooth wheel gives a reduction of 42:1; the same wheel driven by a three start worm gives a ratio of 14:1.

The basic outline of a worked example is given in fig. 149 (see pages 60 and 61 for the method of drawing the helix). Fig. 150 shows a completed drawing of a worm and wheel.

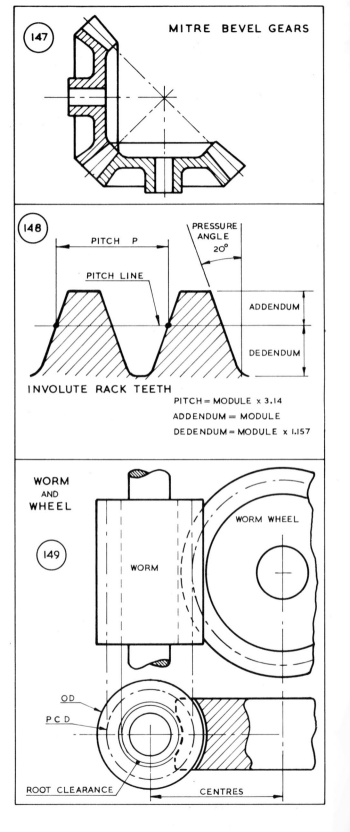

147 MITRE BEVEL GEARS

148 INVOLUTE RACK TEETH

PITCH P

PITCH LINE

PRESSURE ANGLE 20°

ADDENDUM

DEDENDUM

PITCH = MODULE x 3.14
ADDENDUM = MODULE
DEDENDUM = MODULE x 1.157

WORM AND WHEEL

149

WORM

WORM WHEEL

OD

PCD

ROOT CLEARANCE

CENTRES

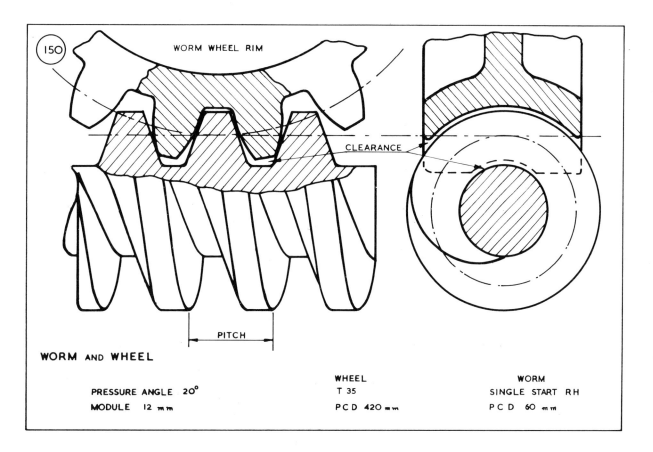

150

WORM WHEEL RIM

CLEARANCE

PITCH

WORM AND **WHEEL**

	WHEEL	WORM
PRESSURE ANGLE 20°	T 35	SINGLE START R H
MODULE 12 mm	PCD 420 mm	PCD 60 mm

EXERCISES

59 Draw two teeth of a spur gear and state the addendum and dedendum (*T* 20, *m* 15 mm).

60 Draw one tooth of a spur gear (*PCD* 10 in, *p* 2.1 in).

61 Draw three consecutive teeth of a spur gear and state the dedendum and addendum (*T* 15, *DP* 1.25 in).

62 Draw four teeth of a pinion (*T* 30, *m* 10 mm). Show them in mesh with an involute rack (draw five rack teeth).

63 Draw five meshing teeth of two spur gears which have a ratio of 2:1 (*T* 30:15, *m* 14 mm). Tabulate all relevant information.

64 Using the dimensions given on page 56 draw a bevel wheel (*T* 18, *m* 8 mm, pitch cone angle 40°).

65 Draw an elevation and sectioned end elevation of a bevel gear (*T* 25, *m* 8 mm, pitch cone angle 45°). Devise appropriate sizes for the shaft, boss, and thickness of the wheel blank.

66 Draw four threads of a single start worm (*p* 48 mm, *PCD* 65 mm, *m* 10 mm).

67 Draw a worm and wheel in a similar position to those shown on this page (*T* 30, *m* 12 mm).

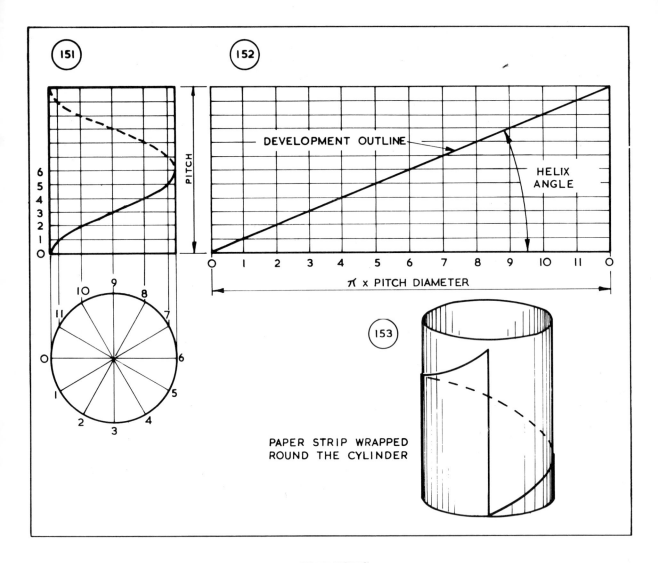

PAPER STRIP WRAPPED
ROUND THE CYLINDER

HELICES

A helix is the locus of a point which simultaneously moves along and around the surface of a cylinder. Both angular and linear velocities are uniform and they are in a constant predetermined ratio.

Pitch is the distance from a point on the helix to a similar point on the next revolution measured parallel to the axis.

Lead is the amount of axial advance during one complete revolution of the helix. In a single thread screw, or one start thread, the pitch and lead are identical. In a two start thread the lead is twice the pitch.

Hand. A helix may be either right-hand (rising towards the right) or left-hand (rising towards the left).

To draw one complete turn of a right-hand helix. Height of cylinder = pitch of helix = 60 mm.

Method (fig. 151). Draw the elevation and plan of the cylinder. Divide the plan circle into twelve equal sectors and project these as generator lines across the elevation. Divide the height of the cylinder into twelve equal slices. The intersection of generator *1* with slice line *1* will give the first point on the helix. The other sections taken in turn will give the line of the complete helix as shown.

Figs. 152 and 153 show the helix treated as a strip of paper unwound from the cylinder. This demonstrates that a helix is a curve of constant slope.

SCREW THREADS

Screw threads and springs are common engineering items which take the form of helices. In standard screws and bolts the thread profile is an equilateral triangle, with the sharp corners at the crests and roots of the threads rounded off for strength and smooth working. Threads carrying heavy loads, such as screw jacks, are cut to a square profile where the depth of the thread equals half the pitch. The first step in drawing an elevation of any screw thread is to set out a helix as follows:

Method (fig. 154). Draw a semicircle and project generators *0* to *6* to intersect the corresponding vertical divisions *0* to *6* which occupy half the lead. A fair curve drawn through these intersections will give the front elevation of one outside corner of the thread. Repeat the process for the other outside corner of the same thread. The root corners of the threads are similarly projected from the root semicircle. The whole process is then repeated for as many threads as are required.

Multiple threads

The amount of axial advance during one complete revolution of a screw is called the lead. In a single thread screw, or one start lead, the pitch and lead are identical. In a two start, or two thread screw, the lead is twice the pitch, in a three start it is three times the pitch and so on. When the design calls for a large axial movement it is common practice to cut two or more parallel threads on the one screw, as too much increase of pitch on a single thread would lead to a significant reduction in root diameter and thus produce a weakened screw.

The multi-start thread (fig. 155) is drawn by the same method as the single start thread (fig. 154).

Note how the root corners run out of view and reappear on the centreline.

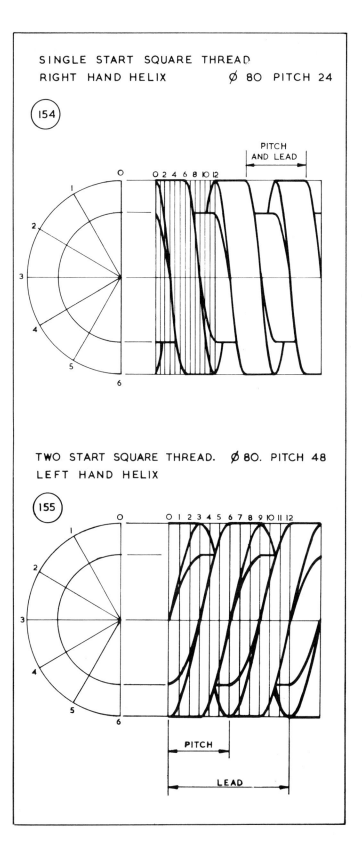

SINGLE START SQUARE THREAD
RIGHT HAND HELIX   ∅ 80 PITCH 24

154

PITCH AND LEAD

TWO START SQUARE THREAD.   ∅ 80. PITCH 48
LEFT HAND HELIX

155

PITCH

LEAD

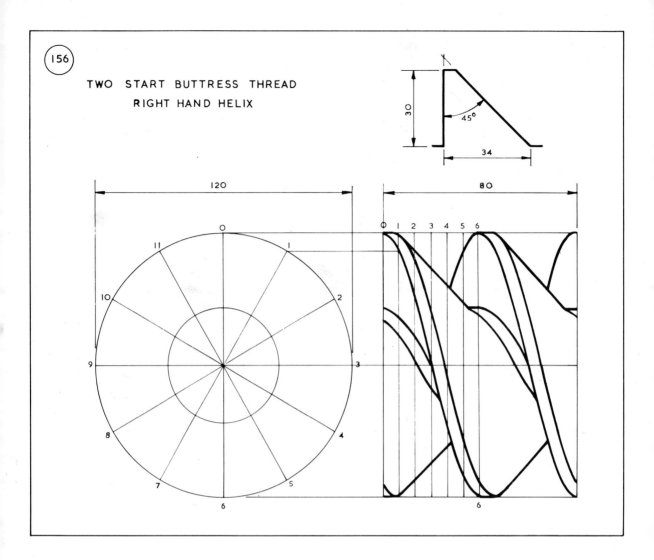

Buttress threads

When screws have to transmit heavy pressure in one direction only a thread profile similar to the one shown above is used. This is called a buttress thread. The sloping flank is designed to permit the easy withdrawal or disconnecting of the nut and a speedy repositioning along the screw as with engineers' parallel vices.

Method (fig. 156). Draw concentric circles of diameters equal to the outside diameter and root diameter of the screw thread. Divide the circles into twelve equal sectors. Project the outer diameter and draw an elevation of a length equal to the lead of the screw. Divide the elevation into twelve equal vertical slices and number them in a similar manner to the circles. Draw a projection line from the point where radius *1* cuts the outer circle to meet vertical slice line *1*. This gives a point on the helix described by the leading outer edge. Repeat with the remaining intersection points and line in the curve from the top of line *0* to the bottom of line *6*. If all seven projection lines are then extended by a distance equal to the thickness of the flat crest of the screw, they will end in points along the parallel helix which is formed by the width of the screw crest. The two helical curves forming the root are similarly projected from the points where the sector lines cross the inner circle.

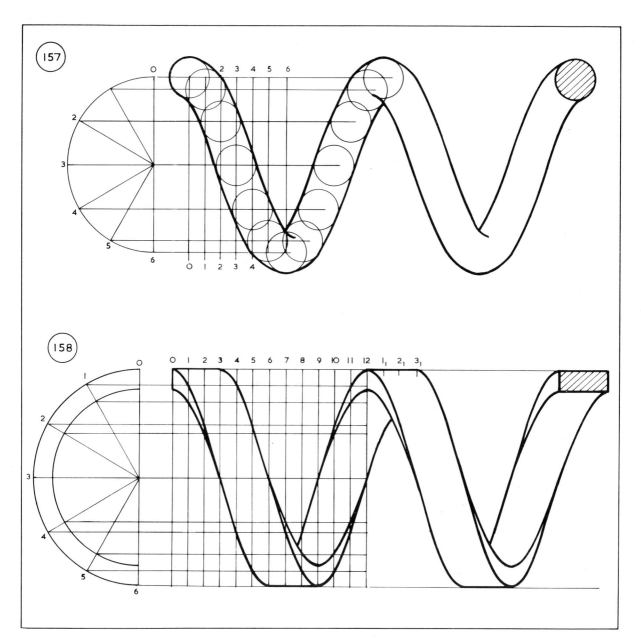

SPRINGS

To draw two coils of a spring which is right-hand wound from wire of 15 mm diameter, with a pitch of 72 mm and an outer diameter of 80 mm

Method (fig. 157). Draw the centreline of the wire as a helix. On this draw circles equal in size to the wire diameter about every point where the helix cuts the generators produced. Draw fair curves tangential to these circles to produce the outline of the spring.

To draw two turns of a spring which is right-hand wound from strip 18 mm × 8 mm with a pitch of 72 mm and an outer diameter of 80 mm

Method (fig. 158). Draw the first outer diameter helix through vertical ordinates 0 to 12 (one pitch). Draw a second helix parallel to the first from ordinate 3 to 3_1. Line in the flat outer surface, top and bottom, of the spring. Project the inner helix from the inner semicircle. Note how the 'thickness' disappears on the centreline reappearing on the opposite side of the strip. Square section springs are drawn in a similar manner.

HELICOIDS

A helicoid is a surface generated by a straight line moving in contact with two co-axial helices.

To draw one convolution of a right helicoid to the given dimensions

Method (fig. 159). Draw the plan and divide into twelve equal parts. Draw an elevation of height equal to the pitch, and of width equal to the plan. Project the plan divisions to form generators on the elevation. Divide the elevation vertically into twelve equal parts. The point where division projector *1* from the plan cuts horizontal slice line *1* in the elevation lies on the outer helix. Draw all the projectors in turn and draw a fair curve through all the intersecting points so obtained. Repeat this procedure with the centre pillar. Project division lines from the same small circle in the plan to cut the horizontal division lines on the elevation of the pillar. Draw this second inner helix. Line in as shown giving due consideration to sight lines and hidden detail.
(*Note:* The generating line in a right helicoid is at right angles to the axis.)

To draw one convolution of an oblique helicoid to the same dimensions as in fig. 159 above, but with the generatrix at 60° to the axis

Method (fig. 160). Draw the centre pillar. Draw the generatrix at the top of the pillar inclined at 60° to the axis. Working from the outer end of this generatrix, step off the lead and draw the generatrix in the bottom position. Divide the lead into twelve equal slices and proceed to draw the outer helix by the method detailed above and on page 60. Repeat with the inner helix round the centre column starting from the inner end of the generatrix. Line in as shown giving due consideration to sight lines and hidden edges.

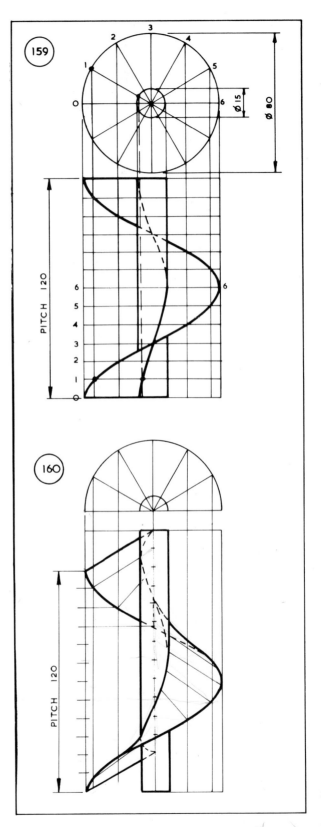

EXERCISES

68 to 71 inclusive

Draw an elevation and plan of one complete convolution of the helicoid generated by a straight line *AB* which is inclined at 30° to the horizontal (60° to the axis). In each exercise start the helix at the front centre of the base.

68 Left-hand helix; inner diameter 30 mm; lead 120 mm; *AB* 40 mm long.

69 Right-hand helix; inner diameter 50 mm; lead 96 mm; *AB* 60 mm long.

70 Left-hand helix; inner diameter 25 mm; lead 120 mm; *AB* 50 mm long.

71 Right-hand helix; inner diameter 20 mm; lead 96 mm; *AB* 50 mm long.

72 Draw an elevation showing two complete turns of a drive screw diameter 90 mm having a right-hand single start square thread (lead 24 mm).

73 Draw two complete turns of a two start square thread (diameter 90 mm; lead 48 mm).

74 Draw two turns of a right-hand wound coil spring (outer diameter 100 mm; lead 50 mm) made from 20 mm square section steel.

75 Draw to a scale of 1:20 a right-hand spiral conveyor elevator designed to carry parcels from the ground floor to the first floor (a height of 3 m). The conveyor (width 1 m) covers this distance in three complete convolutions. A guard (vertical height 200 mm) is fitted to the outer edge. The centre support column is 1 m diameter.

76 Fig. 76 shows a centreline section through a grain elevator screw. Draw a completed elevation to a scale of 1:10.

77 Fig. 77 shows the plan and cross-section of an oblique helicoid (pitch 120 mm). Draw a complete elevation of the given solid including hidden edges.

78 Fig. 78 shows a cross-section of a splined shaft (outside diameter 80 mm). The splines are machined to form a right-hand helix (lead 200 mm). Draw a full size elevation of a part of the shaft (100 mm long). Omit hidden detail.

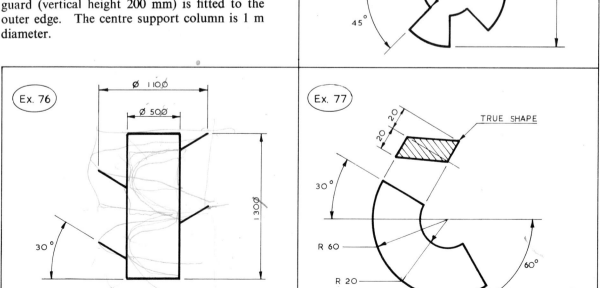

CAMS

Cams are machine parts that are specially shaped to convert rotating motion into reciprocating motion by causing a follower to rise and fall in a predetermined manner.

Cam operated valves are commonly used for the automatic metering of gases and liquids, and cams of all types are extensively used in textile and packaging machinery. The modern car engine incorporates a number of cams; the valves are opened by cams as shown in fig. 161; four- and six-lobed cams govern the spark distribution and many car petrol and oil pumps are cam driven.

DISPLACEMENT DIAGRAMS

Design requirements in the part of the machine under consideration will dictate the type of movement required in the cam follower. This is then translated into the profile of a cam which will give the follower the required motion. When designing this profile the movement of the follower is usually considered in four separate sections: the period when the follower is at the bottom of its movement, called the bottom dwell; the movement required during the rise or lift of the follower; the period when the follower remains at the top of its movement, called the top dwell; and the movement required when the follower returns to the bottom position. There are three different types of follower motion in standard use. The displacement–time graphs of these are given opposite and the explanatory details below.

Uniform velocity, UV (fig. 162)

The straight line slope shows that there are equal displacements of the follower during equal periods of time (equal angles of cam revolution). This type of motion produces abrupt changes of movement in the follower at the beginning and end of both rise and fall. This abrupt change is undesirable as it imposes strain on the mechanism. To overcome this the corners of the graph are rounded off thus giving a cam with a more gradual acceleration and deceleration at the ends of the follower movement.

Simple harmonic motion, SHM (fig. 163)

The displacement diagram is a sine curve and if a cam is produced from this curve only (i.e. devoid of top and bottom dwell) it will have

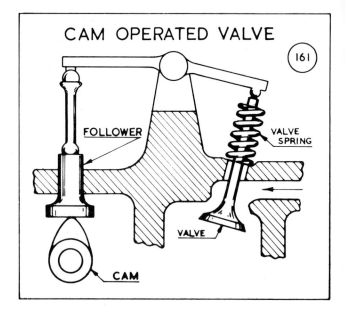

CAM OPERATED VALVE

161

FOLLOWER

VALVE SPRING

VALVE

CAM

lobes of circular form. Consideration shows that this type of cam will give the smoothest change of motion in the follower.

Uniform acceleration and retardation, UAR (fig. 164)

This displacement curve is parabolic. It gives a uniform rate of acceleration from the start to the midpoint and a similar uniform rate of retardation from the midpoint to the end of the movement.

When designing a cam profile it is usual to start with a displacement–time graph for the follower and then project this to the cam centreline and rabat the various points as shown on page 69.

Three such displacement graphs are shown on the opposite page, one for each of the three standard types of follower motion. In each case the diagram indicates a bottom dwell through 90° of cam revolution, a lift through 90°, a top dwell through 90°, and a fall to the bottom position through the remaining 90°. The base line can be of any suitable length that is readily divisible into twelve equal parts for simple cams, and twenty-four parts for more complex cams—120 mm is a useful size. The length of this line can then be taken to represent one revolution of the cam, and its divisions the appropriate number of degrees of turning movement. The height of the diagram is equal to the total lift of the follower movement. The construction of the lift and fall curves are self-explanatory and can be easily seen on examination of the three drawings.

FOLLOWER PERFORMANCE GRAPHS

162 UNIFORM VELOCITY

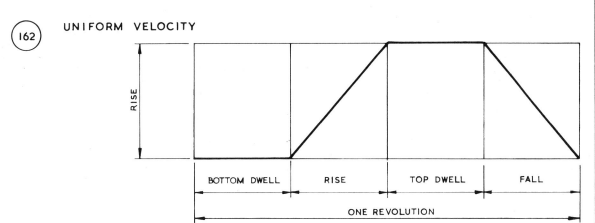

163 SIMPLE HARMONIC MOTION

164 UNIFORM ACCELERATION AND RETARDATION

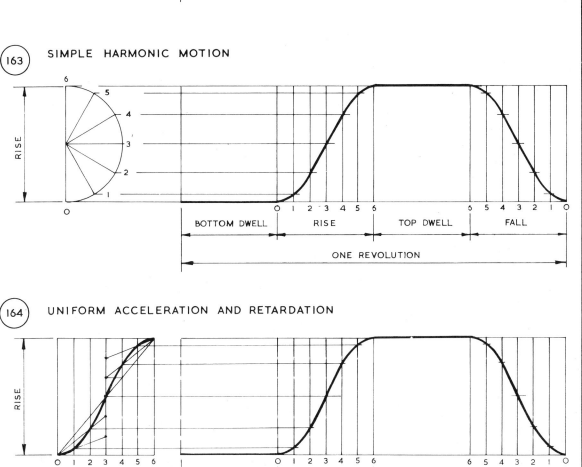

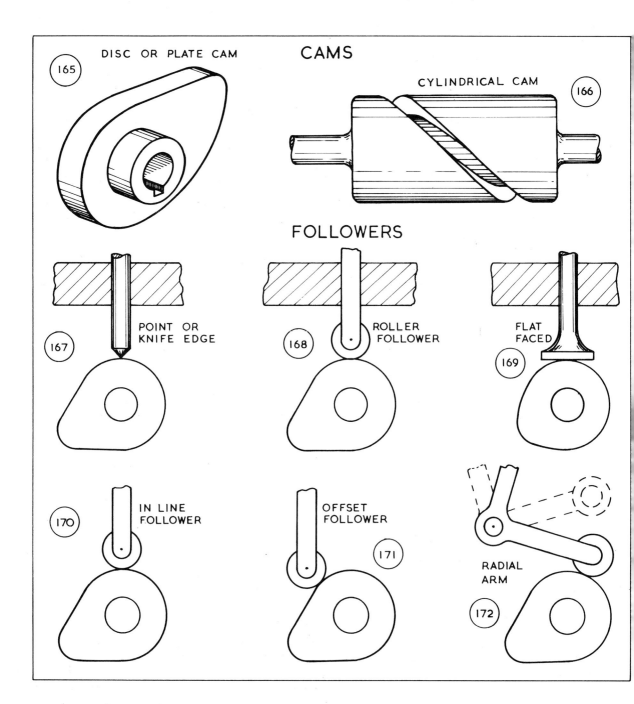

CAMS

DISC OR PLATE CAM
(165)

CYLINDRICAL CAM
(166)

FOLLOWERS

(167) POINT OR KNIFE EDGE

(168) ROLLER FOLLOWER

(169) FLAT FACED

(170) IN LINE FOLLOWER

(171) OFFSET FOLLOWER

(172) RADIAL ARM

TYPES OF CAMS AND CAM FOLLOWERS

Cams are of two main types: disc or radial (as in fig. 165) and cylindrical or drum (as in fig. 166). The follower is kept in contact with the cam either by its work loading or by spring pressure. If the follower has to move positively in both directions it is fitted with a roller end which runs in a groove or slot machined in the cam face.

Followers are of three types: roller ended, flat faced, and point or knife ended. All these types can be mounted in line with the cam centreline (as in figs. 167-9), offset (as in fig. 171) or mounted on a swinging radial arm (as in fig. 172). The knife end follower suffers rapid wear and is little used; a roller end reduces wear considerably.

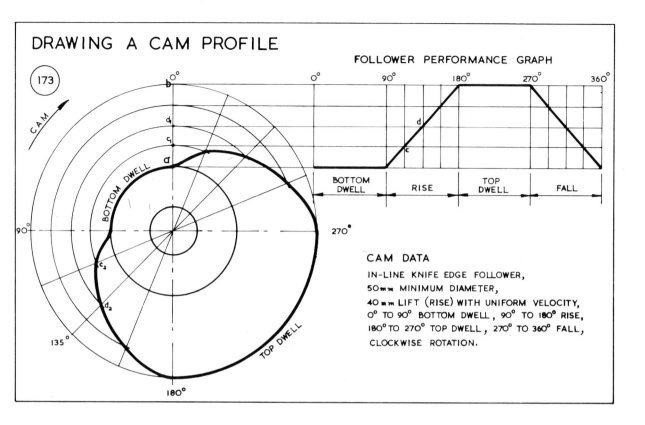

DRAWING A CAM PROFILE

173

CAM

FOLLOWER PERFORMANCE GRAPH

0° 90° 180° 270° 360°

BOTTOM DWELL | RISE | TOP DWELL | FALL

90°

135°

180°

270°

CAM DATA

IN-LINE KNIFE EDGE FOLLOWER,
50 mm MINIMUM DIAMETER,
40 mm LIFT (RISE) WITH UNIFORM VELOCITY,
0° TO 90° BOTTOM DWELL, 90° TO 180° RISE,
180° TO 270° TOP DWELL, 270° TO 360° FALL,
CLOCKWISE ROTATION.

To draw a cam profile to the given data

Method (fig. 173). Draw the two centrelines to position the cam drawing. Mark in the top and bottom limits of follower travel *ab* on the vertical centreline. Draw horizontal projectors of these points to establish the base line and the upper limit of the follower graph. Mark off a convenient distance along the base line or axis of the graph. This distance will represent one revolution of the cam (120 mm is commonly used, as this gives a scale of 10 mm to represent 30°). Draw verticals across the graph at any convenient spacing. Line in the top and bottom dwell on the follower graph and connect the ends of these lines by the specified motion curve (in this case, uniform velocity). Draw the maximum and minimum diameter circles about the cam centre. Divide these radially as required (twelve sectors of 30° for simple cams and twenty-four sectors of 15° for complex cams). Although in practice it is the cam which revolves, we can draw it in a stationary position only. Therefore, to maintain the correct direction of rotation, we must plot the follower moving in the opposite direction round the cam. Project the first increment of rise from a vertical on the graph to the vertical centreline of the cam. Using compasses, swing this point round to cut the appropriate radial division as c to c_1 and then to c_2 and d to d_1 and then d_2. (*Note:* The radial divisions on the cam and the vertical divisions on the graph both carry identical numbering.) Draw smooth curves through all the intersection points taken in due order. These curves should link up with the top and bottom dwell arcs to produce the cam profile. Sometimes the cam performance (follower displacement) is quoted on a time basis (number of revolutions in a given time). To draw a cam to this type of data the figures are converted arithmetically to give the proportion of rise, fall, and dwell in each revolution, and then the cam can be drawn to the method given above.

Roller ended followers

The cam (fig. 174) has similar basic data to the above but differs in the type of follower. The same method is used to set out the cam except that the base of the graph is set in line with the *centre* of the roller follower and the cam curve is drawn tangential to the series of plotted roller circles.

CAM PROFILE ROLLER FOLLOWER WITH SIMPLE HARMONIC MOTION

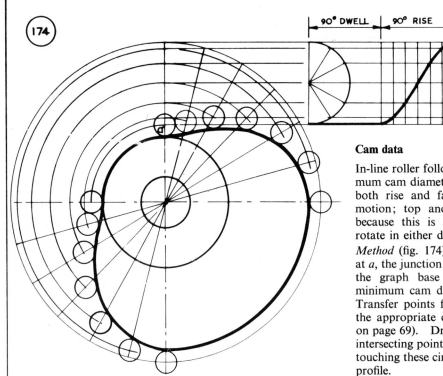

90° DWELL | 90° RISE | 90° DWELL | 90° FALL

Cam data

In-line roller follower, diameter 12 mm; minimum cam diameter 50 mm; total rise 42 mm, both rise and fall having simple harmonic motion; top and bottom dwell as shown; because this is a symmetrical cam it may rotate in either direction.

Method (fig. 174). Draw a 12 mm follower at *a*, the junction of the vertical centreline and the graph base line produced. Draw the minimum cam diameter circle touching this. Transfer points from the graph curve to cut the appropriate cam radial lines (as detailed on page 69). Draw 12 mm circles at all these intersecting points. Draw a continuous curve touching these circles to give the required cam profile.

CAM PROFILE POINT FOLLOWER WITH UAR AND UV MOTION

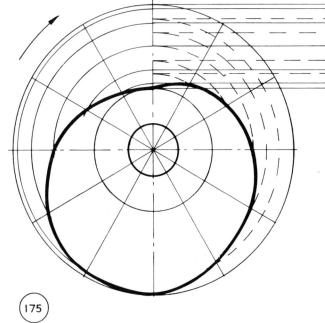

180° | 180°

Cam data

In-line knife edge follower; minimum cam diameter 50 mm; rise 42 mm through 180° with uniform acceleration and retardation; fall 42 mm through 180° with uniform velocity; clockwise rotation.

CAM PROFILE FLAT FACE FOLLOWER WITH UAR MOTION

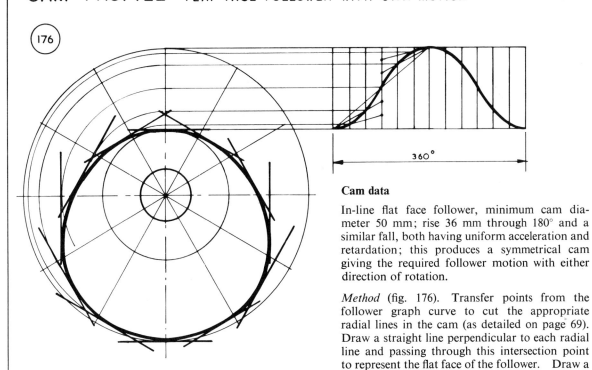

(176)

360°

Cam data

In-line flat face follower, minimum cam diameter 50 mm; rise 36 mm through 180° and a similar fall, both having uniform acceleration and retardation; this produces a symmetrical cam giving the required follower motion with either direction of rotation.

Method (fig. 176). Transfer points from the follower graph curve to cut the appropriate radial lines in the cam (as detailed on page 69). Draw a straight line perpendicular to each radial line and passing through this intersection point to represent the flat face of the follower. Draw a continuous curve to touch these lines and give the required cam profile.

3 CAMS THE THREE TYPES OF FOLLOWER MOTION COMPARED

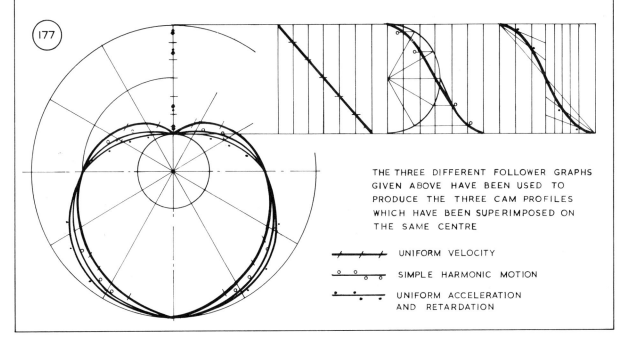

(177)

THE THREE DIFFERENT FOLLOWER GRAPHS GIVEN ABOVE HAVE BEEN USED TO PRODUCE THE THREE CAM PROFILES WHICH HAVE BEEN SUPERIMPOSED ON THE SAME CENTRE

———————— UNIFORM VELOCITY

———o——o——o——— SIMPLE HARMONIC MOTION

———•——•——•——— UNIFORM ACCELERATION AND RETARDATION

71

CAM WITH OFFSET FOLLOWER

Cam data

Minimum cam diameter 50 mm; bottom dwell 0° to 60°; rise 60° to 150°; top dwell 150° to 210°; fall 210° to 300°; and the remaining 60° bottom dwell; total lift 36 mm; uniform velocity; clockwise rotation; roller follower diameter 12 mm; offset 20 mm to the right of the cam centreline.

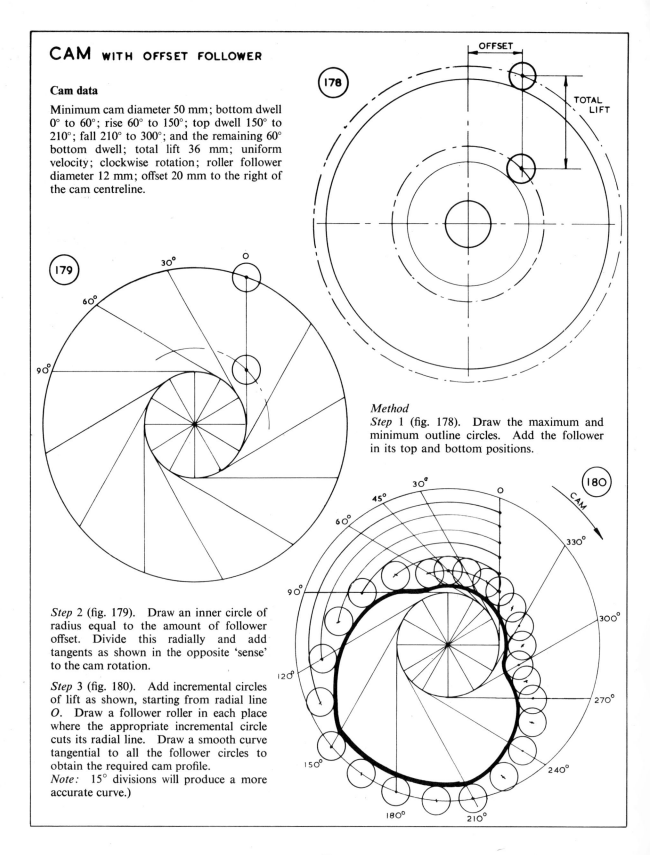

Method

Step 1 (fig. 178). Draw the maximum and minimum outline circles. Add the follower in its top and bottom positions.

Step 2 (fig. 179). Draw an inner circle of radius equal to the amount of follower offset. Divide this radially and add tangents as shown in the opposite 'sense' to the cam rotation.

Step 3 (fig. 180). Add incremental circles of lift as shown, starting from radial line O. Draw a follower roller in each place where the appropriate incremental circle cuts its radial line. Draw a smooth curve tangential to all the follower circles to obtain the required cam profile.

Note: 15° divisions will produce a more accurate curve.)

CAM WITH RADIAL ARM FOLLOWER

Cam data

Roller follower diameter 16 mm; mounted on a radial arm to the dimensions given in fig. 181; full lift of roller 0° to 180°; top dwell 180° to 270°; fall 270° to 360°; uniform velocity; clockwise rotation.

Drawing instructions are given on page 74.

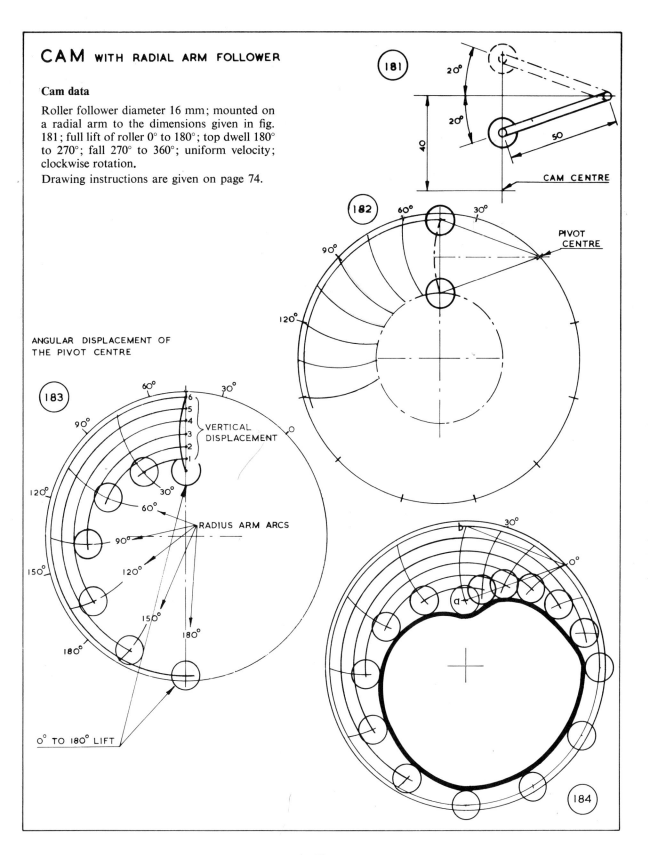

Radial arm follower (page 73)

Method (figs. 181 to 184). Set out the pivot centre and the top and bottom positions of the roller follower. Draw the cam centrelines (as detailed on page 69). Draw a circle concentric with the cam and passing through the pivot centre. Starting from the pivot centre, set out twelve equidistant positions and number them as shown. Using a radius equal to the length of the radial arm (50 mm), and taking each of these twelve points in turn,

draw twelve arcs as in fig. 182. Label them 0° to 360°. Divide the total lift of the follower roller into six equal parts as *1, 2, 3, 4, 5, 6* in fig. 183. From the cam centre strike off arcs from each of these six divisions to cut the appropriate radial arm arcs, e.g. *1* to 30°, *2* to 60°, *3* to 90°, and so on. Draw outline follower rollers centred about each of these intersections. Draw a fair curve tangentially to these circles to develop the cam profile.

Cylindrical cam

Method (figs. 185 and 186). Draw the elevation and end elevation and from these unroll a development of the cam surface. Set out the extreme ends of the follower roller. Divide the development into twelve strips each representing 30° of movement round the end elevation and the cam circumference. Number them as shown. Set out the path of the follower centre according to the given data. Draw a roller circle about each point where the follower movement centreline crosses a numbered generator line. Draw fair curves tangential to all these circles to give the follower groove along the development. Project the division lines from the end elevation to give generators on the elevation. Number these as in the development and end elevation. Project the points where the groove cuts the generators in the development up to the appropriate generator in the elevation. Draw a smaller circle in the end elevation using a radius equal to half the root diameter of the cam. Using the same radial dividers but projecting from the points where they cut the smaller circle, project across to the elevation to intersect the same vertical projectors used earlier. Join all the points so obtained in a fair curve to produce the line of the bottom edges of the groove.

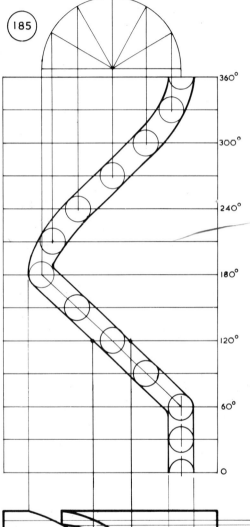

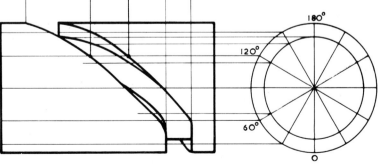

74

EXERCISES

UV = uniform velocity
SHM = simple harmonic motion
UAR = uniform acceleration and retardation

79 Draw a disc or radial cam to give the following performance: anticlockwise rotation; bottom dwell 0° to 150°; UV rise 150° to 210°; top dwell 210° to 270°; UV fall 270° to 360°. Minimum diameter 50 mm; total lift 40 mm; knife edge follower in line with cam centre.

80 Lay out a full-size cam profile to give an in-line follower of 20 mm diameter an SHM rise and fall of 50 mm from a minimum cam diameter of 40 mm.

81 An in-line knife edge follower is to rise and fall 45 mm from a minimum cam radius of 25 mm with UAR during one revolution of a cam. It is to have 30° dwell at top and bottom. Design the cam.

82 Draw a radial cam of 45 mm minimum radius to give a UAR lift and fall of 40 mm in one revolution. (Flat face follower.)

83 A roller ended follower of 20 mm diameter is displaced 25 mm to the left of the cam axis and is given a rise and fall of 60 mm with UV during one anticlockwise revolution of the cam. Draw the cam to include a 60° dwell about top and bottom centres (minimum radius 30 mm).

84 Design a clockwise rotating disc cam to give a 45 mm rise and fall from a minimum radius of 30 mm to a 20 mm diameter follower which is offset 18 mm to the left of the cam centreline. SHM 0° to 180°; UAR 180° to 360°.

85 Design a disc or plate cam to give a vertical rise of 45 mm to a 16 mm diameter roller which is carried at the end of a radial arm 60 mm in length (centres). (Minimum diameter of cam 30 mm; rise and fall SHM with a 30° dwell top and bottom.)

86 A cylindrical cam 50 mm in diameter and 90 mm in length carries a continuous groove 10 mm wide by 8 mm deep. This groove imparts SHM to a roller follower over a total lateral distance of 70 mm. Draw the development and elevation of the cam.

87, 88, 89, 90 Cam profiles are given below. All have 12 mm diameter roller followers. Copy the cam profiles and from these produce appropriate displacement diagrams.

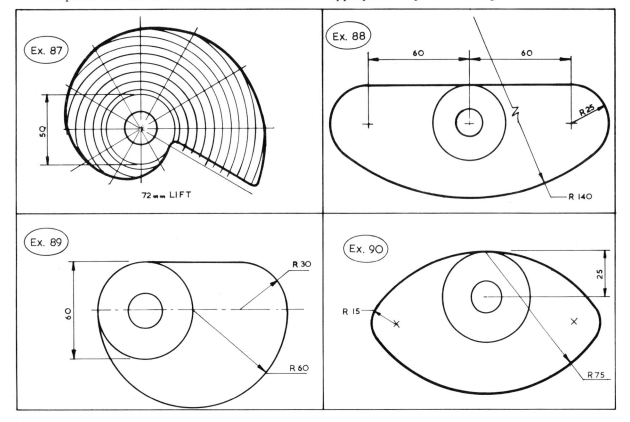

Ex. 87 — 50, 72 mm LIFT

Ex. 88 — 60, 60, R 25, R 140

Ex. 89 — 60, R 30, R 60

Ex. 90 — 25, R 15, R 75

DEVELOPMENTS AND INTERPENETRATIONS

A development drawing is a figure produced by unfolding the surfaces of an object and setting them down on one plane. All lines in a development show true lengths of edges and all surfaces show the true shape and size of the corresponding surfaces in the object.

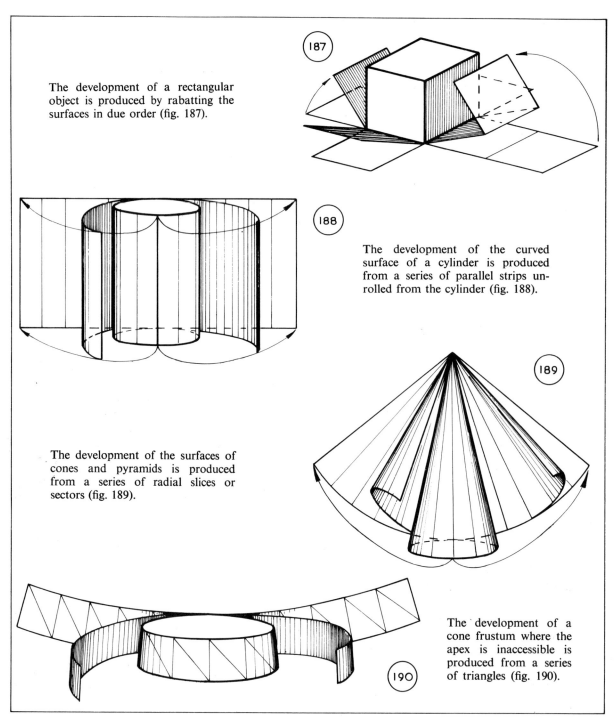

The development of a rectangular object is produced by rabatting the surfaces in due order (fig. 187).

The development of the curved surface of a cylinder is produced from a series of parallel strips unrolled from the cylinder (fig. 188).

The development of the surfaces of cones and pyramids is produced from a series of radial slices or sectors (fig. 189).

The development of a cone frustum where the apex is inaccessible is produced from a series of triangles (fig. 190).

DEVELOPMENTS: BASIC METHODS

Tray

Note that in this example the base is an irregular quadrilateral.

Method (figs. 191 and 192).   Draw the true shape of the base. Draw the two ends in position ensuring that the internal corners form right angles. From point *D*, using radius *DH*, and from point *A*, using radius *AE*, draw arcs to give the true shape of the right-hand side, again ensuring that the internal corners form right angles.   Repeat the same procedure with the left-hand side.   Note that the internal angles again are right angles.   Angles between sides, ends and the base are always right angles if the sides and ends are to be perpendicular to the base.

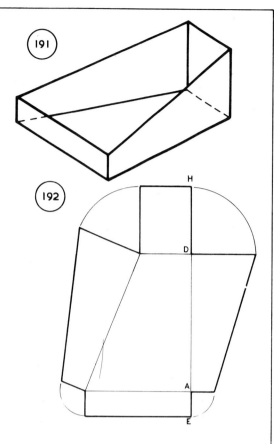

Right square pyramid

Method (figs. 193 and 194).   As the development of the sloping surfaces consists of four adjacent isosceles triangles, the easiest method is to develop first a cone.   But length *OA* in the elevation is not the true slant height.   Consider *OA* in the plan as the hypotenuse of a right-angled triangle with the right angle contained between a vertical line dropped from point *O* to the base and a horizontal one along the base to point *A*.   If this triangle is turned or rabatted about the vertical line until it is parallel to the vertical plane, and then projected to the elevation, it will give the true slant height at Oa_1.

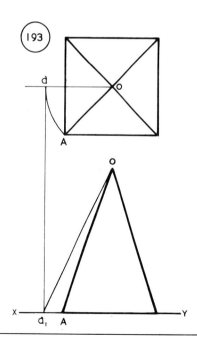

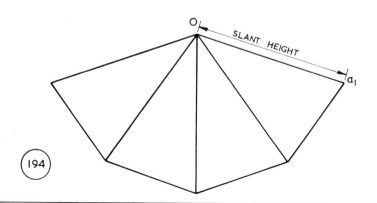

Right cylinder

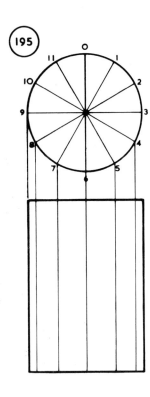

Method (figs. 195 and 196). Draw the elevation and plan of the cylinder. Divide the plan into twelve equal sectors. Number the radial lines. Draw vertical projection lines from these across the elevation. These are termed 'generators' because any one of them revolved about the centreline would trace, or generate, the curved surface of the cylinder. Project the elevation horizontally. Step off along the projectors twelve spaces equal in length to the chordal distances across the twelve arcs. This gives a development 1.1 per cent short but is acceptable for theoretical developments. Accuracy can be obtained by calculation using πD. The rectangle *OABO* is the development of the curved surface of the cylinder.

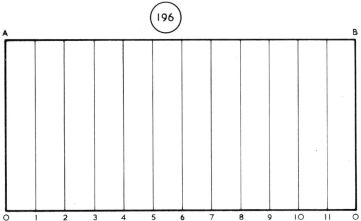

Right cone

Method (figs. 197 and 198). Draw the elevation and plan. Divide the plan into twelve sectors. Number the radial lines. Project them vertically to cut the base of the cone. Join these cutting points to the apex to form generators. The development of the curved surface is obtained by drawing an arc with radius equal to the *slant height* of the cone and length equal to twelve chordal distances taken from the plan circle.

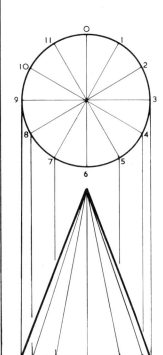

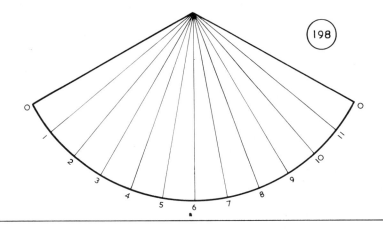

DEVELOPMENTS BY TRIANGULATION

True lengths of oblique lines

In this method the surface to be developed is reduced to a series of triangles, one side of each being usually concurrent with the base or top of the object. The true length of this side is obtained directly from the plan. The true lengths of the other two sides are found by rabatment from the plan. They are swung round in arcs to a line parallel to the *xy* line and projected to the elevation as shown.

Fig. 199 shows the elevation, end elevation and plan of a plane triangular figure which is parallel to both the horizontal plane and the vertical plane. The three sides of the triangle shown in the elevation are all true lengths.

Fig. 200 shows the elevation, end elevation and plan of the same triangular plane figure which has been tilted at 60° to the *VP*. Only the base line now displays its true length.

Fig. 201. It is easier to 'see' the true length of side *AB* if it is considered as the hypotenuse of a right-angled triangle which is turned, or rabatted, about the vertical line running from point *A* to the horizontal plane until it is parallel to the *VP* from *B* to b_1 and then projected to the elevation giving the true length at a_1b_1.

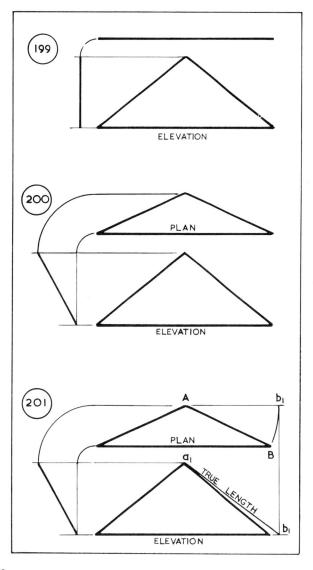

To determine the true shape of a triangular lamina sited in an oblique plane (third angle orthographic projection)

(*Note:* A lamina is a plane figure of negligible thickness.)

Method (fig. 202). With B in the plan as centre and BA as radius, draw an arc bringing A down to a on the xy line (parallel to VP). Project a to a_1 where it cuts a horizontal from A in the elevation. Join a_1 to B thus obtaining the true length of AB.

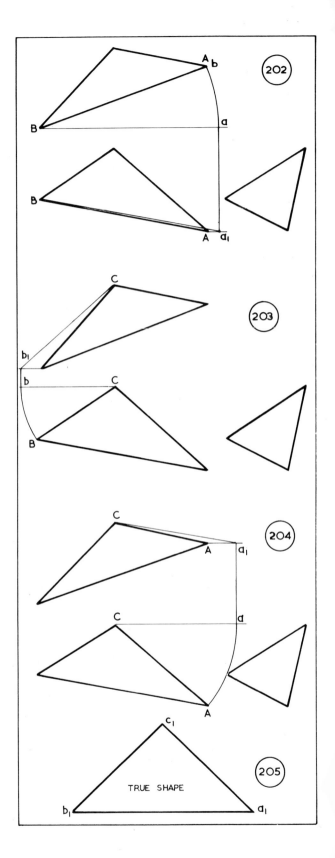

Fig. 203. With C in the elevation as centre, and CB as radius, draw an arc bringing B to cut a horizontal from C (parallel to VP) in b. Project b to b_1 in the plan where it cuts a horizontal from B. Join b_1 to C thus obtaining the true length of BC.

Fig. 204. Follow the same procedure as above with the line CA to obtain its true length.

(*Note:* Lines may be rabatted in either the plan or the elevation, whichever is the most convenient in any particular drawing.)

To draw the true shape

Method (fig. 205). Draw any line equal in length to a_1B in fig. 202. Using B as centre and b_1C from fig. 203 as radius, strike an arc b_1c_1 in fig. 205. Using a_1 as centre and a_1C from fig. 204 as radius, strike another arc cutting the first one in c_1. Draw lines joining b_1 and a_1 to c_1 to complete the true shape.

An alternative method is given on page 14 (fig. 39).

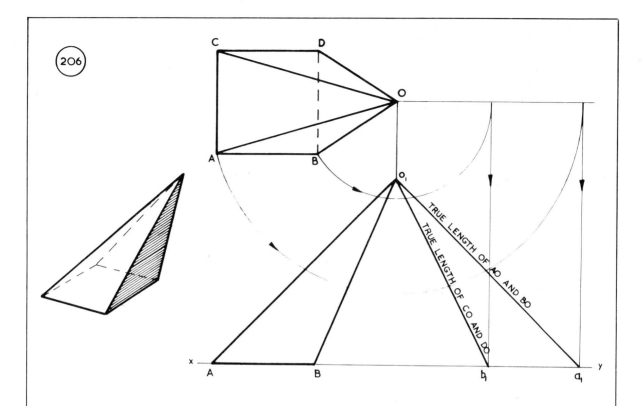

Oblique square pyramid

Method. The true lengths of the edges OA, OB, OC and OD are ascertained by rabatment from the plan. Consider each one as the hypotenuse of a right-angled triangle with the right angle contained between the base and a perpendicular from point O. Taking O in the plan as a centre, from points A, B, C, and D draw arcs to a line parallel to the VP and passing through point O. These rabatted points are then projected to the xy line and joined to O_1 giving the true lengths of the sloping edges. The true lengths of the base lines AB, BC, CD and DA are all taken direct from the plan. The *development* of the pyramid (fig. 207) is drawn by constructing the four triangular sides by the intersecting arcs method. From point O_1 step off the true length O_1d_1. From O_1 draw an arc at b_1 using the true length O_1b_1. Then complete the triangle by cutting this arc in b_1 by stepping off the true length DB. Follow the same procedure with the other three sides.

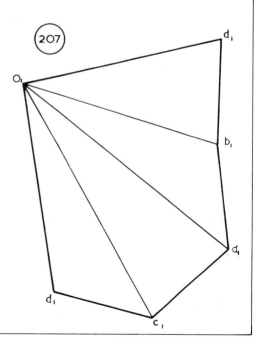

OBLIQUE SQUARE PYRAMID

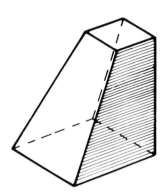

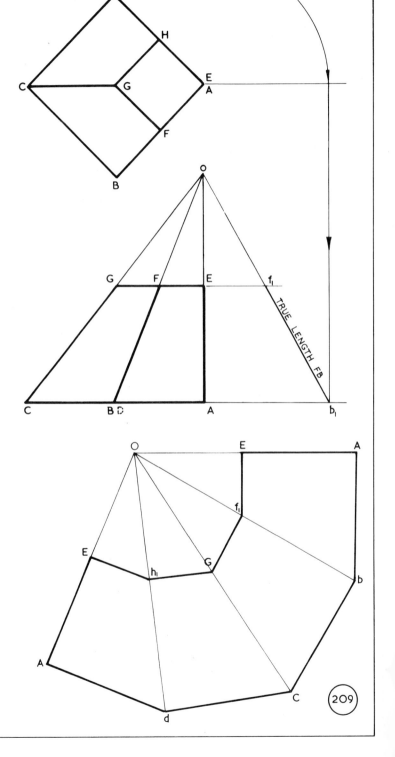

The basic method of development is similar to that given on page 77 (fig. 193).

Note that with this type of layout edges *CG* and *AE* are parallel to the *VP* and thus are of true length in the elevation. To obtain the true lengths of edges *FB* and *HD* rabat them as detailed on page 80. In this case swing *D* in the plan to the *xy* line from point *AE* with *AD* as radius. Drop a vertical to b_1 and join this to *O* as shown.

The *development* is built up by a series of triangles (fig. 209): draw line *OA* and step off distance *OE*; using point *A* as centre and *Ab* from the plan as radius, strike an arc at *b;* using *O* as centre and Ob_1 from the elevation as radius, strike a second arc to cut the first in *b;* draw lines from *A* and *O* to *b* to complete the first triangle; add the other three using the same construction and the appropriate dimensions; finally cut off from point *O* the relevant distances OG, Of_1, Oh_1, OE.

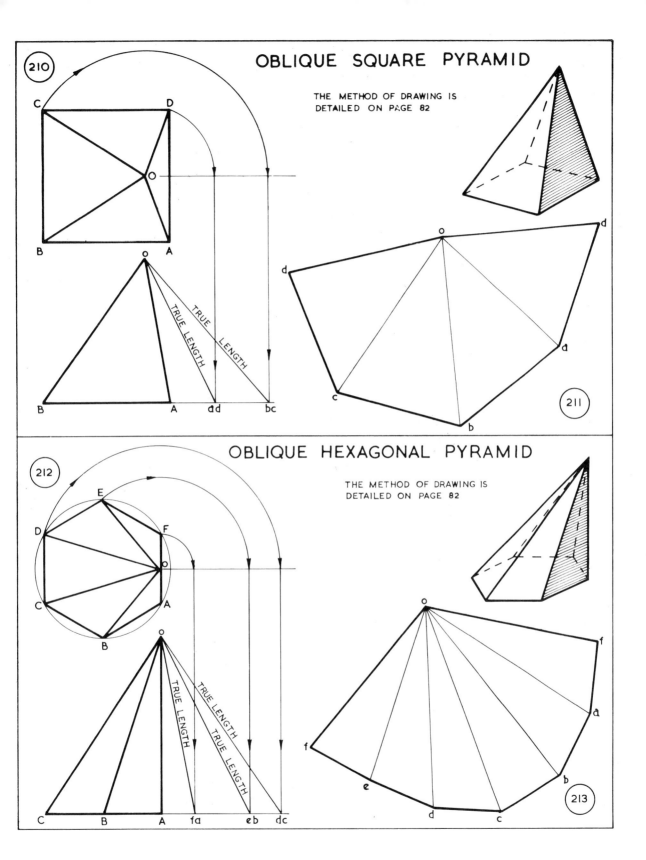

OBLIQUE SQUARE PYRAMID

THE METHOD OF DRAWING IS
DETAILED ON PAGE 82

210

211

OBLIQUE HEXAGONAL PYRAMID

THE METHOD OF DRAWING IS
DETAILED ON PAGE 82

212

213

OBLIQUE CONE

Method (fig. 214). Draw the elevation and plan, and line in the generators as detailed on page 78 (fig. 197).

Development: using *O* in the plan as centre, rabat the points where the generators cut the base circle as shown; drop vertical projectors from the plan centreline to the *xy* line and take these to the apex in the elevation to obtain the true length of each generator.

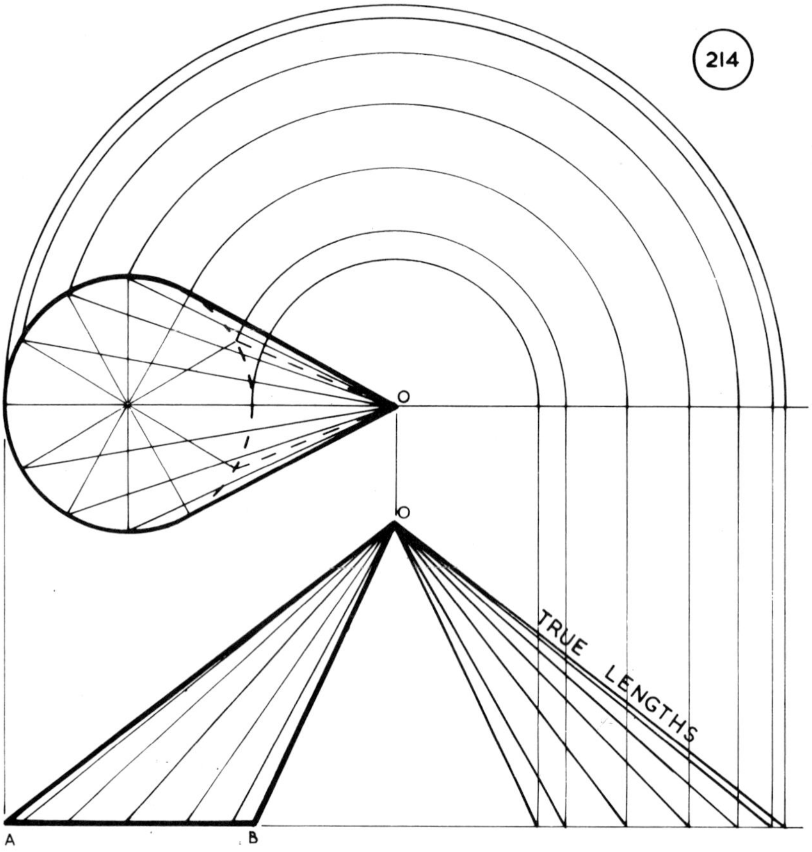

TRUE LENGTHS

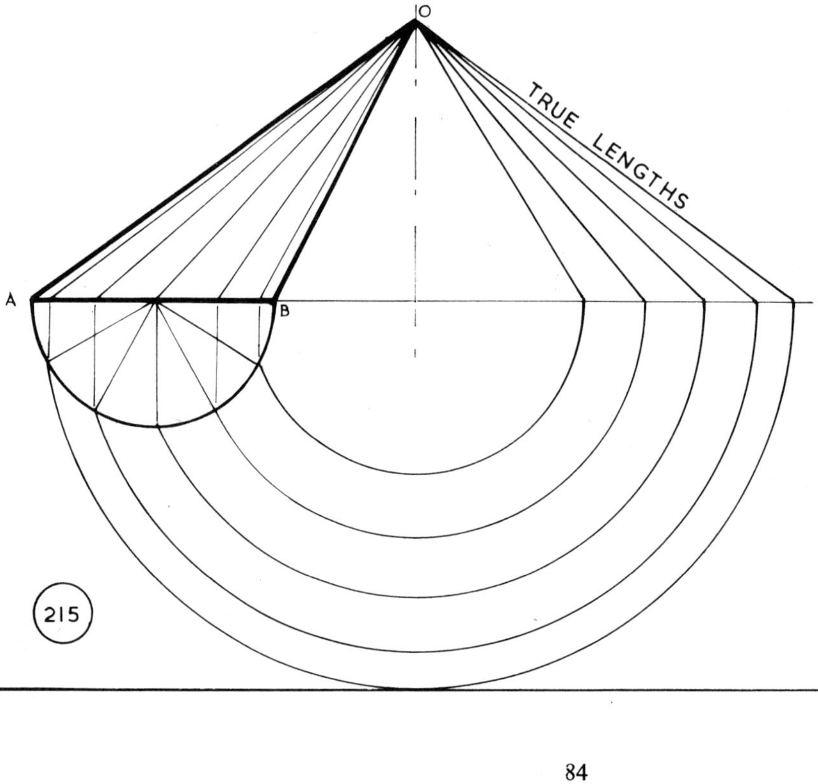

Fig. 215 shows an alternative and much quicker method of obtaining the true lengths of the generators although it is not so easy to 'see' the logical rabatment of the generators in this method. Note that in both drawings *OA* and *OB* are parallel to the *VP* and therefore display their true lengths in the elevation.

DEVELOPMENT OF AN OBLIQUE CONE

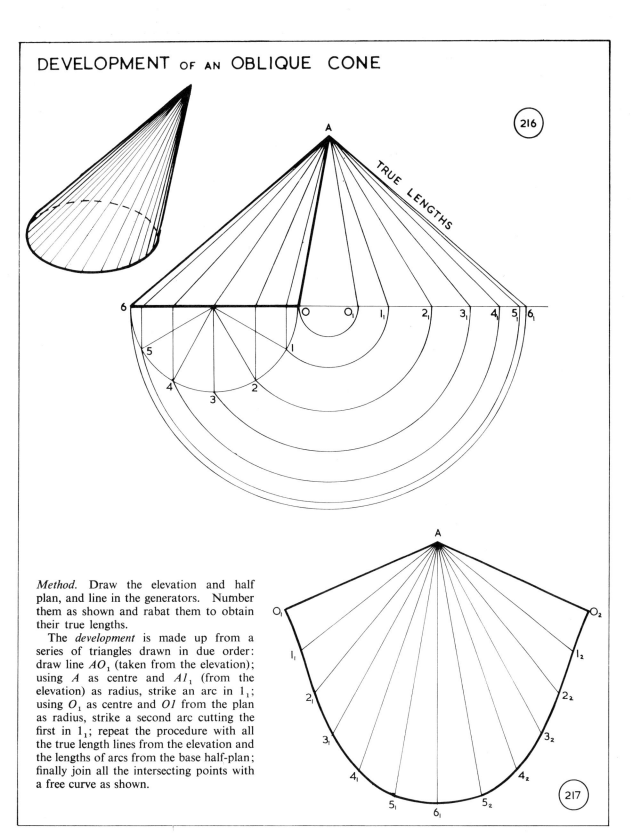

TRUE LENGTHS

216

217

Method. Draw the elevation and half plan, and line in the generators. Number them as shown and rabat them to obtain their true lengths.

The *development* is made up from a series of triangles drawn in due order: draw line AO_1 (taken from the elevation); using A as centre and $A1_1$ (from the elevation) as radius, strike an arc in 1_1; using O_1 as centre and $O1$ from the plan as radius, strike a second arc cutting the first in 1_1; repeat the procedure with all the true length lines from the elevation and the lengths of arcs from the base half-plan; finally join all the intersecting points with a free curve as shown.

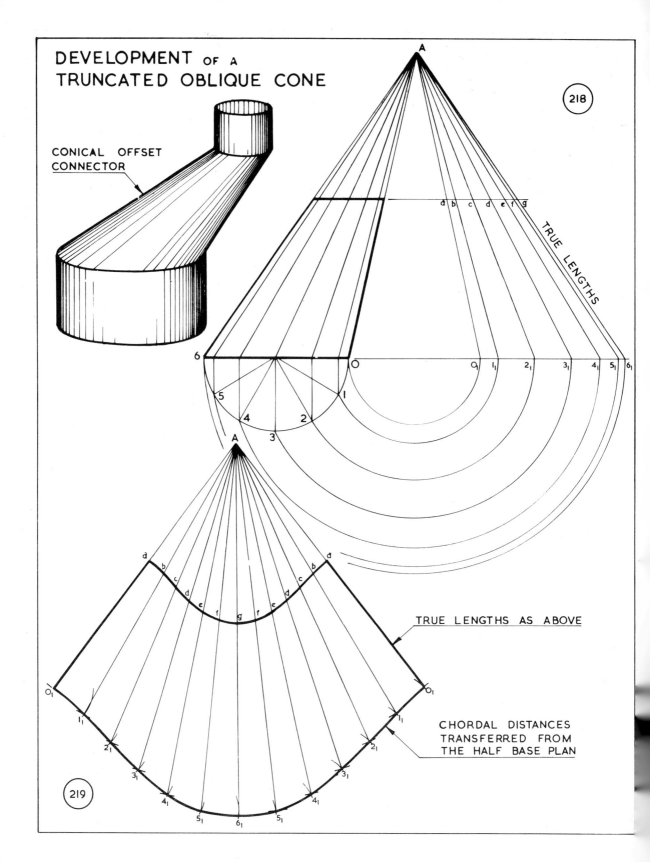

DEVELOPMENT OF A
TRUNCATED OBLIQUE CONE

218

CONICAL OFFSET
CONNECTOR

TRUE LENGTHS

219

TRUE LENGTHS AS ABOVE

CHORDAL DISTANCES
TRANSFERRED FROM
THE HALF BASE PLAN

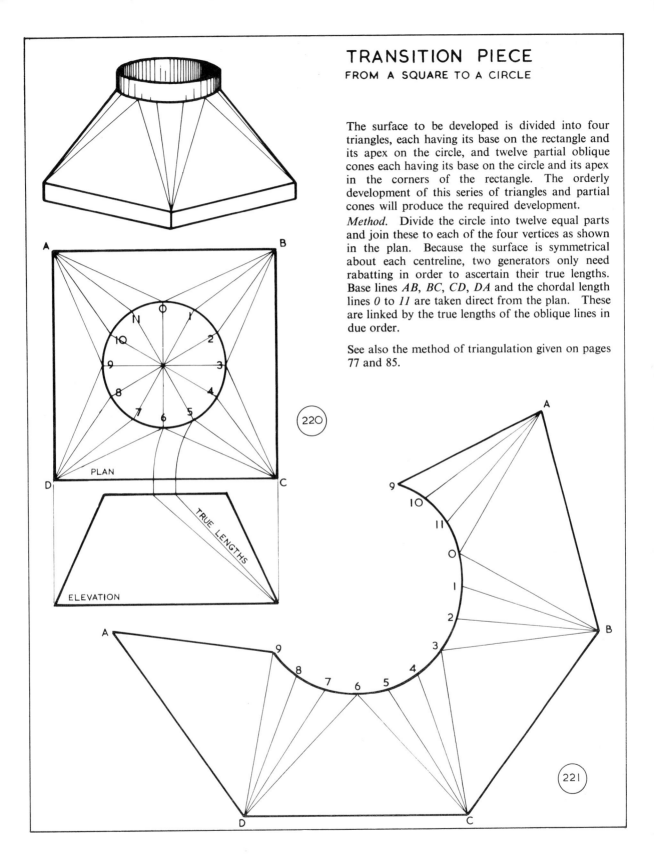

TRANSITION PIECE
FROM A SQUARE TO A CIRCLE

The surface to be developed is divided into four triangles, each having its base on the rectangle and its apex on the circle, and twelve partial oblique cones each having its base on the circle and its apex in the corners of the rectangle. The orderly development of this series of triangles and partial cones will produce the required development.

Method. Divide the circle into twelve equal parts and join these to each of the four vertices as shown in the plan. Because the surface is symmetrical about each centreline, two generators only need rabatting in order to ascertain their true lengths. Base lines *AB*, *BC*, *CD*, *DA* and the chordal length lines *0* to *11* are taken direct from the plan. These are linked by the true lengths of the oblique lines in due order.

See also the method of triangulation given on pages 77 and 85.

PLAN

TRUE LENGTHS

ELEVATION

220

221

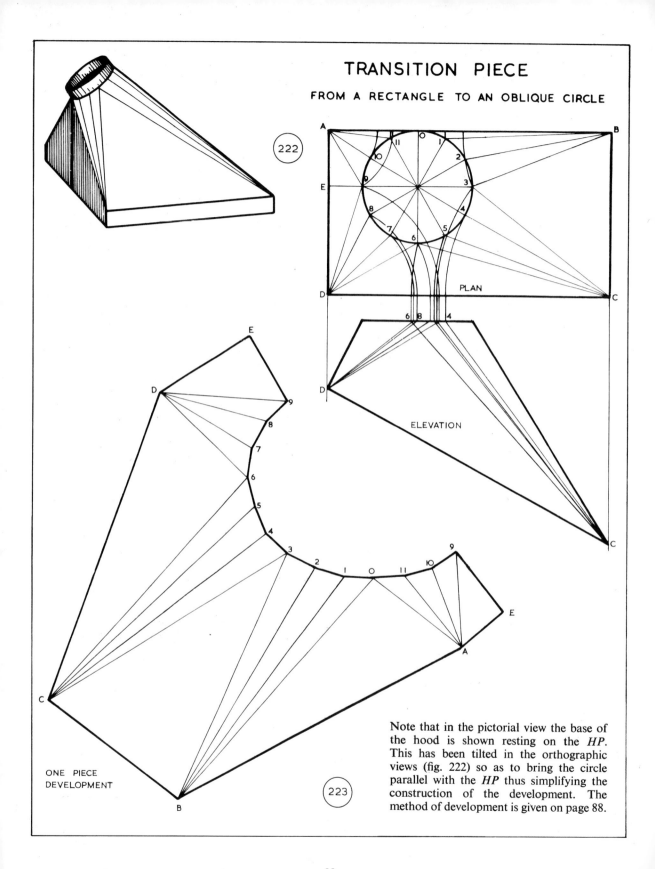

TRANSITION PIECE
FROM A RECTANGLE TO AN OBLIQUE CIRCLE

222

PLAN

ELEVATION

ONE PIECE
DEVELOPMENT

223

Note that in the pictorial view the base of
the hood is shown resting on the *HP*.
This has been tilted in the orthographic
views (fig. 222) so as to bring the circle
parallel with the *HP* thus simplifying the
construction of the development. The
method of development is given on page 88.

INTERPENETRATIONS

When any two or more prisms, pyramids, cylinders, cones or spheres intersect one another the development of their surfaces cannot be produced without first drawing the lines of intersection (interpenetration lines).

Lines produced by the interpenetration of any two prisms or pyramids are simply a series of connected straight lines. Each vertex of these interpenetration lines denotes the point where the edge of one prism penetrates the face of the other prism. It is custom- ary, therefore, so to arrange the drawings that they give the true shape end views of one or both of the prisms. Each point of intersection is in turn projected to the appropriate view where they are all linked together to produce the required lines of interpenetration.

In general, lines produced by the interpenetration of any two curved surfaces will be curved. The simplest general solution is to divide each true shape end view into a number of equal horizontal slices and project the cut widths of these two sets of slices to a common view where they will form a series of intersection points which can be linked to form the curve of interpenetration. Alternatively, the same method can be used with vertical radial slices in place of the horizontal parallel slices.

Square prism penetrating a right square pyramid

Method. Draw the elevation and plan. Add the end view of the square prism to give distance *BD* in the plan. In the elevation project vertical lines from *A* and *C* to cut the rib *O4* in a_1 and c_1. Project a vertical line from the intersection point *Y* in the elevation to cut the rib *O4* in the plan. From this point draw a horizontal section across the pyramid. The intersection of *BD* in the plan with this horizontal section plane gives the remaining points of intersection in b_2 and d_2. Join all these points of intersection with straight lines as shown to produce the lines of interpenetration.

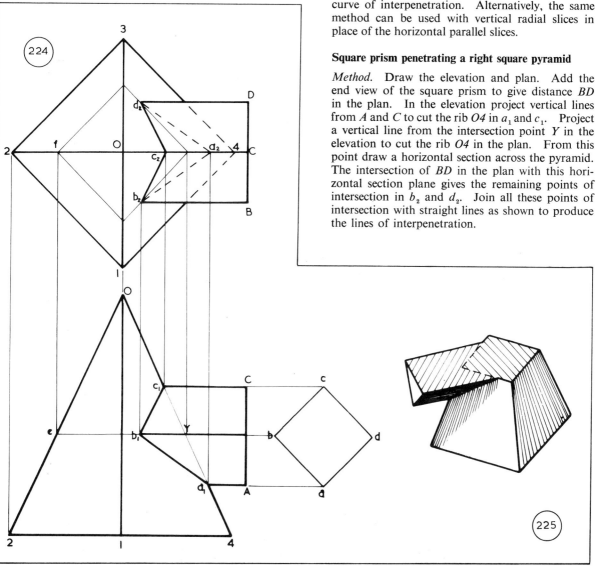

Square pyramid penetrating a hexagonal pyramid

Method. Draw the plan and elevation of both pyramids. Draw an auxiliary end elevation giving the true shape of the base of the square pyramid. Draw vertical projection lines from intersection points *A*, *B*, *C*, *D* in the elevation to give the corresponding intersection points *a*, *b*, *c*, *d* in the plan. On the plan draw a section taken horizontally across the hexagonal pyramid from line *A'A*. This will give the points in the plan where the front and rear edges of the square pyramid *AA* and *AE* penetrate the hexagonal pyramid. These points can then be projected vertically to the elevation. To obtain the linking interpenetration lines where the square pyramid faces cross the edges of the hexagonal pyramid, project cross-sections *FF*, *GG*, *HH* of the square pyramid from the plan to the auxiliary view in *f*, *g*, *h*. Project the intersection points already obtained from the plan to the auxiliary view. Join each point in turn to the appropriate section corner. These lines will cross the edges of the hexagonal pyramid. Draw projection lines from these intersections to cut the same edges in the plan. Join the points thus obtained in the plan to give the lines of interpenetration. Project these points to the elevation to complete the drawing.

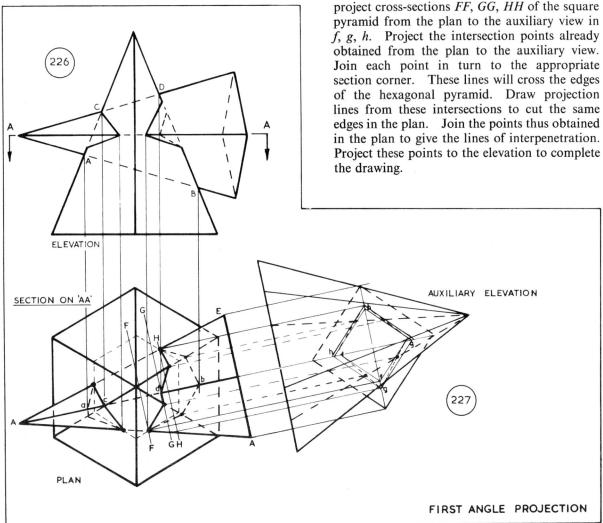

ELEVATION

SECTION ON 'AA'

PLAN

AUXILIARY ELEVATION

FIRST ANGLE PROJECTION

90

DEVELOPMENT of a CYLINDER

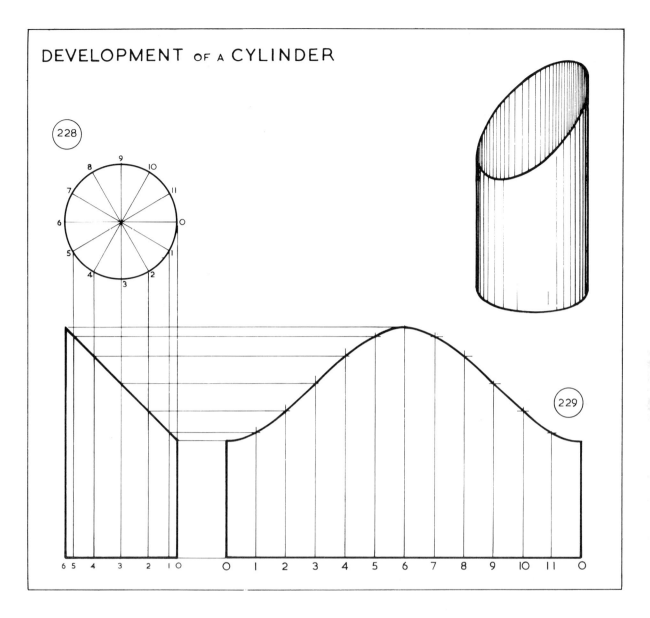

Method. Draw the plan and elevation. Project the overall height of the cylinder to form the basis of the development. Divide the plan into twelve equal sectors and step off the chordal distance of one sector twelve times along the development to give the 'stretchout' line. This method leaves the development 1.1 per cent short but is acceptable for theoretical work.

(Where the exact length is needed it should be calculated using the formula πD.)

Project the sector points from the plan across the elevation to give generators. Project the points where the generators cut the oblique face across to the appropriate generator in the development. Join these intersections by a fair curve to obtain the full development.

RIGHT ANGLED INTERPENETRATION OF CYLINDERS OF EQUAL DIAMETER

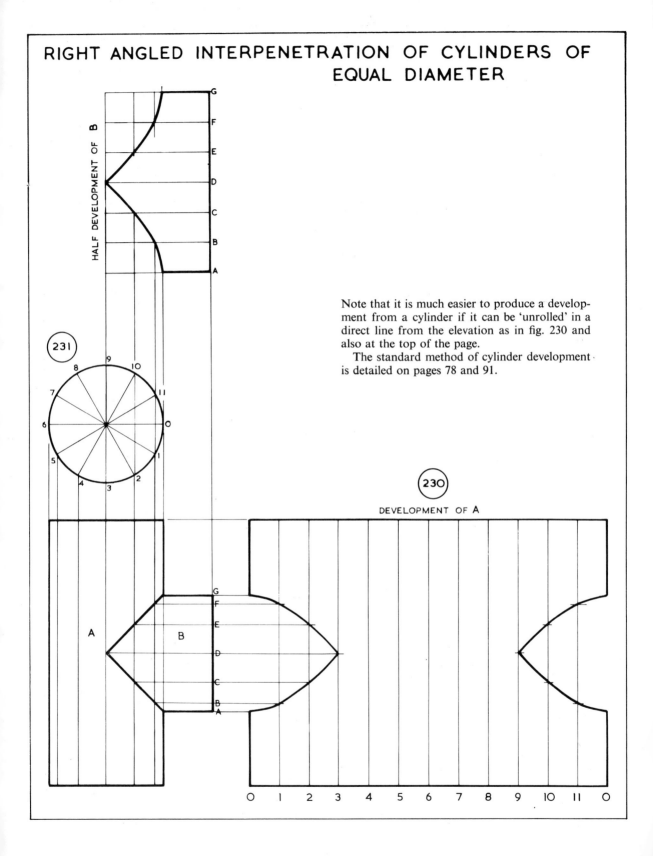

Note that it is much easier to produce a development from a cylinder if it can be 'unrolled' in a direct line from the elevation as in fig. 230 and also at the top of the page.

The standard method of cylinder development is detailed on pages 78 and 91.

INTERPENETRATION. CYLINDERS OF UNEQUAL DIAMETER

Alternative solutions

Method 1 — radial sectors (fig. 233). Draw the elevation, plan (which gives the true shape end view of the larger cylinder) and true shape end views of the smaller cylinder. Divide the latter into twelve equal sectors (six only are shown here). Number them *0* to *11*. Project the points *3, 4, 5, 6, 7, 8, 9* horizontally across to give generators in the elevation of the smaller cylinder. Project points *0, 1, 2, 3, 4, 5, 6* horizontally across to the plan in a similar manner. Take the intersection on the plan of generator *5* and the large circle and from this point draw a vertical projection line to cut the horizontal projection lines *5* and *7* in the elevation. Repeat with lines *0* and *6* in the plan to *6* in the elevation, and *2* and *4* in the plan to *4* and *8* in the elevation. Join all these intersections with a fair curve to obtain the curve of intersection.

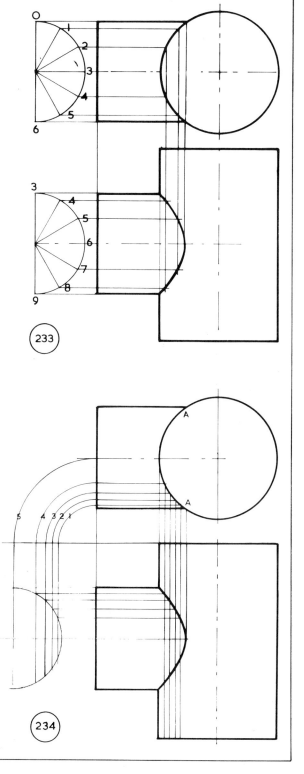

(233)

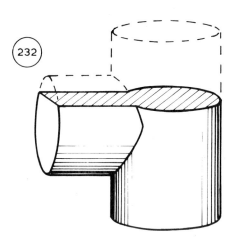

(232)

Method 2 — parallel slices (fig. 234). Draw the elevation, plan and true shape end view of the small cylinder. Divide the arc of intersection marked *A* in the plan into a number of parallel slices. These need not be of exactly the same width. Rabat these and project them to the true shape end view in *1, 2, 3, 4, 5*. Take horizontal projection lines giving the width of these slices across to the elevation. Draw vertical projection lines to cut these from the appropriate intersection points on the arc *A*. Join the cutting points in the elevation by a fair curve of intersection.

(234)

OFFSET CYLINDERS OF UNEQUAL DIAMETERS

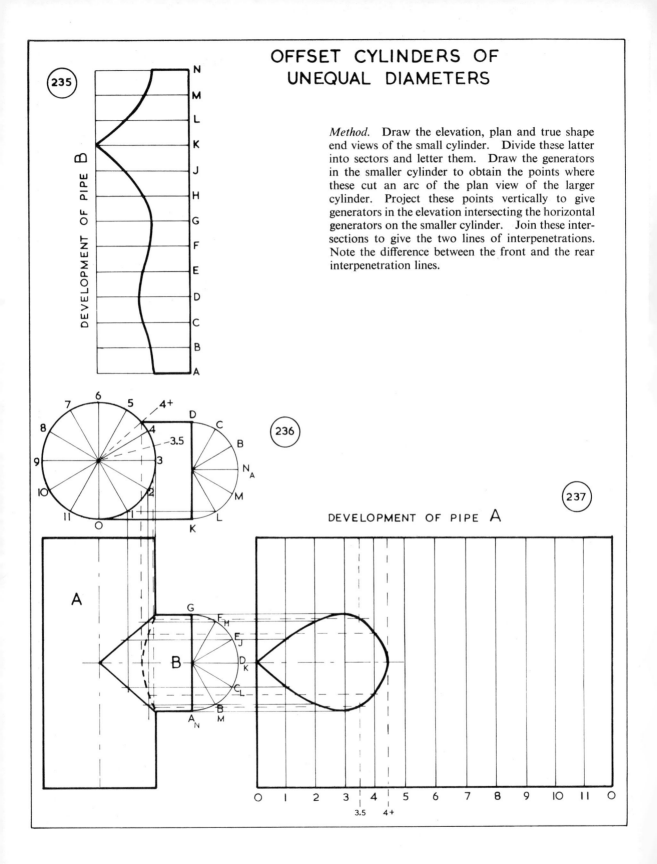

Method. Draw the elevation, plan and true shape end views of the small cylinder. Divide these latter into sectors and letter them. Draw the generators in the smaller cylinder to obtain the points where these cut an arc of the plan view of the larger cylinder. Project these points vertically to give generators in the elevation intersecting the horizontal generators on the smaller cylinder. Join these intersections to give the two lines of interpenetrations. Note the difference between the front and the rear interpenetration lines.

DEVELOPMENT OF PIPE B

DEVELOPMENT OF PIPE A

235

236

237

A

B

ANGLED CYLINDERS OF SIMILAR DIAMETER

Method. Draw the elevation and plan. Divide the plan circle into equal radial slices. Project these to form generators on the plan and elevation. The intersection of these in the elevation will give the lines of interpenetration: draw a vertical line through points *9* and *3* in the plan to give a generator in the elevation; project *9* and *3* horizontally in the plan to give K_1 and D_1 in the branch pipe; draw a vertical projector through these points to the oblique face at *D* and from there parallel to the sides of the branch pipe to cut the vertical generator giving one point of intersection at *x*. Set out the developments as shown using the intersection points obtained (as above and by the method detailed on pages 78 and 87).

DEVELOPMENT OF HALF BRANCH PIPE

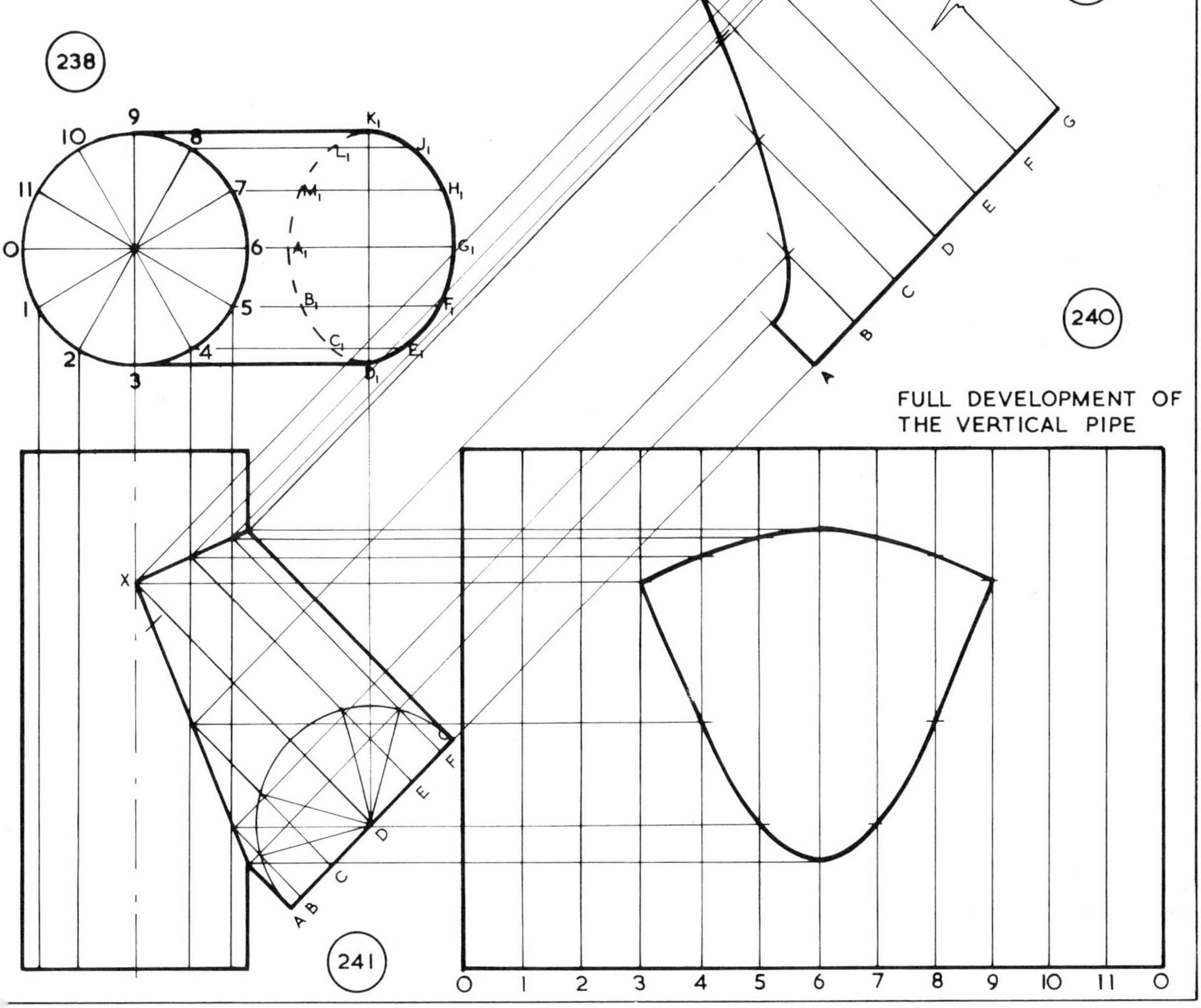

239
238
240
241
FULL DEVELOPMENT OF THE VERTICAL PIPE
0 1 2 3 4 5 6 7 8 9 10 11
K1 J1 H1 G1 F1 E1 D1 C1 B1 A1 M1 L1
A B C D E F G
X
0 1 2 3 4 5 6 7 8 9 10 11 0

CYLINDERS OF UNEQUAL DIAMETERS OFFSET AND ANGLED

Method. Draw elevation, plan and true shape end views of the small cylinder. Divide the small cylinder into twelve sectors. Number and project the generators horizontally in the plan and from there vertically across the elevation to cut the oblique generators giving intersection points. Join these points to obtain the curves of interpenetration.

Set out the overall shapes of the developments. Develop the oblique pipe by the method given on page 95. Divide the larger development into sixteen strips to the chordal distances taken from the plan circle. Project lettered intersection points from this plan circle vertically to the appropriate curve of interpenetration and from there horizontally across to the similarly lettered generator in the development. Join these points to obtain the development.

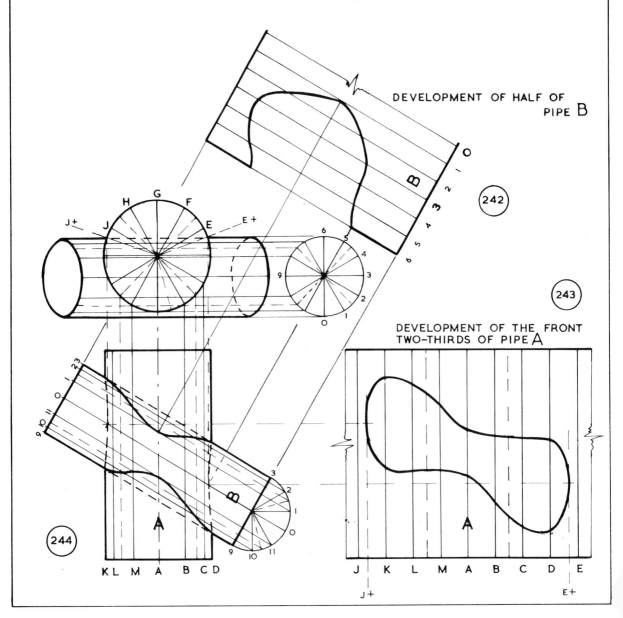

DEVELOPMENT OF HALF OF PIPE B

242

243

DEVELOPMENT OF THE FRONT TWO-THIRDS OF PIPE A

244

CONE PENETRATED BY CYLINDERS

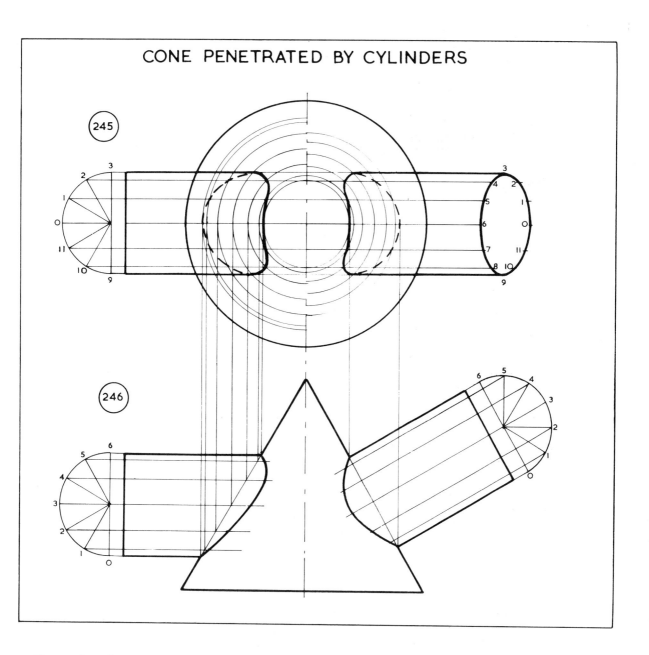

Penetration of a cone by cylinders, one horizontal and the other angled

Method. In both cases draw generators *1, 2, 3, 4, 5* on the cylinders. Erect vertical projection lines from all points where these generators cut the cone surface. Draw sectional circles on the cone plan from every point where these projectors cut the plan centreline. Intersecting points are obtained where these plan section circles cut the cylinder generators. Draw fair curves through these to obtain the plan view of the curves of interpenetration. Draw vertical projection lines from the same points to cut the appropriate cylinder generators in the elevation. These latter intersections will lie on the curves of interpenetration in the elevation.

CYLINDER PENETRATED BY A CONE

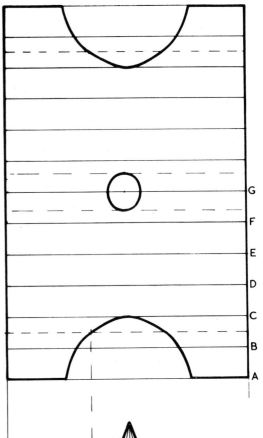

Method. Draw the elevation and end elevation. Add the cone generators projected from the half plans. Draw horizontal projectors to the elevation from the points where these generators cross the true end view of the cylinder. These horizontal projector lines cut the cone generators in the curve of interpenetration.

Development : draw the overall roll out of the cylinder; divide into suitable strips to match the intersections of the cone generators on the end view; transfer these cutting points from the end view to the front view and from there vertically to cut the appropriate strip lines in the development.

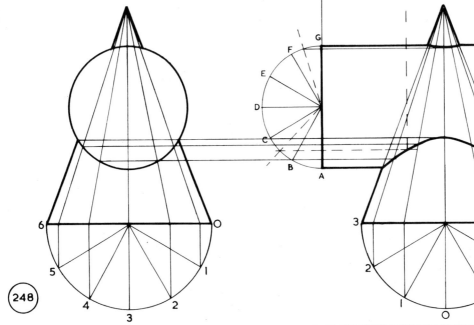

CONE PENETRATED BY A CYLINDER

In this worked example the curves of interpenetration have been established by a combination of the radial sector and the parallel slice methods detailed on page 93. The radial sector method has been used on all the generators except numbers *1* and *7*. It should be noted that it would be necessary to draw an end elevation to find these points of intersection by the radial method. It saves much time however if these two inter-sections are plotted by the horizontal slice method. This can be seen in the plan where the two points *1* and *7* have been rabatted parallel to the *VP* then projected to cut the outermost cone generators and finally projected from these to cut the centre generator numbered *1* in the elevation. Note that all true lengths of generators for the development are taken from these two outer cone lines.

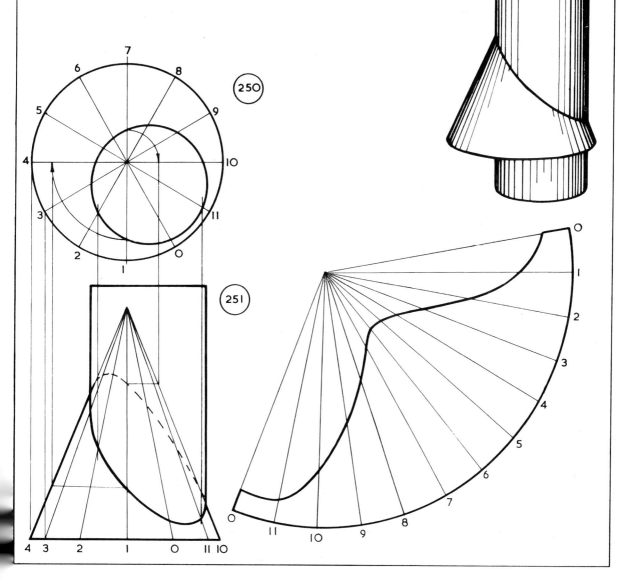

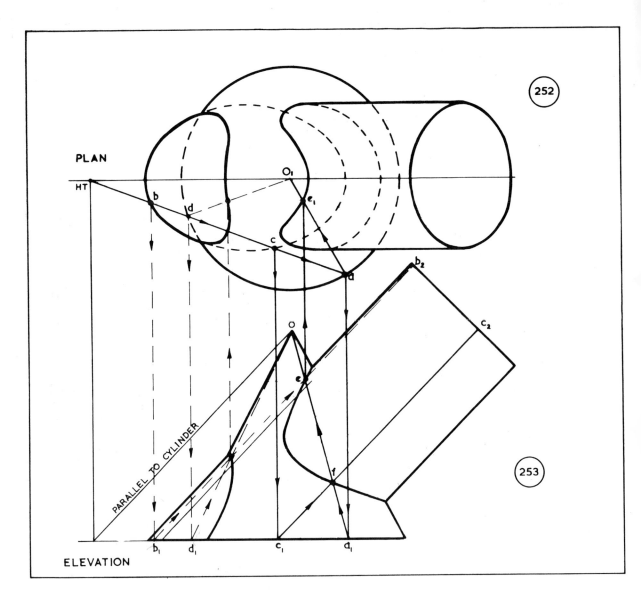

PLAN

HT

O_1

b

d

e_1

c

a

b_2

c_2

O

e

(252)

(253)

PARALLEL TO CYLINDER

f

b_1 d_1 c_1 a_1

ELEVATION

Inclined cylinder penetrating a cone

The curves of intersection pass through a series of points where radial cone generators intersect parallel cylinder generators.

Method. Draw the plan and elevation. Draw a line from the cone apex to the xy line parallel to the sides of the cylinder. This gives the HT. Transfer this to the centreline of the plan. From this point take a convenient number of radial slices, as $HT\,a$. This will be seen to cut the plan of the cylinder at b and c. It also cuts the plan of the cone at d and a. Project all these points to the elevation xy line, as

a to a_1, b to b_1, c to c_1, and d to d_1.

Cylinder generator c_1c_2 will cross the cone generator a_1O in two points on the curve of intersection as shown at e and f. Similarly, b_1b_2 crosses d_1O in one point. One radial slice only has been drawn from the HT to demonstrate the construction. About five more will be needed to complete the full curves in the elevation. To draw the curves in the plan, draw vertical projection lines from the elevation intersection points, as from e to e_1 cutting the cone generator line aO_1.

100

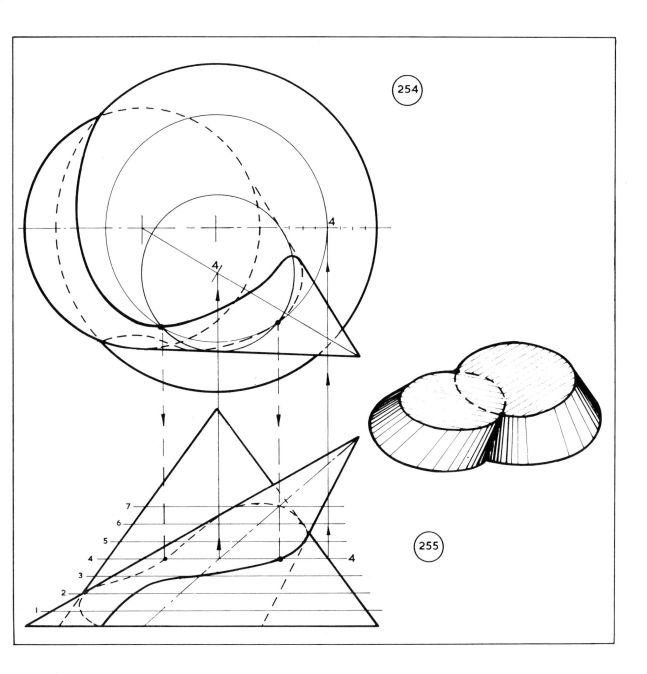

255

Oblique cone penetrating a right cone

Method. Draw the plan and elevation. Cut horizontal section planes across the elevation. Drop vertical projectors where these planes cut the surface of the right cone and draw plan circles of the section planes. Draw centrelines in both the plan and the elevation of the oblique cone. Erect projection lines from the points in the elevation where the centreline cuts the horizontal section planes to cut the centreline

of the oblique cone in the plan. Using these cutting points as centres and radius equal to half the relevant cone section (from the elevation) draw plan circles in the oblique cone. Note how the diameters of these circles diminish in regular amounts the nearer they approach the apex. The points where each pair of plan circles intersect lie on the curves of interpenetration. (This intersection of circular sections is shown in the perspective sketch.)

101

CONES WITH AXES AT RIGHT ANGLES

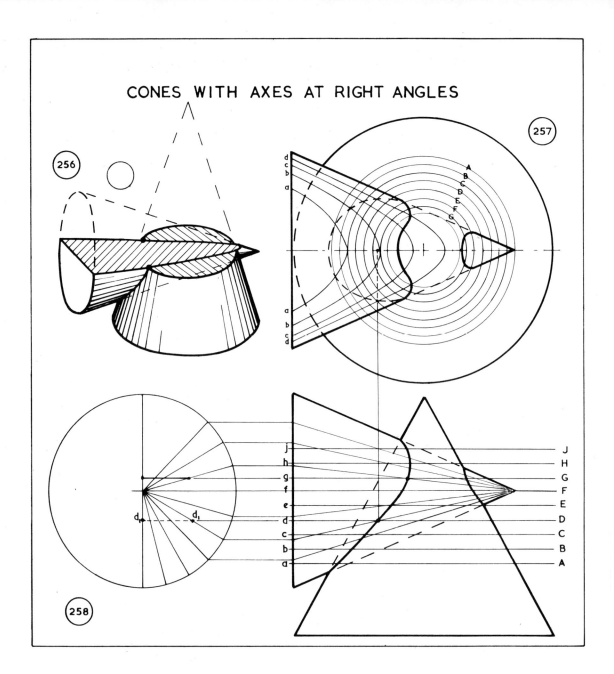

Horizontal slice method

Method. Draw the elevation and plan of the two cones. Draw a true end view of the base of the smaller cone. Divide this into a number of equal sectors and project these to give generators in the elevation. Divide the interpenetration zone in the elevation into a number of horizontal slices. (It facilitates later drawing if these slices are equally spaced on either side of the centreline.)

· When these slices are projected to the plan they appear as circles in the vertical cone and as hyper-bolas in the horizontal cone. Taking one slice at a time, the two points where the circle cuts the hyperbola both lie on the curve of intersection, as in the perspective sketch. A fair curve drawn through all the points so obtained will give the required curves of interpenetration in the elevation. To complete the corresponding curves in the plan take one horizontal plane at a time and erect vertical projectors to the plan from the points where the plane cuts the curves of intersection. These pro-jectors will cut the plan circle of the slice in the plan curves of interpenetration.

CONES WITH AXES AT RIGHT ANGLES

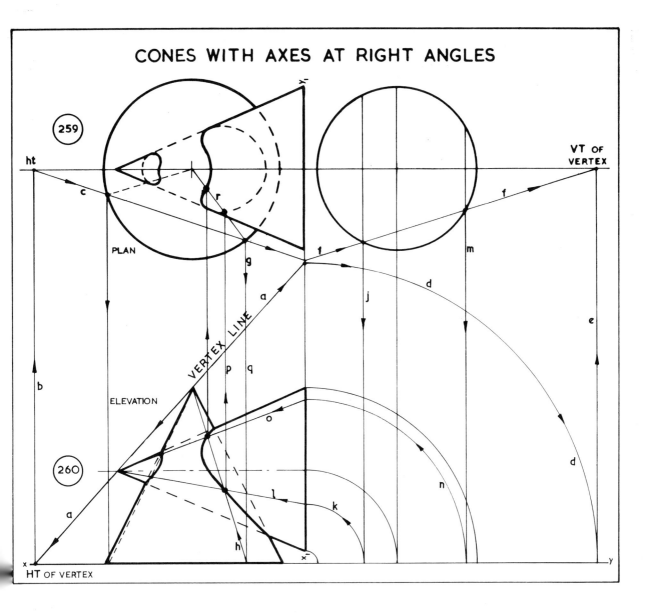

Vertical slice method

An alternative solution to the one shown opposite is to take a number of vertical section planes each cutting through the two plan views (see also page 100).

The method of construction will be easier to follow if the projection lines are drawn in due order as lettered, i.e. *a*, *b*, *c*, *d*, *e*, etc.

Method. Draw the plan and elevation of the two cones and an auxiliary plan of the horizontal cone rabatted from the elevation. Draw the vertex line to cut the *xy* line and its auxiliary x_1y_1 line. Project its traces to *HT* and *VT*, the points of convergence of the cutting planes.

Draw the horizontal trace of a section plane from the vertex *ht* to y_1 and the vertical trace to *VT* cutting the base of both cones.

Draw projectors from these cutting points to the bases of the two cones in the elevation. Draw generators on both cones from these base points. The intersecting points on each pair of generators lie on the curve of interpenetration. Project these intersecting points to the plan where they will cut the generator in the plan curve of interpenetration. Draw a succession of section planes to give sufficient generator intersections for the production of the full curve of interpenetration.

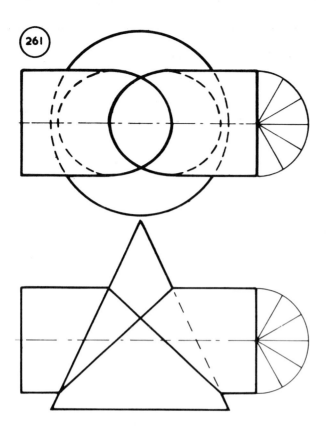

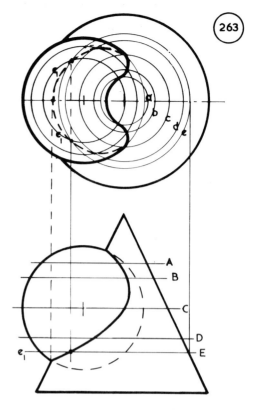

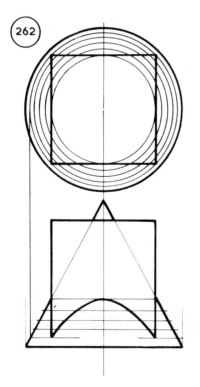

Intersection of a cone and a cylinder with axes at right angles

Method (fig. 261). When the cone and cylinder envelop a common sphere, the lines of intersection are straight in the elevation and elliptical in the plan. These lines are obtained from horizontal sections in the elevation projected to give intersecting circles and rectangles in the plan.

Cone intersecting a square prism

Method (fig. 262). Horizontal sections are taken in the elevation. The plan of these sections gives a series of circles intersecting the plan of the square prism. Vertical projectors taken from the points where the plan circles intersect the square will cut the horizontal section lines in the curve of interpenetration.

Sphere intersecting a cone (fig. 263).

Curves of interpenetration are obtained from a series of intersecting circles in the plan projected from horizontal sections in the elevation. (*Note:* Choose the positions of the elevation section planes to give adequately spaced circles in the plan.)

SPHERE PENETRATED BY A CYLINDER

HORIZONTAL SECTION SOLUTION   VERTICAL SECTION SOLUTION

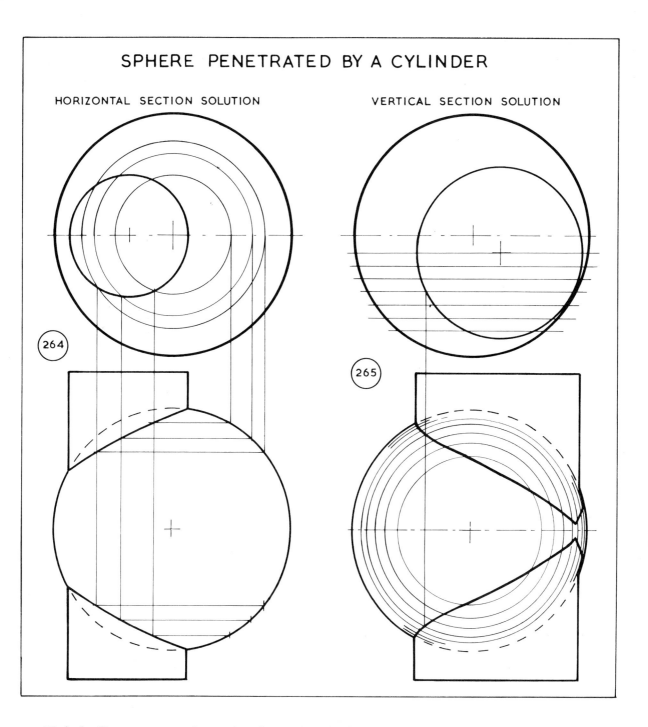

Method. Draw any convenient series of parallel sections through the sphere either horizontally as in fig. 264 or vertically as in fig. 265. In either drawing the plan view of the cylinder will intersect these section lines. Project these intersection points to cut the elevation of its own section plane to produce a series of points on the curve of intersection. (*Note*: Any plane section of a sphere, viewed perpendicularly, is circular in shape.)

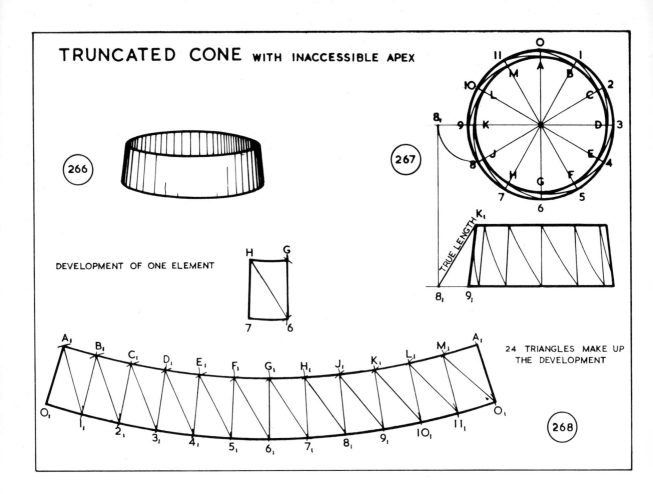

TRUNCATED CONE WITH INACCESSIBLE APEX

266

267

DEVELOPMENT OF ONE ELEMENT

TRUE LENGTH

24 TRIANGLES MAKE UP
THE DEVELOPMENT

268

Method. Divide the base circle into twelve equal sectors. Project these radial lines to the elevation where they will form the plan and elevation of twelve generators. Join the top of each generator to the bottom of the next generator with an oblique line. As all the sectors are of equal size all the oblique lines will be of equal length and it will therefore only be necessary to determine the true length of one of them. Rabat one of these oblique lines, $K8$ in the plan, to $K_1 8_1$ and project to the elevation to give the true length. $K_1 9_1$, being parallel to the VP, gives the true length of the radial lines which are similarly of equal length.

The *development* is built up by constructing a number of adjacent triangles in due order: Draw line $A_1 0_1$ equal in length to $K_1 9_1$; from A_1, using radius $K_1 8_1$, draw an arc at I_1; from 0_1, using as radius the chordal distance from 8 to 9 in the plan, cut the arc in I_1; joining these three points A_1, 0_1 and I_1 produces the first triangle; from A_1, using the chordal distance from K to J in the plan, draw an arc at B_1; from I_1, using radius $K_1 9_1$, cut this arc in B_1; joining these three points produces the second triangle and completes one-twelfth of the development; draw a further eleven similar elements to complete the full development.

OBLIQUE BRANCH PIPES

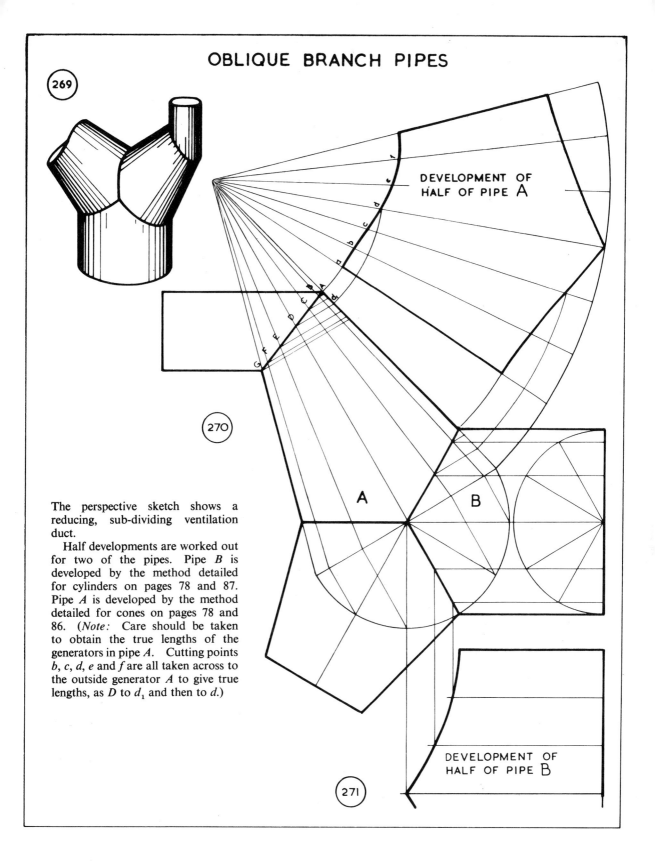

269

DEVELOPMENT OF
HALF OF PIPE A

270

A   B

The perspective sketch shows a reducing, sub-dividing ventilation duct.

Half developments are worked out for two of the pipes. Pipe *B* is developed by the method detailed for cylinders on pages 78 and 87. Pipe *A* is developed by the method detailed for cones on pages 78 and 86. (*Note:* Care should be taken to obtain the true lengths of the generators in pipe *A*. Cutting points *b*, *c*, *d*, *e* and *f* are all taken across to the outside generator *A* to give true lengths, as *D* to d_1 and then to *d*.)

DEVELOPMENT OF
HALF OF PIPE B

271

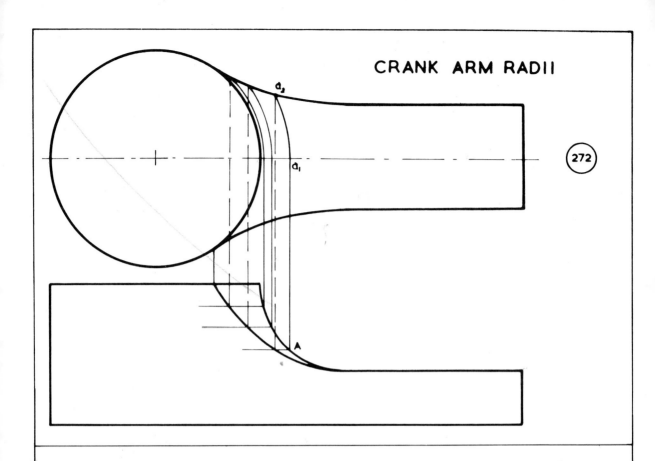

CRANK ARM RADII

(272)

PALMATE SECTION

Method. Draw a series of horizontal section planes across the zone occupied by the change of profile in the elevation, i.e. across the curve where the circular and rectangular cross-sections merge. From the points where the section lines cut the outer surface, as at *A*, drop vertical projectors to the plan centreline a_1. Draw in the plan circles of the section planes. From the points where these plan circles cross the outline of the plan a_2, draw return vertical projectors to cut the appropriate horizontal section planes in the elevation. All these latter intersection points lie on the curve of interpenetration.

(273)

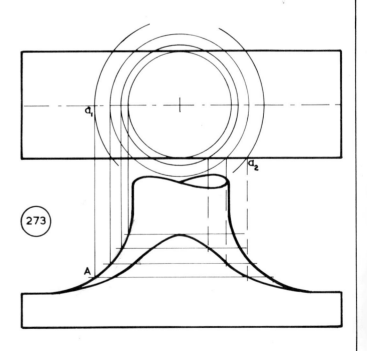

EXERCISES

Draw developments of the surfaces of the geometric shapes. Omit the bases.

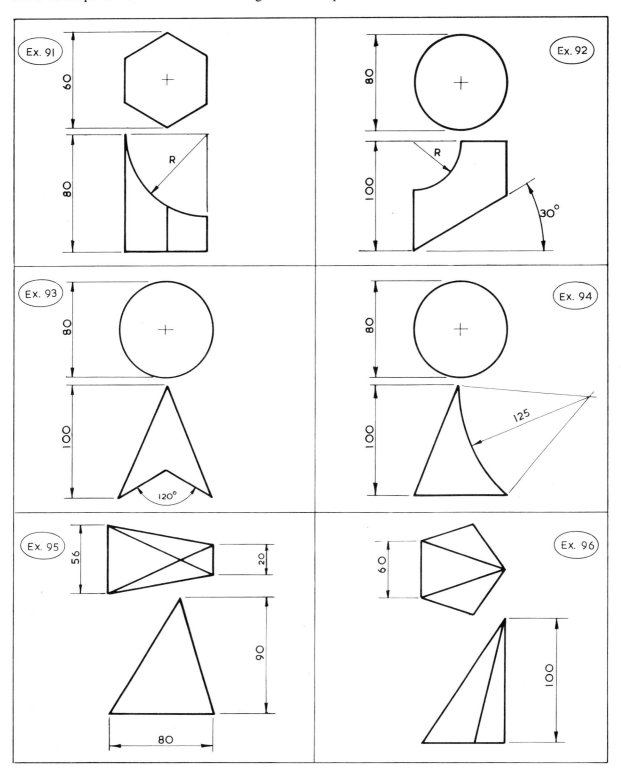

EXERCISES

Draw the intersection lines of the geometric solids.

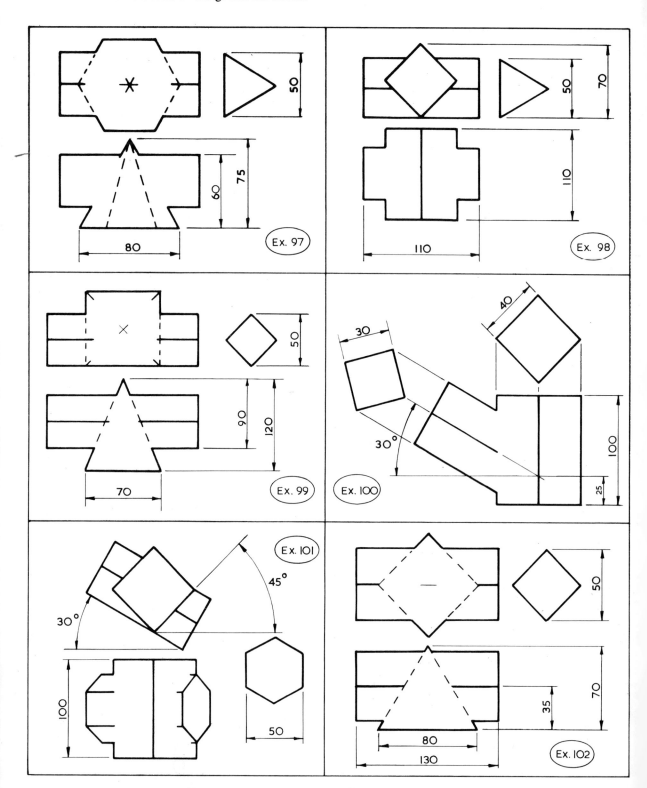

Ex. 97

Ex. 98

Ex. 99

Ex. 100

Ex. 101

Ex. 102

EXERCISES

Draw the curves of interpenetration of the geometric solids.

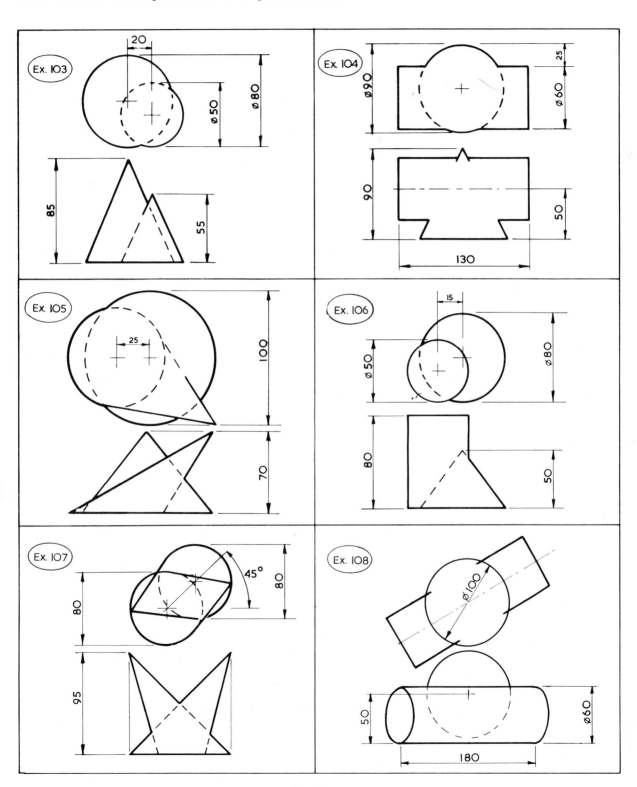

FORCES IN BEAMS AND FRAMEWORKS

GRAPHICAL RESOLUTION OF FORCES

Engineering design often requires the resolution of forces acting upon structures, for example the forces imposed by loading on the jib of a crane or on a girder bridge. All these loads have magnitude, line of application and direction. Forces having three components such as these can be conveniently shown on a drawing by a vector line. Using a suitable scale the length of this line represents the size of the load, the inclination of the line represents the direction or line of application of the force, and an arrowhead inserted on the line indicates its sense, i.e. pushing out or pulling in. When a force is set out in a drawing it is customary to identify the line by capital letters and its accompanying vector by the small version of the same letters, as in fig. 274 opposite.

Triangle of forces

Fig. 275 shows a picture suspended from a nail *A* (one point) by two cords *AB* and *AC*. The distribution of the load can be found by drawing a vector diagram, as shown in fig. 275A: draw a line of suitable scale length to represent the load *a*; from each end of this line draw lines parallel to *AB* and *AC* respectively as *b* and *c*; the scale length of each line will then represent its share of the load.

Fig. 276 shows another example of the same type of problem. A given weight is suspended from the jib of a wall crane. The separate loads carried by the jib and the tie can be found by making a vector drawing to a suitable scale, as shown in fig. 277. This latter drawing is called a **triangle of forces.** The so-called law of the triangle of forces states that three forces in equilibrium acting at a point can be depicted in magnitude and direction by the three sides of a triangle taken in due order.

Parallelogram of forces

The loads or forces *ab* and *ac* carried by the picture cords in fig. 275 can be drawn to a suitable scale and at the same inclinations as the lines *AB* and *AC* to form two sides of the parallelogram *abcd* (fig. 278). Taken in the sense from *a* to *d* the diagonal line becomes the scale resultant, or the equivalent, of the two forces *ab* and *ac*. Consideration of the space drawing (fig. 275) and the vector drawing (fig. 275*b*) will show that this resultant may completely replace forces *ab* and *ac*. To maintain the picture in equilibrium this resultant *a* to *d* must be balanced by an equal and opposite reaction taken in the sense from *d* to *a*. This construction, the **parallelogram of forces,** can only be used where the magnitude and direction of the forces are known. Three factors make up the complete parallelogram: the total combined force, the proportionate division of this and the angle of application of the forces. Any one of these factors can be determined by the use of this construction if the other two are known.

Polygon of forces

If a number of forces act at the same point they can be shown in magnitude and direction by the sides of a polygon of forces. Fig. 279 shows the junction of a number of loaded girders as in a suspension bridge. When these loads are drawn vectorially in due order (i.e. one after the other round the junction point) they produce the force polygon (fig. 280). This was drawn by starting with force *1*, adding force *2*, then *3* and so on clockwise, ending with force *5*. Since the polygon is complete or 'closed' it indicates that the junction of girders is in equilibrium.

Note how the arrow heads which indicate the 'sense' of the forces flow round the polygon.

When a 'dead' load is applied to any structure it is commonly thought of as a 'weight', as for instance a loaded motor lorry coming to a halt in the centre of a bridge. If the lorry and its load totalled 10 tonnes then it is usual to say that the bridge is supporting an applied load of 10 tonnes. It would be more appropriate to regard the 10 t as a force tending to push the bridge downwards, and therefore convert the 10 t to kilonewtons: 1 tonf = 9.964 kN; an easy approximation is 1 tonf = 10 kN (see page 157). This point, however, does not affect the graphical solution of the loading problems that follow and they can be worked in either tonnes or newtons. Examples are given in both notations.

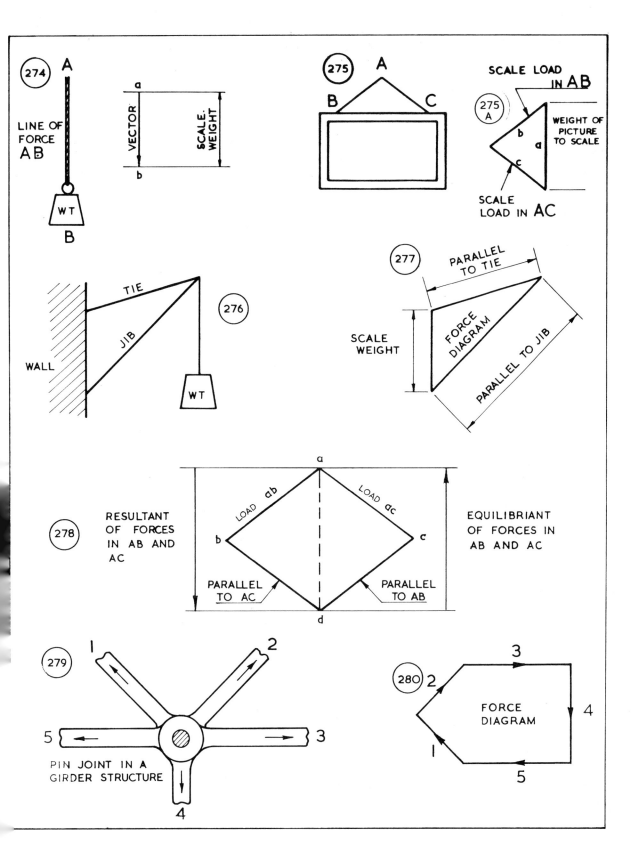

(274) A
LINE OF FORCE AB
WT
B

a
VECTOR
b
SCALE. WEIGHT

(275) A
B C

(275 A)
SCALE LOAD IN AB
b
a
c
WEIGHT OF PICTURE TO SCALE
SCALE LOAD IN AC

(276)
TIE
JIB
WALL
WT

(277)
PARALLEL TO TIE
FORCE DIAGRAM
SCALE WEIGHT
PARALLEL TO JIB

(278)
RESULTANT OF FORCES IN AB AND AC
a
LOAD ab
LOAD ac
b
c
PARALLEL TO AC
PARALLEL TO AB
d
EQUILIBRIANT OF FORCES IN AB AND AC

(279)
1
2
5
3
4
PIN JOINT IN A GIRDER STRUCTURE

(280)
2
3
1
4
5
FORCE DIAGRAM

CO-PLANAR FORCES

Concurrent forces

When a number of forces act about a common point they are called **concurrent.** If they act in the same plane they are **co-planar.** Fig. 281 shows four concurrent co-planar forces acting about point *O*. A fifth, unknown, force is needed as an equilibriant. This may be obtained from the closing line of the force polygon as shown in fig. 282. Start by drawing vector *a* to fully represent force *A*. The vector must be drawn parallel to the line of action of the force and of suitable scale length to represent its magnitude. To the outward end of *a* add vector *b* which fully represents force *B*. Similarly add vectors *c* and *d* representing forces *C* and *D* respectively. The vector *e*, which joins the outer end of *d* to *O*, and completes the polygon, will then fully represent the equilibriant in both direction and scale magnitude. Note how when the arrowheads of sense are added they flow round the polygon. This is a further proof of equilibrium.

Non-concurrent forces

Fig. 283 shows a system of four non-concurrent co-planar forces, i.e. forces that are in the same plane but do not act through a single point. Fig. 284 shows the four forces drawn vectorially in a force diagram, from which can be obtained the magnitude and direction of the equilibriant but not its position relative to the other forces in the system. This is determined from a link or funicular polygon.

Polar diagram and link polygon

Construct the space diagram (fig. 283). Label the spaces between the forces, using capital letters, starting from the left and working clockwise as shown. This method of labelling is known as **Bow's notation.** It is used to simplify the identification of forces and their vectors, e.g. the force *F1* is called 'force *AB*' or simply *AB* and its vector is *ab*. Note that while the force lines of action are labelled with capital (upper case) letters, the vectors are labelled with small (lower case) letters. Draw the polygon of forces (fig. 284), labelling each vector according to Bow's notation as shown. Select any pole, point *O*, and join it to all corners of the polygon (fig. 285). This is the polar diagram. Draw the space diagram (fig. 286, similar to fig. 284). From any point in line *AB* draw a line across space *B* and parallel to line *Ob* in the polar diagram. From the point where this line cuts the line of action *BC* draw across space *C* a line parallel to *Oc* in the polar diagram. Repeat with parallel line *Od* across space *D*. From the cutting points on lines *AB* and *DE* draw parallel *Oa* and *Oe* respectively. These will intersect at the point of application of the equilibriant force line *AE* (shown as a broken line).

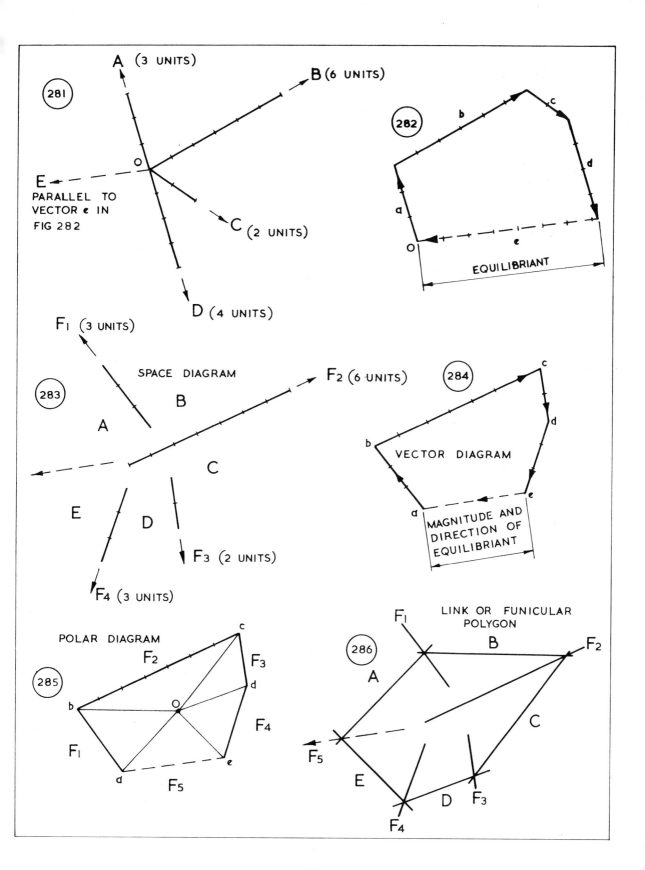

281

A (3 UNITS)

B (6 UNITS)

O

E ←
PARALLEL TO
VECTOR e IN
FIG 282

C (2 UNITS)

D (4 UNITS)

282

b

c

a

d

O

e

EQUILIBRIANT

F₁ (3 UNITS)

SPACE DIAGRAM

F₂ (6 UNITS)

283

A

B

284

C

c

d

b

VECTOR DIAGRAM

E

D

a

e

F₃ (2 UNITS)

MAGNITUDE AND
DIRECTION OF
EQUILIBRIANT

F₄ (3 UNITS)

POLAR DIAGRAM

c

F₂

F₃

285

b

O

d

F₄

F₁

e

d

F₅

LINK OR FUNICULAR
POLYGON

F₁

B

F₂

286

A

C

F₅

E

D

F₃

F₄

115

To find the magnitude, direction, and position of the equilibriant of a series of parallel co-planar forces

The space diagram below (fig. 287) represents a series of parallel forces. Drawn to a suitable scale these give the force diagram drawn on the right (fig. 288).

When the force diagram is a straight line, as *ae*, the magnitude of the equilibriant is represented by the closing line *ea* which overlies the vectors *ab*, *bc*, *cd* and *de*, and is equal to the algebraical sum of the loads.

Method — polar diagram (fig. 289). Draw the force line *ae*. From any convenient point *O* draw lines to points *a*, *b*, *c*, *d* and *e*.

Method — funicular or link polygon (fig. 290). Produce the force lines and letter the spaces *A*, *B*, *C*, *D* and *E*. Through any point on line *AB* draw a line of convenient length and parallel to the line *aO* in the polar diagram. Through the intersection on *AB* and through space *B* draw a line parallel to the line *bO* in the polar diagram to cut line *BC*. Through this intersection and across space *C* draw a line parallel to line *cO* in the polar diagram to cut line *CD*. Repeat the process through space *D* with polar line *dO*. Finally draw a line parallel to the polar line *eO* through the intersection point in line *DE*. This final line will cut the *aO* line in O_1, the point of equilibrium.

The equilibriant passes through this point and is opposite in direction to the series of parallel forces.

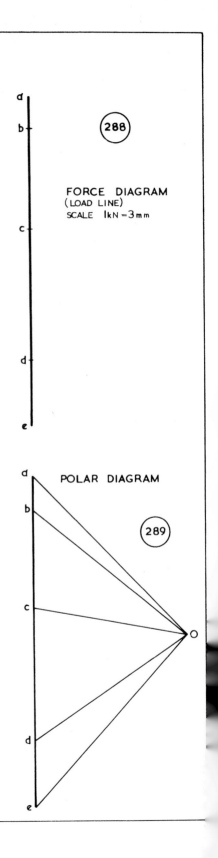

FORCE DIAGRAM
(LOAD LINE)
SCALE 1kN = 3mm

POLAR DIAGRAM

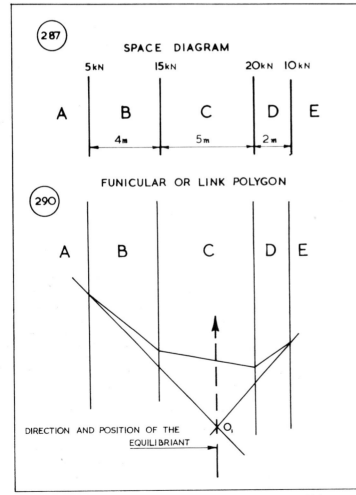

SPACE DIAGRAM

5kN   15kN   20kN 10kN

A | B | C | D | E

4m   5m   2m

FUNICULAR OR LINK POLYGON

A | B | C | D | E

DIRECTION AND POSITION OF THE
EQUILIBRIANT

EQUILIBRIANT AND REACTIONS TO PARALLEL FORCES ACTING ON A BEAM

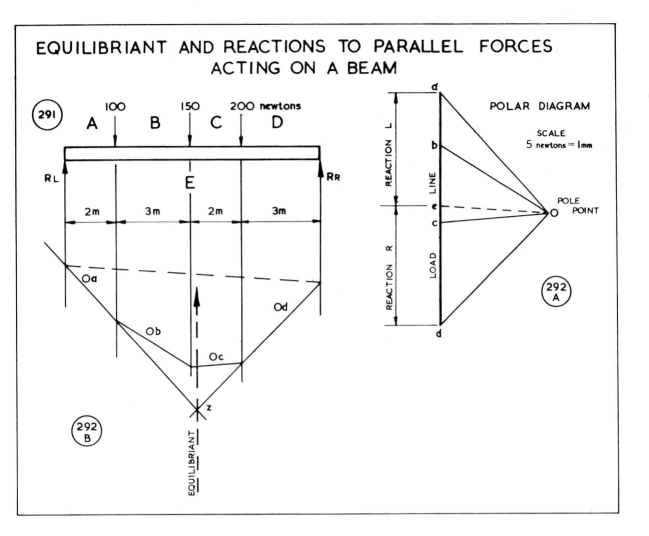

Reactions may be determined by either scale drawings or calculation using moments. The moment of a force about a point is the product of the magnitude of the force and its distance from the point.

Reactions by calculation

Moments about R_L

$$2 \times 100 = 200$$
$$5 \times 150 = 750$$
$$7 \times 200 = 1\,400$$

$$\overline{2\,350 \text{ Nm}}$$

Reaction at $R_R = \dfrac{\text{total moments about } R_L}{\text{total distance } R_L \text{ to } R_R}$

$$= \frac{2\,350}{10} = 235$$

Reaction at R_L = total load — 235

$$= 450 - 235 = 215 \text{ Nm}$$

Reactions by scale drawing

Method. Draw the beam to a suitable scale and insert the arrows at the exact points of loading. Letter the spaces between the forces according to Bow's notation (see page 114). Add the arrows denoting the left- and right-hand reactions, R_L and R_R. Draw the load line to scale. Select any pole point O and join this to a, b, c and d. Produce the space diagram load and reaction lines. Through any point in line R_L and across space A draw a line parallel to polar diagram line Oa. From the point where this line intersects load line AB draw a line across space B parallel to Ob in the polar diagram. Repeat with Oc across space C and Od across space D. Lines Oa and Od will intersect in the line of equilibrium. As the force lines are parallel the equilibriant must also be parallel, and opposite in sense. Join the upper ends of Oa and Od to close the force polygon. Draw a line Oe across the polar diagram parallel to this closing line. Load line distances ea and ed are scale magnitude reaction R_L and R_R respectively.

REACTIONS WHEN LOADS OVERHANG SUPPORTS

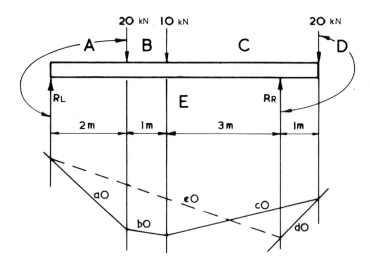

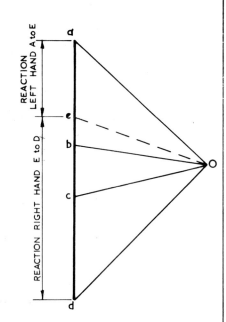

(293) *Note:* The closing line *eO* of the link polygon runs from the intersections of *aO* and *dQ* with the support lines.

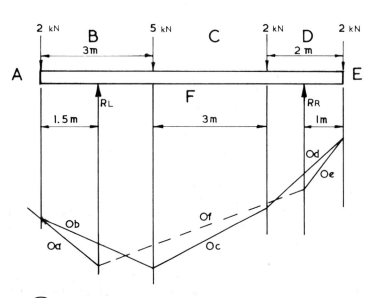

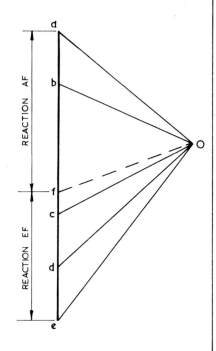

(294) *Note:* The closing line *Of* of the link polygon runs from the intersections of *Oa* and *Oe* with the support lines.

SHEAR FORCE AND BENDING MOMENT IN A LOADED BEAM

Shear force

The shear force in a loaded beam is the force which will cause the beam to shear at a given section plane. It is equal to the algebraic sum of the loads on one side of the shear section. By convention it is called positive shear if the right-hand end of the beam tends to move downwards relative to the left, i.e. a clockwise movement of the beam; it is called negative shear if the tendency is for the right-hand end to move upwards, i.e. anticlockwise. This method of labelling is occasionally reversed in special cases.

Shear force can be calculated by obtaining the algebraic sum of all the forces to one side of the section. Graphically, the shear force can be read to scale directly from a shear force diagram ordinate at the given section.

Bending moment

The bending moment in a loaded beam is the bending effect at a given section plane caused by the application of loading. In equilibrium this bending is resisted and balanced by the material of the beam. By convention the bending moment is called positive if it causes the beam to sag, and negative if it causes the beam to 'hog' or bend upwards.

The bending moment can be calculated by obtaining the algebraic sum of all the moments on one side of the given section plane. Graphically the bending moment is read from the bending moment diagram to the following formula: space diagram distance in metres × polar distance in millimetres × load line scale in tonnes (or newtons); i.e. the link polygon is proportional to the bending moment.

Cantilever beam

Fig. 295 shows a cantilever beam projecting from a wall support. The beam carries a concentrated load at the free end.

Bending moment. Because there is no loading on either side of the terminal point there can be no moment at that point. Hence the b.m. diagram starts with zero value at the left-hand end as shown. As the load exerts an anticlockwise turning influence on the beam, the bending moment is a negative one. Consideration shows that there must be an equal and opposite support reaction at the other end of the beam in order to maintain equilibrium. Therefore this support must be length × load.

Shear force. The shear force diagram takes the form of a rectangle as shown when there is one concentrated load as in this example.

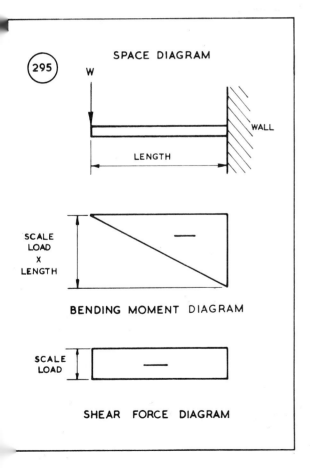

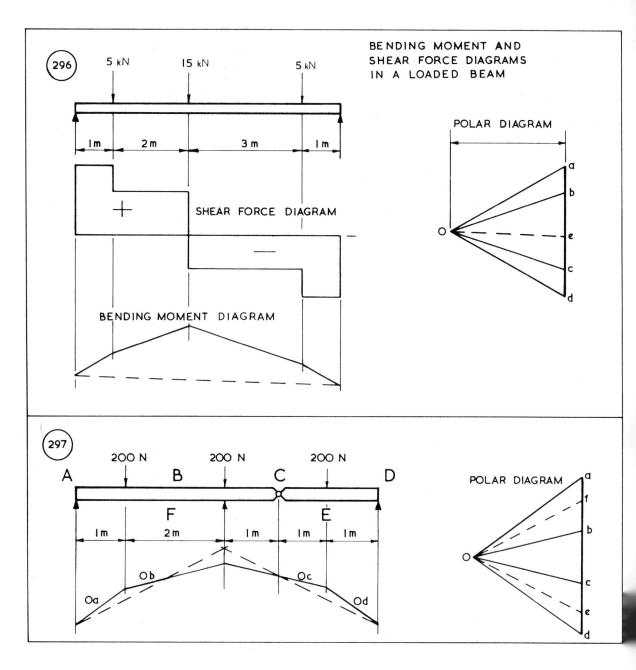

BENDING MOMENT AND SHEAR FORCE DIAGRAMS IN A LOADED BEAM

(296)

5 kN   15 kN   5 kN

1 m   2 m   3 m   1 m

POLAR DIAGRAM

SHEAR FORCE DIAGRAM

BENDING MOMENT DIAGRAM

(297)

A   200 N   B   200 N   C   200 N   D

F   E

1 m   2 m   1 m   1 m   1 m

POLAR DIAGRAM

Ob   *Oc*

Oa   *Od*

Reactions and bending moment diagram of a hinged beam

Method (fig. 297). Draw the space diagram, the load line, and the polar diagram. Draw the link lines *Oa*, *Ob*, *Oc*, *Od* in the funicular polygon parallel to the vectors *Oa*, *Ob*, *Oc*, *Od* in the polar diagram. The remaining links *Of* and *Oe*

must commence at the intersections of *Oa* and *AF* and *Od* and *ED* respectively, and also line *Oe* must intersect *Oc* on the vertical from the hinge as there is no value of bending moment at this point.

Reactions *AF*, *FE* and *ED* can be read to scale from intersections of the vectors *Of* and *Oe* with the load line in the polar diagram.

Beams supporting distributed loads

The beam shown in fig. 298 is freely supported at both ends and carries a load of 12 t. This is evenly distributed over its length at a rate of 2 t/m.

To draw the shear force diagram

The total downward loading being 12 t, the upward reactions at the ends must, by symmetry, be of 6 t each. The shear force in the mid-point of the beam can be calculated by the following formula: reaction − distance from beam end to centre × load per metre $(6 - (3 \times 2) = 0$ t). Therefore the diagram must indicate zero shear force at that point.

Method. Draw the beam line to a suitable scale. Erect a perpendicular at the left end to give a scale reaction of 6 t. Join the top of this line to the mid-point of the beam to indicate zero shear force and continue the sloping line to cut a downward vertical from the right-hand end of the line.

To draw the bending moment diagram

Method. Divide the beam into a number of sections of convenient length. In the example shown each section carries 2 t. For convenience in drawing it is assumed that each load is concentrated at the centre of gravity of each section. Draw force lines through these points. Letter the spaces as in Bow's notation. Draw a force line *ag* and its polar diagram (see page 116 for details of the method). Transfer parallels from the polar diagram to the force lines, *Oa* across *A*, *Ob* across *B*, and so on. Draw a free curve through all the cutting points. This curve should be parabolic.

Bending moment scale
If the space diagram is drawn to the scale of
　　space diagram　　　　10 mm = 1 m
　　load line　　　　　　10 mm = 2 t
　　polar distance *O* to *A*　　= 50 mm
then the bending moment diagram = $1 \times 2 \times 5$ (in t/m).
(*Note:* Maximum bending moment, positive or negative, coincides with the point at which shear force is at zero.)

Fig. 299 illustrates a similar load applied to a cantilever beam.

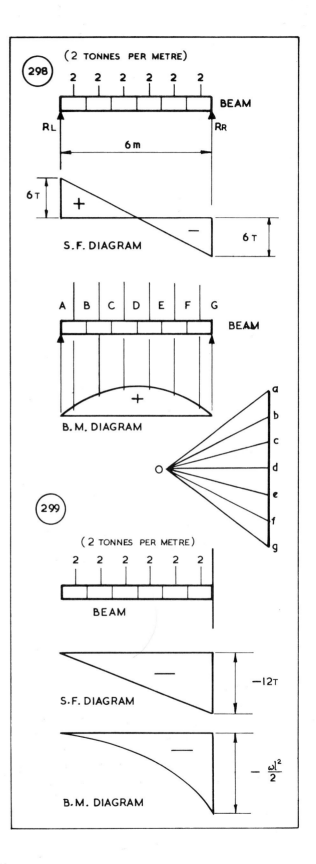

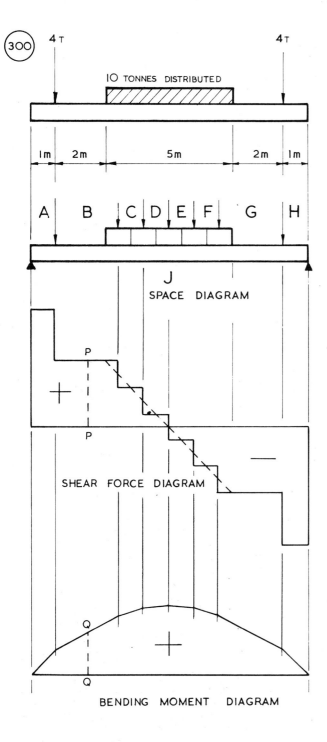

300

4 T   10 TONNES DISTRIBUTED   4 T

1m | 2m | 5m | 2m | 1m

A | B | C | D | E | F | G | H

J

SPACE DIAGRAM

+

P

P

SHEAR FORCE DIAGRAM

−

Q

+

Q

BENDING MOMENT DIAGRAM

To draw the shear force and bending moment diagrams

Method. Split the distributed load into a number of equal portions and treat each portion as a separate concentrated load. The area over which the load is applied must also be divided and each portion of the load must be applied at the centre of its particular section of the beam. This construction results in a stepped form diagram. This should then be corrected by drawing the mean through the series of steps as shown by the broken line.

Shear force at a section
The shear force at any given section, e.g. at *PP*, is proportional to the ordinate *PP* read from the load line scale.

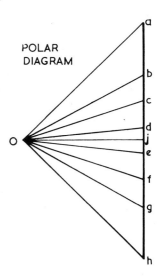

POLAR DIAGRAM

a
b
c
d
j
e
f
g

O

h

Bending moment at a given section
If the beam diagrams are drawn to the scale of

space diagram
1 mm = x metres
load line forces
1 mm = y tonnes (or newtons)
polar distance O to *ah*
= z mm

then 1 mm in any ordinate, e.g. *QQ*, in the bending moment diagram
= xyz tonnes per metre
or   = xyz newtons per metre

122

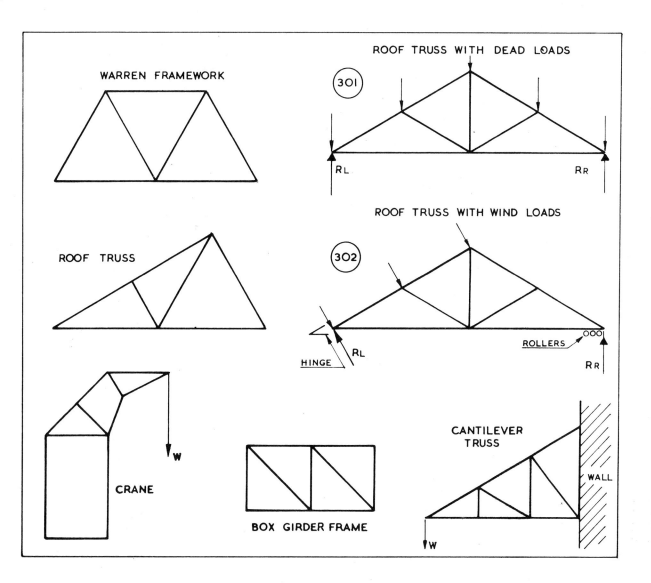

WARREN FRAMEWORK

ROOF TRUSS WITH DEAD LOADS

301

R_L R_R

ROOF TRUSS

ROOF TRUSS WITH WIND LOADS

302

HINGE R_L

ROLLERS R_R

CRANE

BOX GIRDER FRAME

CANTILEVER TRUSS

WALL

W

W

FORCES IN FRAMEWORKS

Many engineering structures are built up from steel girders which have been secured together to form a series of triangular frames. Some examples are shown above: roof trusses, Warren frame bridges, and cranes. These carry a number of loads including structural dead weight, superimposed loads, and loading by wind forces. In order to maintain the structure in a state of equilibrium these loads must of course be balanced by opposite and equal forces. These opposing forces are called reactions. The sum total of all the loads and reactions needs to be analysed to determine the forces in each separate frame member before a satisfactory overall design can be produced. In this analysis it is assumed that

the loads are carried at the joints only.

Steel framework expands and contracts with variations in temperature and due allowance has to be made for this in the design. This is done by securing one end of the frame to a hinge and allowing the other to 'float' on rollers. In determining the reaction at the supports it is assumed that the reaction at the roller end is always perpendicular to the centreline of the rollers, as in fig. 302, R_R (reaction right). The line of reaction at the hinge end is influenced by the line of action of the loads. Dead loading is assumed to be vertical and its resulting reaction will also be vertical. Wind loading is assumed to be perpendicular to the roof surface and will result in an oblique line of reaction at the hinge—fig. 302, R_L (reaction left).

To determine the reactions at the supports and the forces in the members of a roof truss

Fig. 303 opposite shows the outline of a simple roof truss drawn to a suitable scale. This drawing is called a space diagram and it should be noted that it really is a diagram and that single lines are used to denote girders and forces. The framework is simply supported at the ends and it carries three separate loads. Because these are dead loads they are applied vertically and their resultant reactions will also be vertical, as shown at R_L (reaction left) and at R_R (reaction right). These reactions, together with the forces in each frame member, can be determined by drawing vector diagrams for each joint in the frame taking the appropriate members in due order, as in fig. 280, page 113. For convenience in drawing it is usual to combine the polygons necessary for each joint into one composite vector diagram for all the forces acting on the framework.

Solution taken point by point starting from space A: Because the frame outline and the distribution of the loads are symmetrical it follows that the reactions at the supports will be equal (in this case 150 units each, i.e. half the total load).

Method (fig. 304). Draw a vector *ab* parallel to *AB* and to a scale of 100 units in length. From *b* draw a line *bf* of any length parallel to *BF*. The next step should be to draw a vector from *f* parallel to *FE* but vector point *f* is unknown so point *e* must be established first and the diagram worked from *e* backwards to *f*. From *a* draw a line *ae* parallel to reaction *AE* and to a scale of 150 units in length. From *e* draw a line parallel to *FE* cutting *bf* in *f*. This completes the triangle of forces for point *ABFE*. Similarly, fig. 305 is the triangle of forces for point *BCF* and fig. 306 for point *CDEF*. It is usual to superimpose these three drawings (figs. 304, 305 and 306) to give a composite force diagram for the whole frame, as in fig. 307.

Consideration will show that some frame members are in tension while others are under compression. These may be differentiated by inserting the arrows of 'sense' (fig. 280, pages 112 and 113) in due order round each force triangle. To insert these arrows around point *ABFE* follow a clockwise path around its accompanying force diagram (fig. 304).

Method. Start at *a* and move to *b*, then to *f* and to *e*, and back again to *a* as follows:

Stress diagram (fig. 308)		Force diagram (fig. 304)
A	*B*	from *a* to *b* the movement is vertically downwards, therefore the load arrow *AB* points in the same direction.
B	*F*	from *b* to *f* the movement is obliquely downwards to the left, therefore the arrow *BF* must also point obliquely down to the left.
F	*E*	from *f* to *e* the movement is horizontally to the right, therefore the arrow *FE* must point horizontally to the right.
E	*A*	from *e* to *a* the movement is vertically upwards therefore the reaction arrow *EA* points in the same direction.

This procedure is then repeated with the other two framework points—*BCF* and fig. 305 and *CDEF* and fig. 306.

Note:
(1) The arrows 'flow' round the triangles of forces indicating equilibrium.

(2) Arrowheads are *not* inserted in the composite force diagram (fig. 307) as the same line is often traversed in different directions when analysing forces in different points, e.g. from *b* to *c* downwards in *BCF*, and *e* to *a* upwards in *EABF*.

(3) The arrowheads are always in matching pairs in the complete stress diagram (fig. 308).

Struts and ties

Girder *BF* has outward pointing arrowheads. This indicates that the force *inside* the girder is tending to stretch or increase its length. To maintain equilibrium there must be an equal and opposite force *outside* each end of the girder to work against this expansion.

This opposing force must be a compressive one. The girder is then under compression and is called a **strut**. The same applies to girder *FC*. On the horizontal girder *FE* the arrowheads point inwards so that the opposing *outside* forces must be pulling. Therefore the girder is in tension and is called a **tie**. The forces acting against and inside ties and struts are shown in fig. 309.

ROOF TRUSS

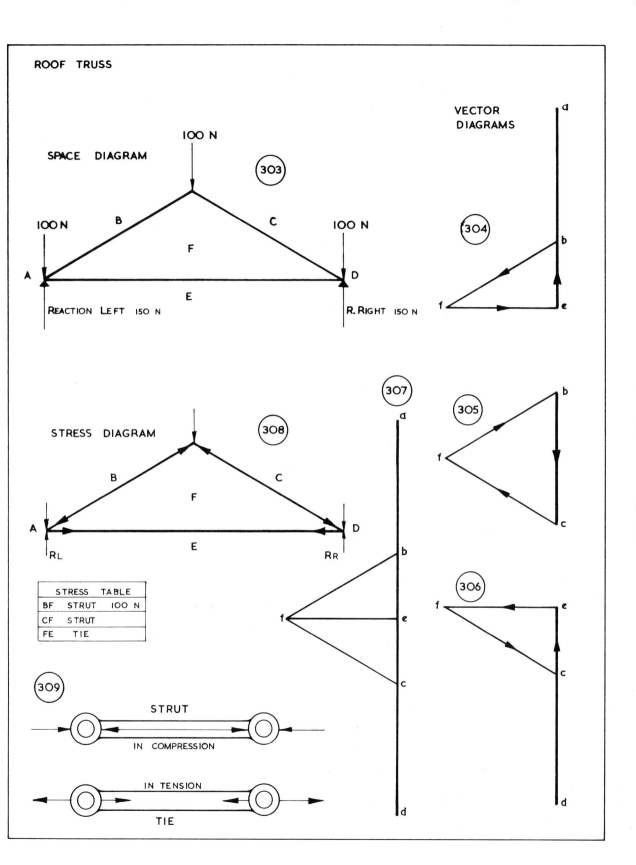

SPACE DIAGRAM

100 N

100 N

B

C

F

A

D

100 N

E

REACTION LEFT 150 N

R. RIGHT 150 N

(303)

VECTOR DIAGRAMS

(304)

STRESS DIAGRAM

(308)

B

C

F

A

D

E

RL

RR

(307)

(305)

(306)

STRESS TABLE

BF	STRUT	100 N
CF	STRUT	
FE	TIE	

(309)

STRUT

IN COMPRESSION

IN TENSION

TIE

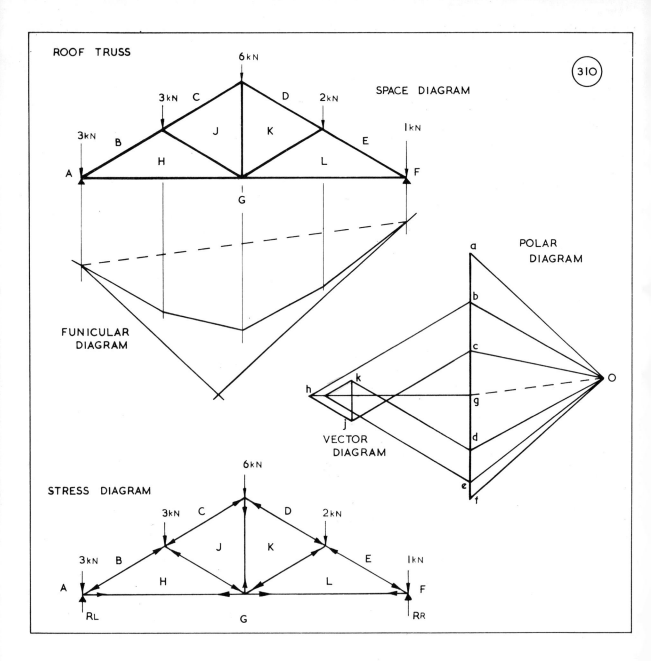

The roof truss shown above is more complicated than the one in fig. 303, page 125. It contains three interior members and also carries uneven loading as in a roof having one side tiled and the other covered with translucent glass-fibre sheets.

Method. The magnitude of the reactions can be determined by drawing a load line, polar diagram and funicular polygon as detailed on page 117. Transferring the closing line from the funicular polygon to the polar diagram will establish point *g* on the load line. Start from *b* on this line and draw a vector line parallel to *BH* and of any length. From point *g* draw a vector *gh* parallel to *HG*. The

intersection of these two lines will establish the position of point *h*. Take each loading point of the truss in turn and treat in a similar manner to produce a composite vector diagram covering the whole frame. Trace a path round each triangle of forces contained in the vector diagram and insert the appropriate arrowheads in the stress diagram as each force is determined. The length of each vector in the combined vector diagram is the scale of magnitude of the force in that particular member, e.g. the length of vector *bh* can be read to the scale used on the load line to give the stress magnitude in member *BH*.

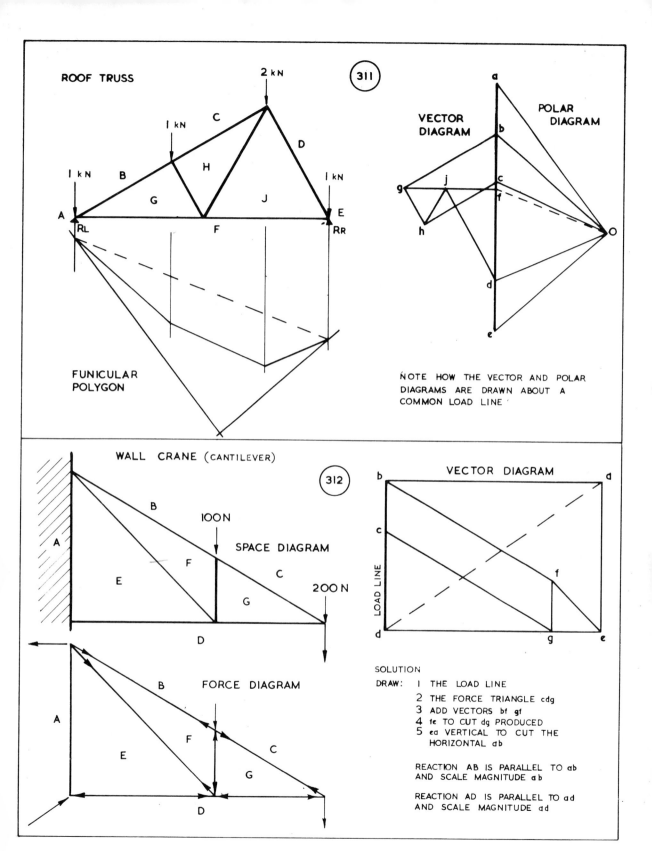

ROOF TRUSS

2 kN

311

VECTOR DIAGRAM

POLAR DIAGRAM

1 kN

C

D

1 kN

B

H

1 kN

A
RL

G

J

F

E
Rr

FUNICULAR POLYGON

NOTE HOW THE VECTOR AND POLAR DIAGRAMS ARE DRAWN ABOUT A COMMON LOAD LINE

WALL CRANE (CANTILEVER)

312

VECTOR DIAGRAM

B

100N

SPACE DIAGRAM

A

F

C

E

G

200 N

D

LOAD LINE

FORCE DIAGRAM

A

B

F

C

E

G

D

SOLUTION

DRAW: 1 THE LOAD LINE
2 THE FORCE TRIANGLE cdg
3 ADD VECTORS bf gf
4 fe TO CUT dg PRODUCED
5 ea VERTICAL TO CUT THE HORIZONTAL ab

REACTION AB IS PARALLEL TO ab AND SCALE MAGNITUDE ab

REACTION AD IS PARALLEL TO ad AND SCALE MAGNITUDE ad

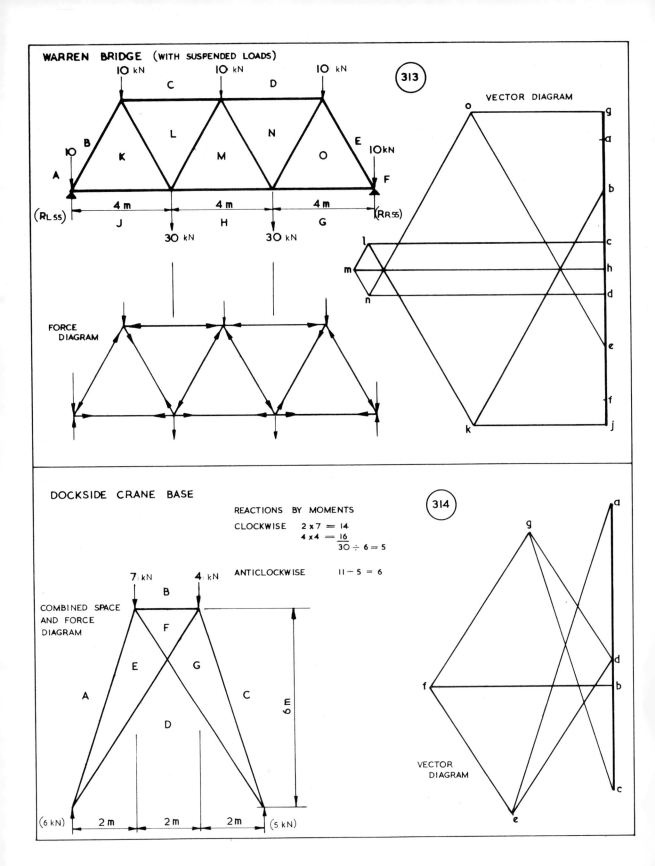

WARREN BRIDGE (WITH SUSPENDED LOADS)

313

VECTOR DIAGRAM

10 kN   10 kN   10 kN

C   D

B   L   N   E   10kN

A   K   M   O   F

4 m   4 m   4 m

(RL 55)   (RR 55)

J   H   G

30 kN   30 kN

FORCE
DIAGRAM

DOCKSIDE CRANE BASE

314

REACTIONS BY MOMENTS

CLOCKWISE   2 x 7 = 14
             4 x 4 = 16
             ─────────
             30 ÷ 6 = 5

ANTICLOCKWISE   11 − 5 = 6

7 kN   4 kN

B

COMBINED SPACE
AND FORCE
DIAGRAM

F

E   G

A   C

D   6 m

(6 kN)   2 m   2 m   2 m   (5 kN)

VECTOR
DIAGRAM

128

CRANE FRAMEWORK

315

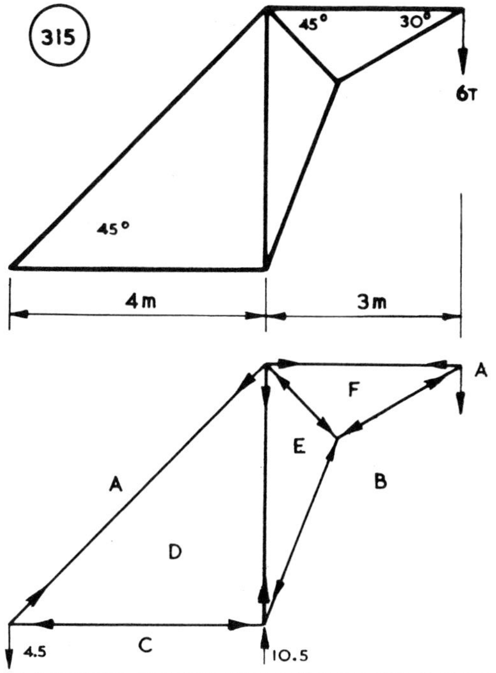

45°   30°

6T

45°

4m   3m

A

F

E

B

A

D

C

4.5   C   10.5

REACTIONS BY MOMENTS

CLOCKWISE 7×6 = 42   42 ÷ 4 = 10.5

ANTICLOCKWISE 3 × 10.5 = 31.5 ÷ 7 = 4.5

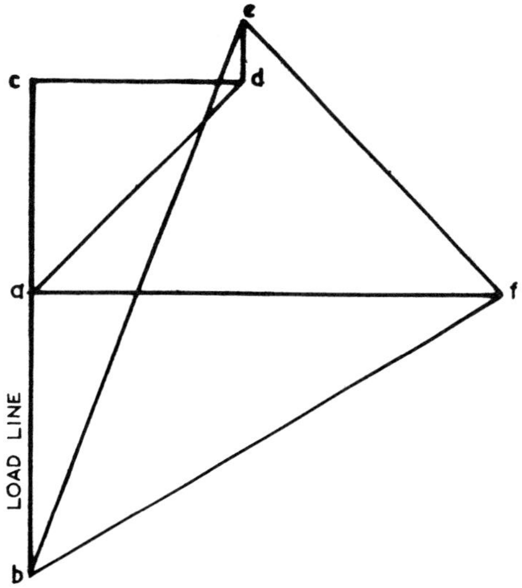

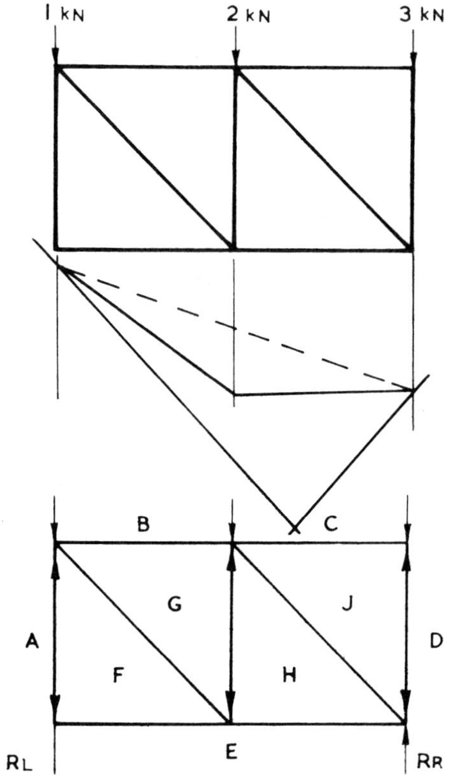

c   e   d

a   f

LOAD LINE

b

---

1 kN   2 kN   3 kN

BOX GIRDER FRAME

316

COMBINED VECTOR AND POLAR DIAGRAMS

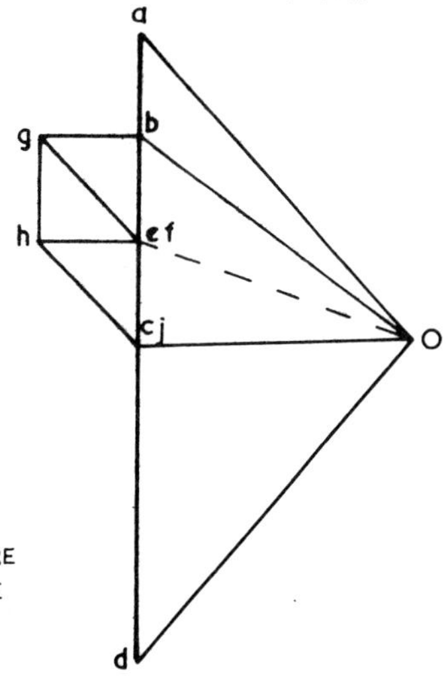

a

g   b

h   e f

c j   O

d

B   C

G   J

A   D

F   H

RL   E   RR

MEMBER	STRUT TIE	UNIT LOAD
A F	STRUT	2
G H	STRUT	1
J D	STRUT	3
B G	STRUT	1
H E	TIE	1
F G	TIE	1.4
H J	STRUT	1.4
C J	REDUNDANT	
F E	REDUNDANT	

NOTE MEMBERS CJ AND FE ARE
CLASSIFIED 'REDUNDANT' BECAUSE
THEY CARRY NO LOAD IN THE
GIVEN ARRANGEMENT

THE EFFECT OF WIND LOADING ON FRAMEWORKS

Fig. A shows the outline of a simple roof truss supporting a single oblique (wind) load. Dead loads have been ignored in order to simplify the drawing. The left-hand end of the frame is secured by a hinge and the right-hand end 'floats' on rollers (fig. 302, page 123).

Fig. B. The vertical reaction at the roller end is projected to cut the line of action of the oblique loading in a point of equilibrium *O*. The left-hand line of action from the hinge must also pass through this equilibrium point, thus establishing the angle of the latter reaction.

Fig. C shows a similar roof truss to that of fig. A, only the positions of the rollers and hinge have been changed end for end while the oblique loading is still applied along the same line of action. It will be readily seen that if the reactions and the load resultant are to meet in a common point then this point must lie above the truss as in fig. D and not below as in fig. B.

Fig. E shows the same simple roof truss carrying an oblique load distributed evenly over one side.

(*Note:* It is conventional to assume that the load is carried at the 'nodes' or joints only.)

Fig. F is the vector diagram of the truss in fig. E. It should be noted that with this pattern of loading *h* and *j* occupy the same point in the vector diagram, thus indicating that member *HJ* carries no stress. When this occurs the member is termed 'redundant'.

Fig. G shows the same frame supporting both oblique wind loads and vertical dead loads. These may be treated in the vector diagram as separate loads, when they will produce a load line similar to *ag* in fig. J, or they may be integrated in pairs by either a parallelogram of forces or a triangle of forces, as in fig. K (see pages 112 and 113), when they will produce the simplified load line *ad* in fig. H.

To simplify the working of the problem the whole of the applied loads may be integrated to form a single force. This force, together with the reactions in the supporting points, will form a system of concurrent co-planar forces (see page 117). To maintain equilibrium in the structure these load and reaction lines must all pass through one point.

WIND LOADING

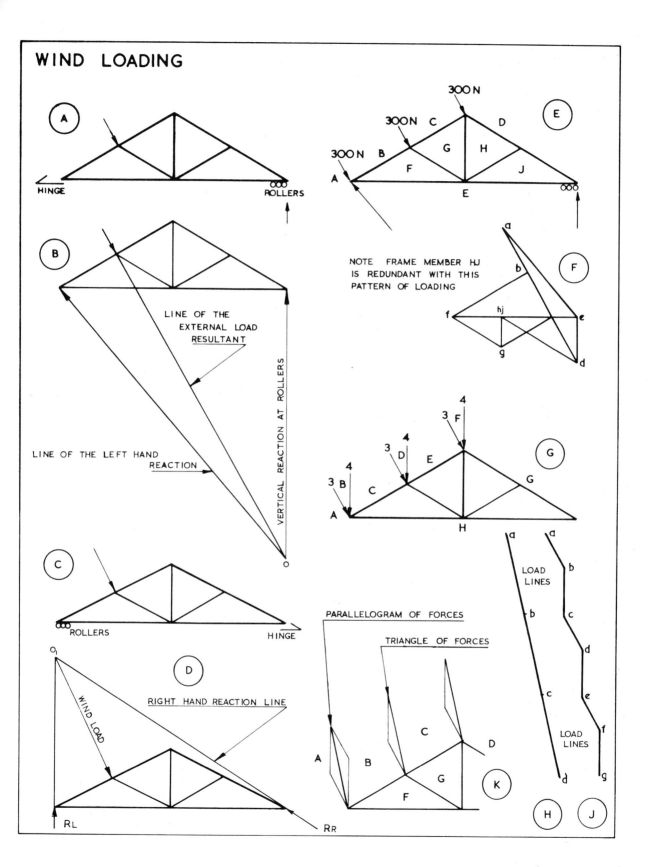

A HINGE ROLLERS

B LINE OF THE EXTERNAL LOAD RESULTANT
LINE OF THE LEFT HAND REACTION
VERTICAL REACTION AT ROLLERS
O

C ROLLERS HINGE

D O₁ WIND LOAD RIGHT HAND REACTION LINE RL RR

E 300N 300N C D 300N B G H A F E J
ROLLERS

NOTE FRAME MEMBER HJ IS REDUNDANT WITH THIS PATTERN OF LOADING

F a b f hj e g d

G 3 B 4 3 D 4 3 F 4 A C E H G

K PARALLELOGRAM OF FORCES TRIANGLE OF FORCES A B C F G D

H LOAD LINES a b c d

J a b c d e f g LOAD LINES

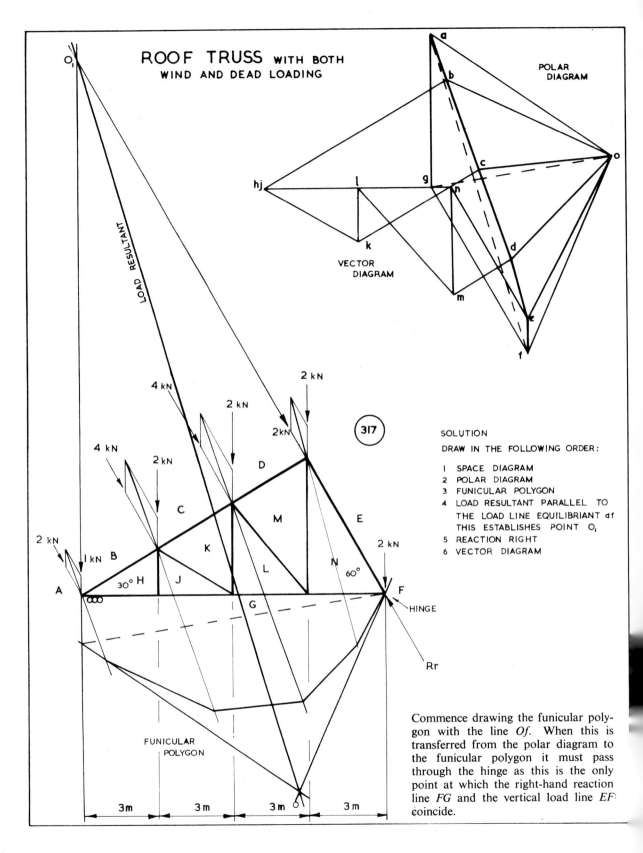

ROOF TRUSS WITH BOTH WIND AND DEAD LOADING

POLAR DIAGRAM

VECTOR DIAGRAM

LOAD RESULTANT

4 kN

2 kN

2 kN

4 kN

2 kN

2 kN

2 kN

D

C

M

E

K

L

N

2 kN

1 kN B

30° H

J

A

G

F

HINGE

Rr

FUNICULAR POLYGON

3 m   3 m   3 m   3 m

317

SOLUTION

DRAW IN THE FOLLOWING ORDER:

1 SPACE DIAGRAM
2 POLAR DIAGRAM
3 FUNICULAR POLYGON
4 LOAD RESULTANT PARALLEL TO THE LOAD LINE EQUILIBRIANT of THIS ESTABLISHES POINT O₁
5 REACTION RIGHT
6 VECTOR DIAGRAM

Commence drawing the funicular polygon with the line *Of*. When this is transferred from the polar diagram to the funicular polygon it must pass through the hinge as this is the only point at which the right-hand reaction line *FG* and the vertical load line *EF* coincide.

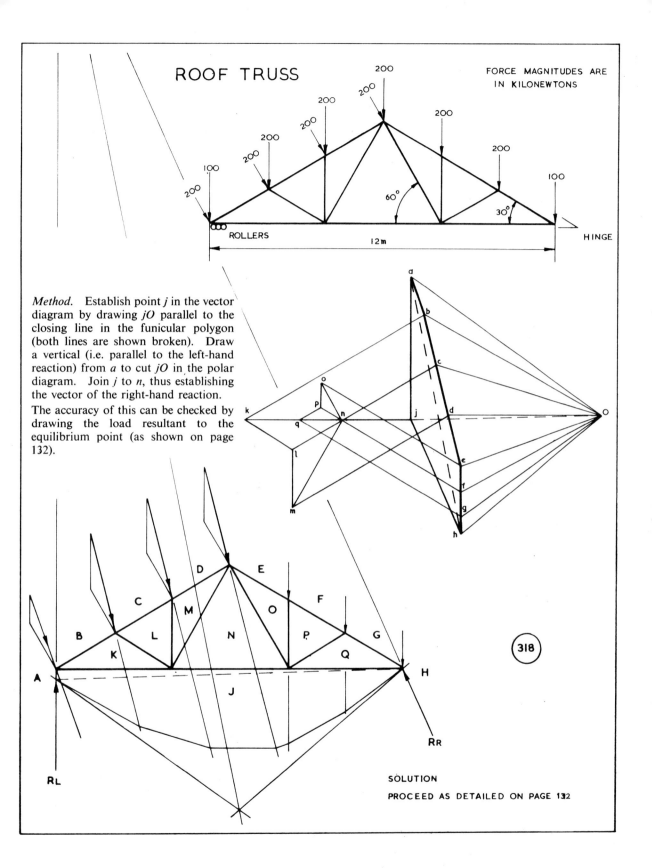

ROOF TRUSS

FORCE MAGNITUDES ARE IN KILONEWTONS

Method. Establish point *j* in the vector diagram by drawing *jO* parallel to the closing line in the funicular polygon (both lines are shown broken). Draw a vertical (i.e. parallel to the left-hand reaction) from *a* to cut *jO* in the polar diagram. Join *j* to *n*, thus establishing the vector of the right-hand reaction.

The accuracy of this can be checked by drawing the load resultant to the equilibrium point (as shown on page 132).

318

SOLUTION

PROCEED AS DETAILED ON PAGE 132

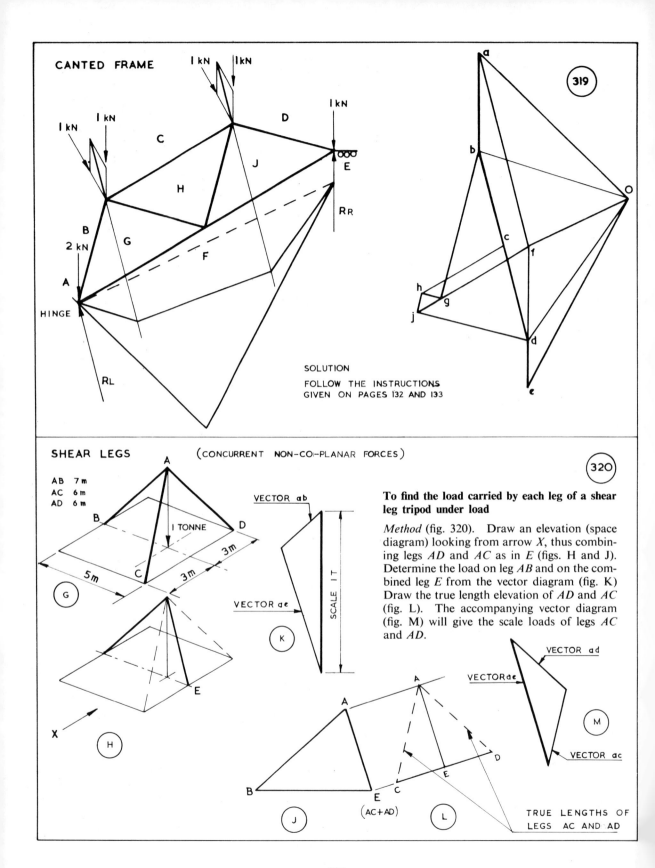

CANTED FRAME

1 kN 1 kN

1 kN

1 kN 1 kN

C   D

J

H   E

B   RR

2 kN   G

F

A

HINGE

RL

(319)

a

b

O

c

f

h

g

j

d

e

SOLUTION
FOLLOW THE INSTRUCTIONS
GIVEN ON PAGES 132 AND 133

SHEAR LEGS   (CONCURRENT NON-CO-PLANAR FORCES)

(320)

AB 7 m
AC 6 m
AD 6 m

A

B   D

I TONNE

5 m   C   3 m

3 m

G

E

H

X

VECTOR ab

VECTOR ae

SCALE I T

K

To find the load carried by each leg of a shear leg tripod under load

Method (fig. 320).   Draw an elevation (space diagram) looking from arrow X, thus combining legs AD and AC as in E (figs. H and J). Determine the load on leg AB and on the combined leg E from the vector diagram (fig. K) Draw the true length elevation of AD and AC (fig. L).   The accompanying vector diagram (fig. M) will give the scale loads of legs AC and AD.

VECTOR ad

VECTORae

VECTOR ac

M

A

A

D

B   E C   E

(AC+AD)

J   L

TRUE LENGTHS OF
LEGS AC AND AD

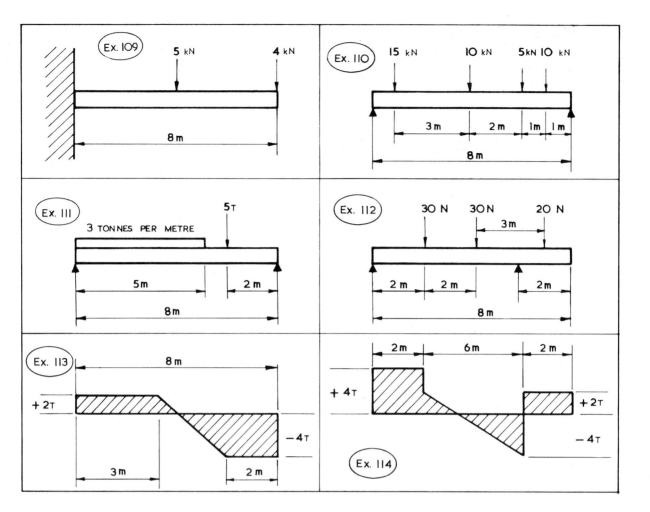

EXERCISES

109 Draw the shear force and bending moment diagrams for the cantilever beam.

110 Determine the equilibriant and reactions at the supports, and draw the shear force and bending moment diagrams for the loaded beam shown.

111 Fig. 111 shows a simply supported beam which carries a load of 15 t evenly distributed over 5 m together with a concentrated load of 5 t. Determine the reactions at the supports using graphical means only.

112 The loaded beam shown in fig. 112 overhangs the right-hand support. Draw the shear force and bending moment diagrams and also determine the reactions at the supports.

113 Fig. 113 shows a shear force diagram. Deduce from this the loading pattern on the

beam. Draw the space diagram and the bending moment diagram.

114 Fig. 114 shows a shear force diagram. Working from this, draw a fully dimensioned space diagram and determine the value of the support reactions.

115 A beam is 7 m in length and is freely supported at the ends. It carries a uniformly distributed load of 2 t/m over the full length. In addition, it carries a concentrated load of 5 t at the right-hand end. Determine the reactions at the supports by graphical means. Draw the shear force diagram.

116 A 10 m beam of uniform density weighs 1 t/m. It is hinged at a distance of 3 m from the left-hand end. It has simple supports at each end and a third support 6.5 m from the right-hand end. Using graphical means determine the reactions in the three supports.

EXERCISES

In each of the following problems draw the framework, insert the forces and the reactions, give the magnitude of the force in each member and state whether it is a strut or a tie.

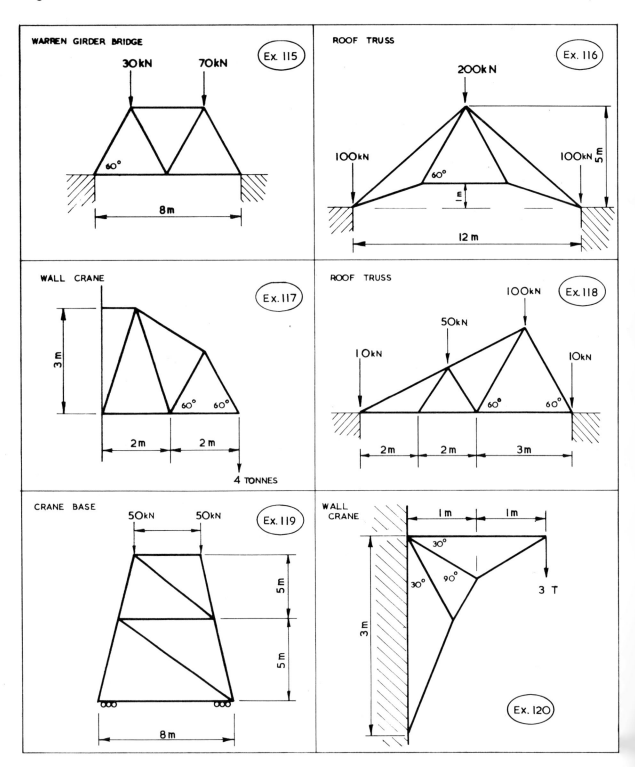

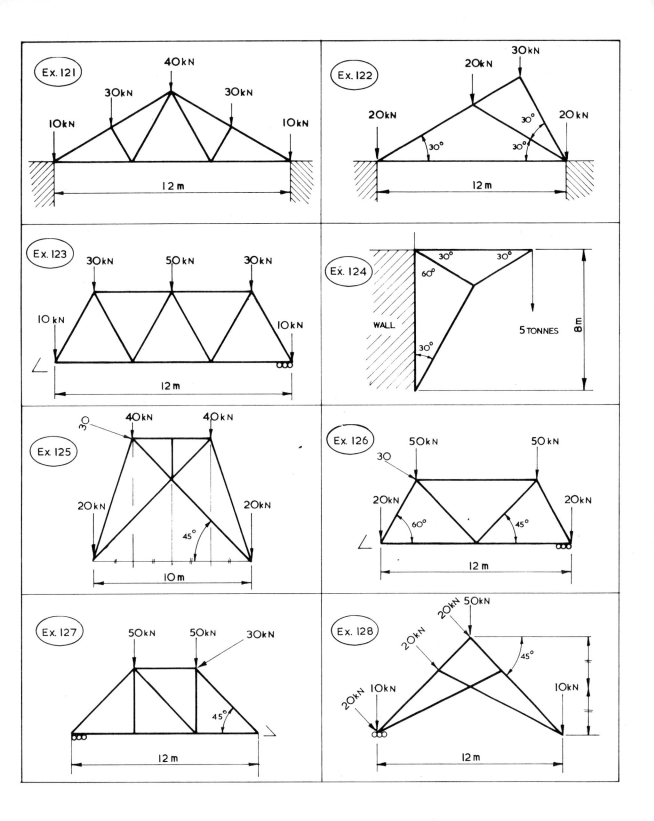

Ex. 121

40kN

30kN   30kN

10kN   10kN

12 m

Ex. 122

30kN

20kN

20kN   30°   20kN

30°   30°

12 m

Ex. 123

30kN   50kN   30kN

10 kN   10kN

12 m

Ex. 124

30°   30°

60°

WALL   5 TONNES   8m

30°

Ex. 125

30   40kN   40kN

20kN   20kN

45°

10 m

Ex. 126

50kN   50 kN

30

20kN   20kN

60°   45°

12 m

Ex. 127

50kN   50kN   30kN

45°

12 m

Ex. 128

20kN 50kN

20kN

20kN 10kN   45°

10kN

12 m

137

CENTROIDS

The centroid of an area is the centre point of balance or average mid-point of all the elements which make up the given plane area. It should be noted that a theoretical plane area can have no mass, therefore a centroid cannot be described as a centre of gravity.

Centroid of regular figures

The centroid is at the geometric centre of each of the regular plane figures shown opposite (fig. 321).

Centroid of a trapezium

The centroid must be on the centreline connecting the two parallel sides, and is situated at the intersection of the diagonal from B_1 (produced from A) to A_1 (produced from B) as shown (fig. 322).

The trapezoid may also be divided into two triangles, and the centroid will then be located at the intersection of the centreline AB and the line joining the centroids of the two triangles.

Centroid of a triangle

The centroid lies at the intersection of the medians. (A median is a line joining the mid-point of any side to the opposite vertex.)

Because the medians intersect at a point two-thirds of their length from the apex, the centroid may be found by measurement along any one median as shown (fig. 323).

The perpendicular distance from the centroid to any one of the sides is equal to one-third of the perpendicular height.

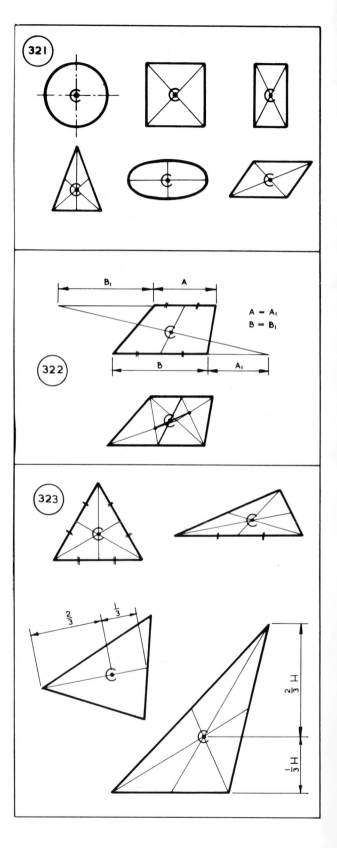

Centroid of an irregular quadrilateral

Method (fig. 324). Divide each side of the quadrilateral into three equal parts. Take each corner in turn and draw a straight line through the two points nearest the corner, one on each side of the quadrilateral. These four lines will then form a second, derived quadrilateral. Draw the diagonals of this second figure. The diagonals intersect one another in the centroid of the first quadrilateral.

Re-entrant quadrilateral

Method (fig. 324A). The same method as used above will determine the centroid. Note that the re-entrant corner is treated similarly to all the other corners.

Centroid by medians

If a shape is readily divisible into a number of triangles, the centroid can be determined by an extension of the median method detailed on page 138 (fig. 323).

Method (fig. 325). Draw a diagonal line dividing the quadrilateral into two triangles as in step 1. Find the centroid of each triangle by the median method. Draw a straight line joining the two centroids. The centroid of the combined figure must lie on this line. Draw a second diagonal dividing the quadrilateral into its other two triangles and repeat the above procedure as in step 2. The centroid lies at the intersection of the two straight lines which join the triangle centroids, as shown in the complete drawing.

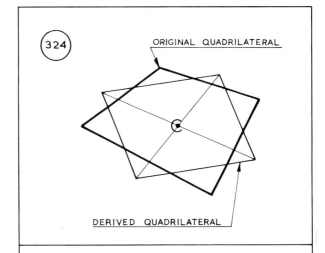

ORIGINAL QUADRILATERAL

DERIVED QUADRILATERAL

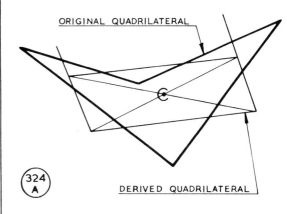

ORIGINAL QUADRILATERAL

DERIVED QUADRILATERAL

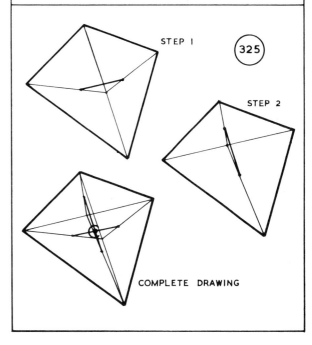

STEP 1

STEP 2

COMPLETE DRAWING

To determine the centroid of an area which is readily divisible into two rectangles

Method (fig. 326). Draw the diagonals of each rectangle to obtain the two centroids. Consideration will show that the centroid of the whole figure must lie on the straight line joining these two. Join the two centroids by a straight line. Divide this in proportion to the area of each rectangle. Note that the centroid is nearer the larger of the two rectangles, as shown.

Area of $X = 40 \times 20 = 800$
Area of $Y = 40 \times 30 = 1\,200$

ratio $\dfrac{2}{3} = 5$ parts

To determine the centroid of an area which is readily divisible into three rectangles

Method (fig. 327). Proceed as above to determine the position of the centroid in any two of the rectangles. Join the centroid of the two combined rectangles to that of the third. Divide this line into the ratios of the areas as before.

Area of $X + Y = 2\,000$
Area of $Z \qquad = \quad 500$

ratio $\dfrac{4}{1} = 5$ parts

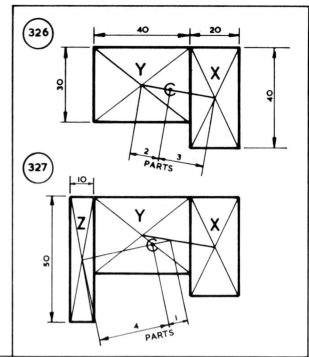

To determine the centroid by funicular (link) polygons

Method (fig. 328). Divide the figure into three rectangles, finding their separate centroids from the diagonals.

Polar diagram A
Draw a force line *abcd* to a convenient scale so that *ab* represents area *X*, *bc* represents area *Y* and *cd* represents area *Z*. Join these points to any convenient pole point *O*.

Funicular polygon A
Draw straight lines from all three centroids parallel to the force line *abcd* in polar diagram A. At any point in line *X* draw a line parallel to *aO*. From the intersection of *aO* and *X* draw a line parallel to *bO* intersecting line *Y*. From this intersection draw a line parallel to *cO* intersecting line *Z*. From this intersection draw a line parallel to *dO* intersecting line *aO* to give point R_1. The resultant of the three areas passes through this point in a direction parallel to force line *abcd*. Draw this line.

Repeat the procedure to produce polar and funicular diagrams B from a force line set at approximately right angles to the first. The two resultant lines intersect in the centroid of the combined areas (see page 116 for a further use of this construction).

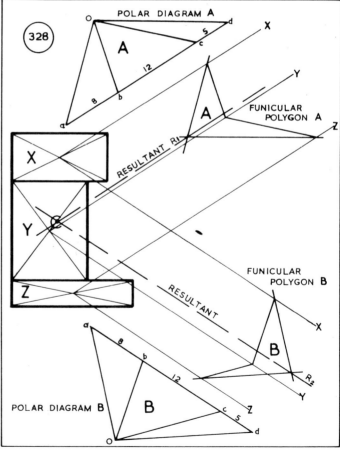

140

To determine the centroid by moments

In a symmetrical figure the centroid will be positioned on the centreline. Its exact distance from any convenient axis, such as XX in fig. 329, can be found from the following formula:

$$\bar{y} = \frac{Aa + Bb}{A + B}$$

(*Note:* The sign $\bar{y}$ (bar y) is commonly used to denote the perpendicular distance from the axis to the centroid.)

Area A = 800 mm²
Area B = 1 200 mm²
Distance a = 70 mm
Distance b = 40 mm

$$\bar{y} = \frac{(800 \times 70) + (1\,200 \times 40)}{800 \quad \times \quad 1\,200} = 52 \text{ mm}$$

When the given figure is not symmetrical, as fig. 330, the position of the centroid can be established by setting out two axes XX and YY at approximately right angles to each other:

$\bar{y} = 52$ mm as above
$$\bar{x} = \frac{(800 \times 40) + (1\,200 \times 45)}{800 \quad + \quad 1\,200} = 43 \text{ mm}$$

$\bar{y}$ is the distance XX to centroid
$\bar{x}$ is the distance YY to centroid

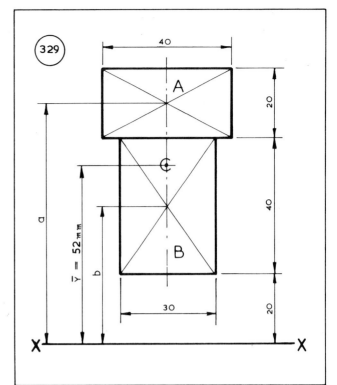

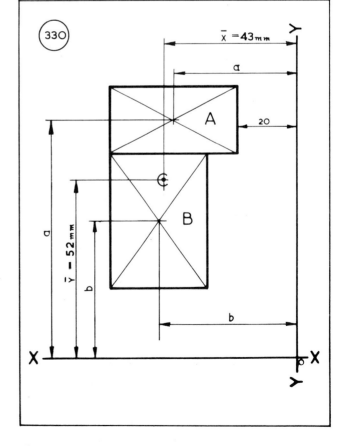

141

Centroid of an irregular figure

When a plane figure is not divisible into rectangles or triangles the methods detailed in the preceding pages cannot be applied. In these cases the centroid may be determined by finding the areas of the original figure and its first derived figure and then applying these in the formula:

$$XX \text{ to } y = \frac{A_1}{A} \times H$$

where
  $\bar{y}$ is the distance of the centroid above XX
  A is the area of the original figure
  A_1 is the area of the first derived figure
  H is the height of the figure XX to AB

If the figure is symmetrical about a vertical centreline (as in fig. 331) the centroid must lie on the centreline and application of the above formula will give the height of the centroid above XX. If the figure is not symmetrical (as in fig. 332) it will be necessary to repeat the process from a second axis YY set approximately at right angles to the XX axis. Thus $\bar{y}$ equals the distance of the centroid above axis XX and $\bar{x}$ equals the distance of the centroid above axis YY. Ordinates drawn at these distances will intersect one another in the centroid, as in fig. 330 (page 141).

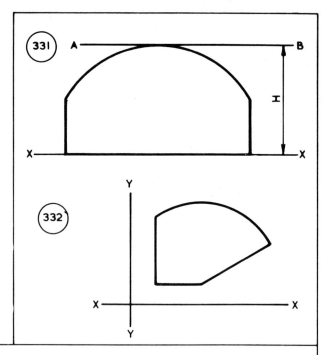

To determine an area by graphical integration

Method (fig. 333). Divide the area into strips of equal width. Draw a mid-ordinate in the centre of each strip. Project each mid-ordinate height in turn to the YY axis and from its intersection with this axis join it to a convenient pole P on the XX axis. That part of the diagram lettered POY is a funicular and will be used again in the next diagram. Project the strip divisions to a new axis O_1X_1. Draw a line sloping upwards from the pole O_1 (make it parallel to the line P_1 in the funicular) to cut the vertical *1*. From its intersection with this vertical draw a line across the space *1* to *2* parallel to the funicular P_2. Repeat the procedure taking lines in their numerical order from the funicular and drawing parallels across similarly numbered spaces in the second diagram. The integration line will end on vertical *8*. Multiply this height with the pole distance to obtain the area of the figure. (The area of the original figure is shown integrated to a rectangle of equal area.)

AREA BY GRAPHIC INTEGRATION

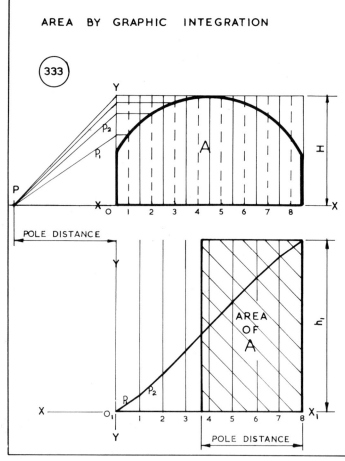

142

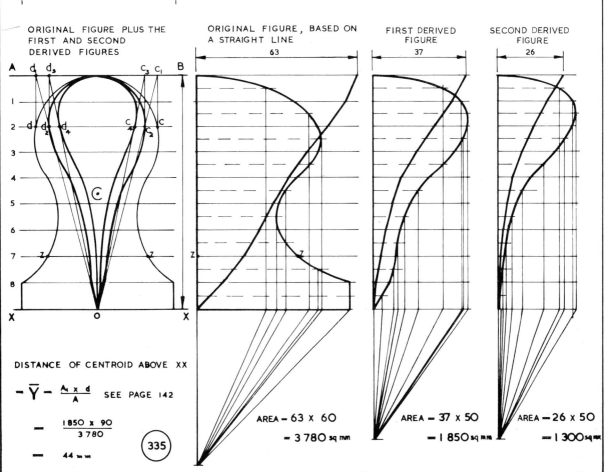

To determine the centroid of the conveyor rail section

Method. Draw an axis XX and a parallel AB at a convenient distance from XX. Divide the figure into even strips parallel to XX. Line 2 will be seen to cut the figure in d. From d draw a perpendicular to cut AB in d_1. Join this to O in XX. The line d_1 to O will cut the horizontal line 2 in d_2, which is on the outline of the first derived figure. Likewise, c to c_1 and back to O establishes a second point on the outline. Repeat this construction from all the parallel lines to obtain a number of other points on the outline of the first derived figure. Draw a fair curve through all the points thus obtained.

The area of the second derived figure is not needed for this solution but is included because it follows logically in the study of strength of materials and is therefore often included in this type of question. The same process as above is repeated using the first derived figure as a base, i.e.: erect a perpendicular from d_2 to cut AB in d_3; join this to O cutting line 2 in d_4, a point on the outline of the second derived figure.

(*Note:* The widths of the figures below have been transferred by ordinates from fig. 335 to straight base lines to facilitate graphical integration of each figure to a rectangle of equal area, as fig. 333.)

ORIGINAL FIGURE PLUS THE FIRST AND SECOND DERIVED FIGURES

ORIGINAL FIGURE, BASED ON A STRAIGHT LINE

FIRST DERIVED FIGURE

SECOND DERIVED FIGURE

DISTANCE OF CENTROID ABOVE XX

$$-\overline{Y} = \frac{A_1 \times d}{A} \quad \text{SEE PAGE 142}$$

$$= \frac{1850 \times 90}{3780}$$

$$= 44 \text{ mm}$$

AREA = 63 × 60 = 3 780 sq mm

AREA = 37 × 50 = 1 850 sq mm

AREA = 26 × 50 = 1 300 sq mm

143

To determine the centroid of a hollow beam section

This example differs from the previous ones by containing a negative area, i.e. the central hole. In cases such as this the figure is treated first as a solid section, and then the negative area is subtracted by means of transferred ordinate lengths, as shown below.

Method. Copy the given figure to a scale of 1:10. Using the method detailed on page 143 draw a first derived figure using the outer profile of the beam as a base. By the same method add a first derived figure using the central hole as a base (fig. 337). Transfer the overall widths of the ordinates from fig. 337 to fig. 338 (as detailed on page 143) in order to set out the two areas on the straight base lines OY and O_1Y_1. Subtract the negative area in each case by similarly transferring the hole widths, as aa to a_1a_1 and bb to b_1b_1. Determine the areas of the two figures by graphical integration (as detailed on page 143) and apply the areas to the formula to find $\bar{y}$ as shown at the foot of the page.

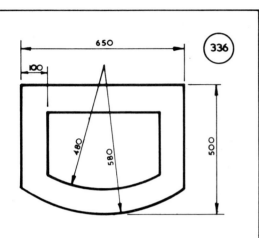

Formula for moment of areas

Area of section	$= A$
Area of first derived figure	$= A_1$
Area of second derived figure	$= A_2$

Distance of centroid to XX axis $= \bar{y} = \dfrac{A_1 \times d}{A}$

Second moment of area about $XX = A_2 d^2$

Second moment of area about an axis through the centroid $= A_2 d^2 - A\bar{y}^2$

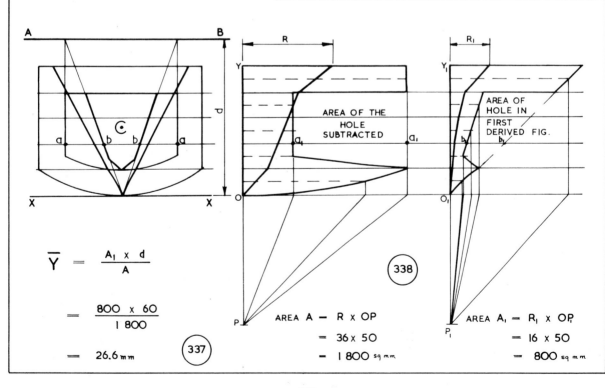

$$\bar{Y} = \frac{A_1 \times d}{A}$$

$$= \frac{800 \times 60}{1\,800}$$

$$= 26.6\,\text{mm}$$

AREA A — R x OP

= 36 x 50

= 1 800 sq mm

AREA A_1 — R_1 x OP_1

= 16 x 50

= 800 sq mm

SIMPSON'S RULE

This is a simple method for computing an area by the use of ordinates.

Method (fig. 339). Divide the figure into an even number of equal strips by ordinates. Subdivide each strip by a mid-ordinate as shown in broken line opposite. Add together the lengths of all the mid-ordinates and multiply by the width of the strip, or apply the following formula:

$$\frac{S(A + 4B + 2C)}{3}$$

where

A = the sum of the end ordinates
B = the sum of the even ordinates
C = the sum of the odd ordinates
S = the width of the space

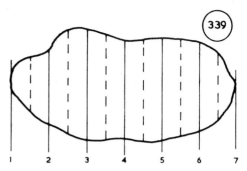

(*Note:* The end ordinates are not included in either the odd or even sets B or C. Obviously, the larger the number of strips, the greater the degree of accuracy.)

EXERCISES   DETERMINE THE CENTROID

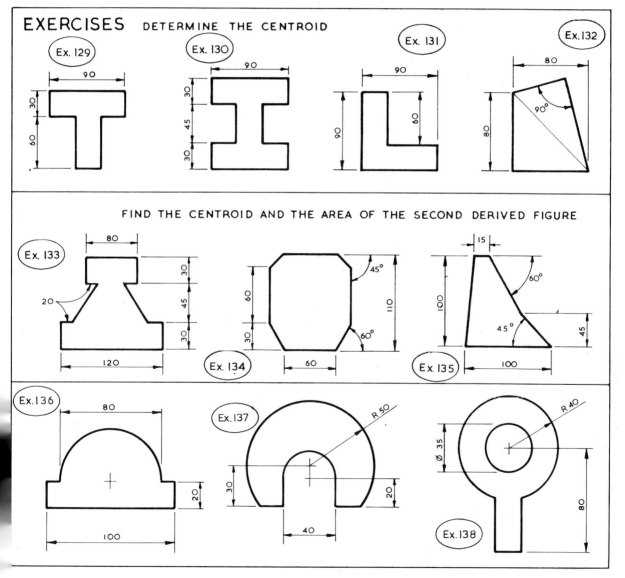

FIND THE CENTROID AND THE AREA OF THE SECOND DERIVED FIGURE

VELOCITY DIAGRAMS

Relative velocity

The velocity of a body is the vector quantity of the magnitude of its speed and direction. All velocity is relative, never absolute. For example the motion of an aircraft is usually regarded relative to a given point on the earth's surface. Yet this surface is not stationary, it is in motion round the earth's axis, and, of course, the earth is in motion round the sun.

If a mass X is moving in a straight line its velocity can be represented vectorially, as shown opposite. Where the line is parallel to the path of movement, the arrowhead denotes the sense or direction of movement and the length of the line represents, to scale, the velocity of the mass.

If a mass Y is moving in a straight line it can be similarly represented.

Velocity triangle

If X and Y are not moving in the same straight line or direction, the velocity of X relative to Y and the velocity of Y relative to X may be found by constructing a velocity diagram.

To determine the relative velocities of the two forces detailed above

Method (fig. 342). Mark in point O. This is always considered to be at rest relative to the earth. Draw Ox parallel to velocity vector x and of length to represent vx magnitude. Draw Oy parallel to vector y and of length to represent vy magnitude. (Note that both vector lines must be drawn to the same scale.) Join x to y. Then x to y represents the velocity of Y relative to X in both direction and scale magnitude, as if X was a fixed point. y to x similarly represents the velocity of X relative to Y in both direction and scale magnitude, as if Y was a fixed point.

Velocity diagrams applied to machine links

A link is a rigid bar which transmits motion in a machine. If AB is a machine link, the distance AB is fixed. If the link rotates about A then B can have a velocity relative to A and vice versa. Since the distance AB is fixed, any motion is considered to be in a direction perpendicular to line AB as otherwise the distance A to B would have to contract or expand.

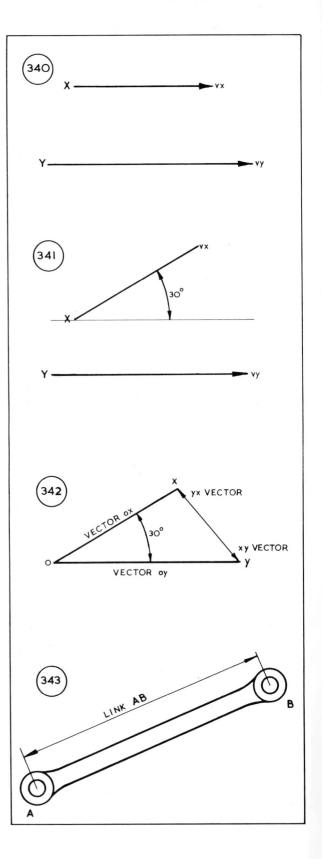

GRAPHICAL DETERMINATION OF VELOCITIES

Two aircraft are on a converging flight path. At the exact moment when they are 6 000 metres apart, aircraft B turns through 45° to starboard.

To determine their nearest closing distance when passing and also the distance travelled by aircraft B to this point from the moment of change of course

Aircraft speeds: A 130 metres per second; B 200 metres per second.

Method (figs. 344 and 345). Draw Oa parallel to AB and of scale length to represent 130 m/s. Draw Ob at 45° to Oa and of scale length to represent 200 m/s. Then vector ab represents in both velocity and direction the velocity of B to A as seen from A. Transfer ab to the space diagram fig. 345 and erect a perpendicular from ab to A. The scale distance BC is the distance travelled by B to the nearest closing point and scale distance CA is the nearest distance at the moment of passing.

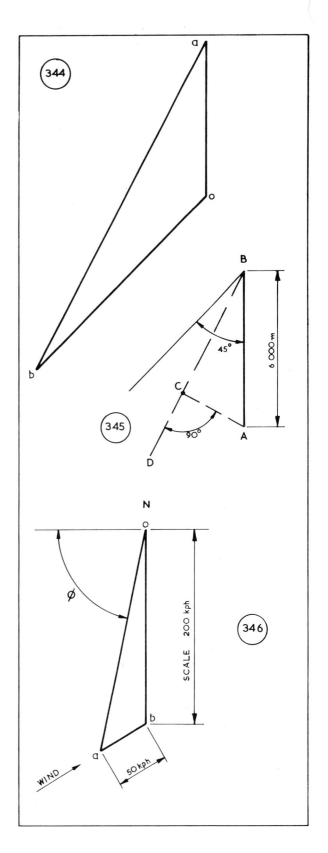

A light aeroplane is scheduled to fly 600 km due south at 200 kph. The wind is blowing steadily from 60° west of south at 50 kph.

To determine the time needed for the flight and also the course to be steered

Method (fig. 346). Draw vector ab parallel to the wind force and of suitable length to represent 50 kph. Draw a vertical line from b (due north) to O and to the same scale as ab. Then Ob represents to scale the flying speed per hour in still air. Oa represents to scale the actual flying speed per hour in the given wind. θ represents the direction of the flight.

ANGULAR VELOCITIES

Angular velocity of a line

If a sheet of carbon paper is inserted face down between two sheets of plain paper and a straight line *AB* is drawn on the top sheet a carbon copy of this line will be produced on the bottom sheet. If the top sheet is then moved over a short angular distance relative to the bottom sheet an angle will be produced between the lines as shown (fig. 347). This is similar to the movement of a crank arm. In moving from *AB* to *ab* the angular velocity ω of *AB* is

$$\omega = \frac{x \; rad}{xt}$$

where *xt* is the time taken in seconds for the movement and *x rad* is the angular measurement in radians. (*Note:* Angular velocity is measured in radians per second (rad/s).)

A radian is an angle at the centre of a circle which includes an arc equal in length to the length of the radius. Since one revolution, or 360°, is equal to 2π radians, 180° is equal to 3.1416 radians. Therefore the angular velocity of a link is

$2\pi \times$ revolutions per second $= N$ rad/s.

The linear velocity of the revolving end is the angular velocity $\times$ radius in metres, expressed in metres per second (m/s).

Angular velocity of a link

Fig. 348. The velocity of *A* is known in magnitude and direction, say 8 m/s at 40° to the link centreline. The velocity of *B* is known only in direction, say at 145°.

To determine the magnitude of *vb* and the angular velocity of *AB*

Method (fig. 349). Take any convenient point of origin and mark it *O*. Draw vector *Oa* parallel to *va* and of suitable length to represent 8 m/s. Draw vector *Ob* parallel to *vb* and of indefinite length. Draw *ab* perpendicular to *AB* from the end of *Oa* to cut *Ob* giving the position of *b*. Then *Ob* is the vector magnitude and direction of the velocity of *B*, the magnitude being read to the same scale as used for *Oa*. Therefore the angular velocity ω of the link is

$$\omega = \frac{vba}{AB} = \frac{ab}{AB}$$

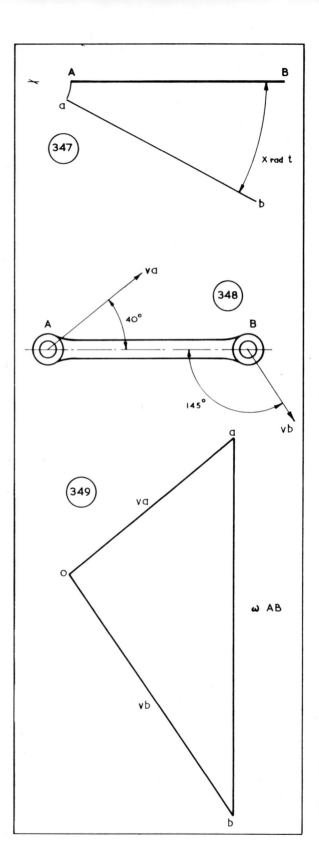

APPLICATION OF VELOCITY DIAGRAMS TO MECHANISMS

Fig. 350 shows an engine crank OA which turns at 4 000 rpm in an anticlockwise direction. The length of the crank is 80 mm and the connecting rod AB is 160 mm in length.

To determine the piston velocity and the angular velocity of the connecting rod

The first step is to determine the angular velocity of the crank arm OA which will lead to the linear velocity of the pin A.

Angular velocity of crank OA is
$$\omega = \frac{2\pi \times 4\,000}{60} = 418.88 \text{ rad/s}$$

Linear velocity of A is
$$vOA = \frac{418.88 \times 80}{1\,000} = 33.5 \text{ m/s}$$

As point A has circular movement around point O, the velocity of A is tangential to the crank circle. Therefore vector Oa should be perpendicular to OA and its 'sense' is in the direction of crank rotation.

Method (fig. 351). Establish a convenient point of origin O. From O draw vector Oa perpendicular to crank OA and of a length to represent scale value of its velocity, say 33.5×5 (scale 5:1) $= 167.5$ mm. Draw vector Ob of indefinite length and parallel to OB. As the velocity of B relative to A is perpendicular to the centreline of the connecting rod, draw a vector from a perpendicular to AB cutting Ob, thus establishing the length of this latter vector. Then the linear velocity of B (the piston) is equal to the length of the vector Ob read to the above scale, and expressed in m/s.

Angular velocity of $AB = \dfrac{ab}{AB}$ in rad/s

Proportional velocities

Figs. 352 and 353. If a point C is established at a convenient point along the connecting rod AB as shown, its velocity can be determined by dividing the vector acb in the same proportion as the rod ACB:

$ac : cb$ as $AC : CB$
Oc = scale velocity of point C

(*Note:* In the vector diagrams (figs. 351 and 353) Oa rises to the left to match the anticlockwise rotation of the crank arm.)

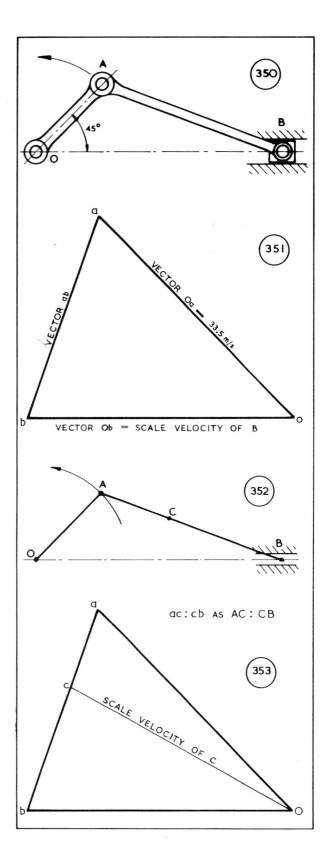

Velocities in a quadratic crank linkage

Fig. 354 shows in skeleton form a four-bar pin-jointed mechanism. *AB* is a revolving crank arm. *BC* and *CD* are pin-jointed links which follow the movement initiated by *AB*. *DA* is a rigid non-moving base link. This type of mechanism is called a quadratic crank.

Drawn to a reducing scale the mechanism shown has the following dimensions: *AB* 40 mm, *BC* 120 mm, *CD* 78 mm, *AD* 150 mm. The crank *AB* revolves clockwise at 300 rpm. At the moment under consideration angle *BAD* is 60°

To determine the angular velocity of links *BC* and *CD* and also the linear velocity of *C*

Method (fig. 355).

$$\text{Angular velocity of } AB = \frac{2\pi \times 300}{60}$$
$$= 31.42 \text{ rad/s.}$$
$$\text{Linear velocity of } B = \frac{31.42 \times 40}{1\,000}$$
$$= 1.26 \text{ m/s.}$$

Draw *OB* perpendicular to *AB* and of a suitable length to represent the linear velocity of *B*, say 126 or 189 mm. Draw *bc* perpendicular to *BC* and of indefinite length. Draw *Oc* perpendicular to *CD* to cut *bc* in *c*. Then

$$\text{angular velocity of } BC = \frac{bc}{BC}$$
$$\text{in rad/s anticlockwise}$$
$$\text{angular velocity of } CD = \frac{cd}{CD}$$
$$\text{in rad/s clockwise}$$
$$\text{linear velocity of } C = Oc \text{ to scale in m/s.}$$

Proportional velocities in a quadratic crank linkage

The four-bar mechanism (fig. 356) consists of two rocking levers, *OA* 100 mm long and *BD* 125 mm long. These are connected by a link *AB* which is 300 mm long. Lever *OA* rotates in a clockwise direction about *O* while lever *BD* rocks about point *D* which is 350 mm from *O*. *OD* is a rigid base link 315 mm long. At the moment under consideration *OA* is at 45° to *OD* and turning at 700 rpm.

To determine the angular velocity of rod *AB* and the linear velocity of *C* on rod *AB*

Method (fig. 357).

$$\omega OA = \frac{2\pi \times 700}{60} = 73.3 \text{ rad/s}$$
$$vA = \frac{73.3 \times 100}{1\,000} = 7.33 \text{ m/s}$$

Draw *Oa* perpendicular to *OA*, of scale length to represent 73.3 rad/s and of similar 'sense', i.e. downwards to the right. Draw *Ob* perpendicular to *BD* and of indefinite length. Draw *ab* from *a* perpendicular to *AB* to cut *Ob* in *b*. Insert point *c* on *ab* proportional to *C* on *AB*. Join *Oc*. Then

$$\omega AB = \frac{ab}{AB} \text{ in rad/s}$$
$$vC = \text{scale reading } Oc \text{ in m/s.}$$

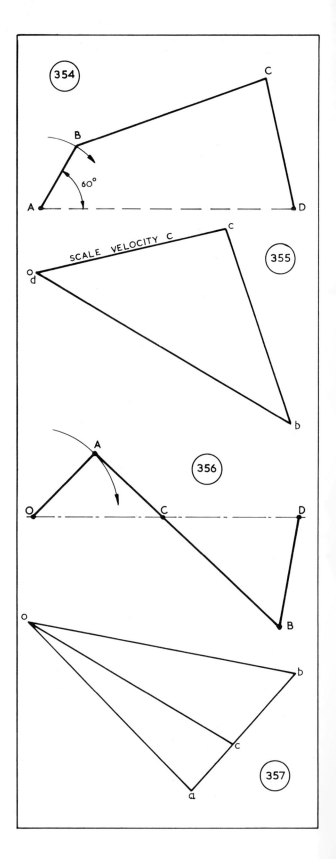

150

The mechanism shown in fig. 358 consists of five pin-jointed links. OA is a crank arm which revolves around O in an anticlockwise direction at 900 rpm. The lever BD rocks about point D and is actuated by OA through link AB. Connecting rod CE is suspended from the mid-point of AB and terminates in a piston E which moves vertically in its cylinder. The links have the following lengths: OA 100 mm, AB 120 mm, BD 100 mm, OD 200 mm, CE 140 mm. At the moment under consideration crank OA is at 45° as shown.

To determine the linear velocity of E and the angular velocity of CE and BD

$$\omega OA = \frac{2\pi \times 900}{60} = 94.2 \text{ rad/s}$$

$$vA = \frac{94.2 \times 100}{1\,000} = 9.42 \text{ m/s}$$

Method (fig. 359). Draw Oa perpendicular to OA to represent v 9.42 m/s anticlockwise. Through d, which is coincident with O, draw db perpendicular to DB and of indefinite length. Draw ab perpendicular to AB. As C is the mid-point of AB mark c mid-point in ab. Draw Oe vertical as the velocity of E is vertical. Cut this vector in e by a line taken from c and perpendicular to CE. Then

$$vE = \text{scale } Oe \text{ in m/s}$$

$$\omega CE = \frac{ce}{CE} \text{ in rad/s}$$

$$\omega BD = \frac{bd}{BD} \text{ in rad/s}$$

Proportional velocities with two pistons in a single crank linkage within a quadratic crank chain

The mechanism shown in fig. 360 consists of two compression pistons driven from the crank OA through coupled connecting rods AB and CD. AB is 800 mm long, CD 500 mm, OA 200 mm, BC 260 mm. The length of the centreline of piston D to O is 500 mm. At the moment under consideration the crank, which turns clockwise at 600 rpm, is at 60° to OA, as shown.

To determine the linear velocities of both pistons

Method (fig. 361). Draw to a suitable scale, say 1 : 10. Follow the method given in previous exercises to find ωOA and vA. Draw Oa perpendicular to OA and of scale length 62.8 rad/s. Draw Ob parallel to OB and of indefinite length. Draw ab from a perpendicular to AB and cutting Ob in b. Mark in c proportional to ab as C is to AB. Join c to O. Draw vertical Od of indefinite length and cut this vector in d by the line cd drawn perpendicular to CD. Then

$$vB = \text{scale } Ob$$

$$vD = \text{scale } Od.$$

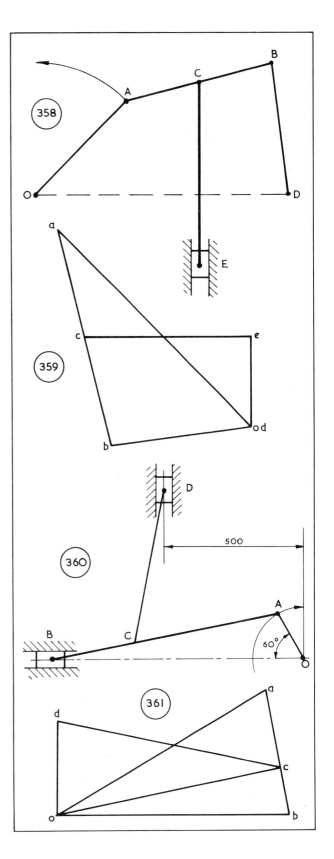

Velocity of a sliding coupling on a link

Fig. 362 shows a sliding coupling free to move up and down the driving crank OA but constrained to move horizontally by the trunnion guides. Let x be the known angular velocity of the crank about O. B_1 is a point on the crank arm which is coincident with B, the position of the slider at the moment under consideration. vb is the known direction of the velocity of the slider.

To determine the linear velocity of the slider

Method (fig. 363). Draw Ob_1 perpendicular to OBA and of scale length to represent ωOA, as the angular velocity of B_1 relative to O must be perpendicular to OBA. Draw Ob of indefinite length and parallel to vb, the known direction of the velocity of the coupling relative to O. Draw b_1b parallel to OBA. This gives the direction of the velocity of the slider along OA at the moment under consideration. The line b_1b will cut vector Ob in b, thus establishing b. Then vector bb_1 gives the scale linear velocity of the slider.

Velocity of a point connected to a link

If the ends of a rigid link AB are moving with the velocities va and vb respectively, the relative velocities of A to B and B to A can be found graphically from the velocity diagram, fig. 364. If a point C is connected to the link as shown in fig. 365 the relative velocity of C can be determined as follows.

Method (fig. 366). Draw the velocity diagram for the link: vector Ob parallel to vb and of suitable scale length; vector Oa parallel to va and of scale length; join b to a. Join the point C to A and B in the space diagram. Draw a vector from b of indefinite length parallel to BC. Draw another vector from a parallel to AC cutting vector bc in c. Join c to O. This vector will then give the scale velocity of point C.

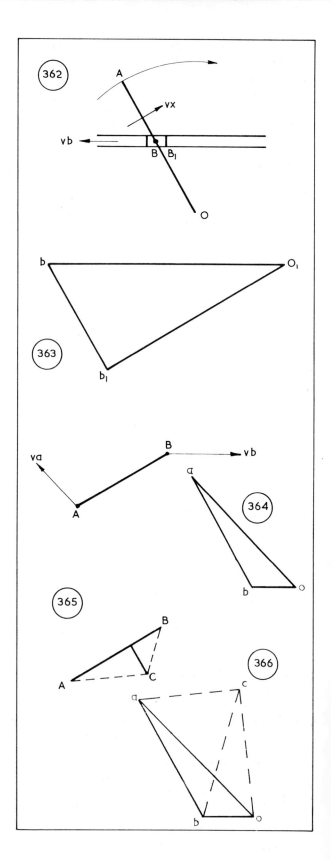

Velocities in a mechanism actuated by a sliding coupling

Fig. 367 shows a shaping machine ram D which is connected to the rocker arm BA by the connecting rod BD. The linkage is driven by the crank OC working through the pin and slider block C. At the moment under consideration the crank OC is at 45° to the horizontal. OC revolves clockwise at a uniform speed of 300 rpm. Drawn to a reducing scale the mechanism has the following dimensions: AB 120 mm, BD 120 mm, OC 30 mm, OA 70 mm.

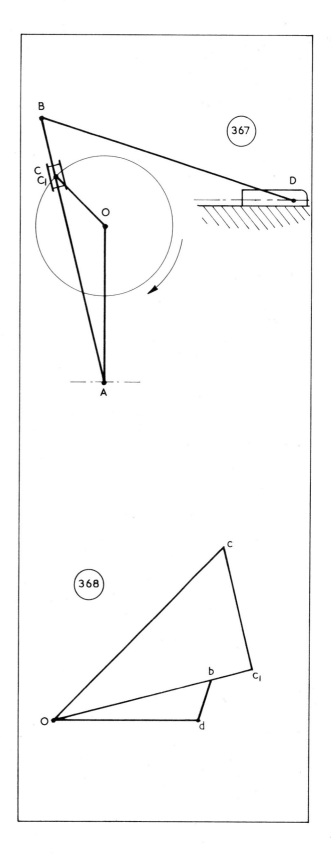

To determine the linear velocity of D

Method (fig. 368).

$$\omega OC = \frac{2\pi \times 300}{60} = 31.4 \text{ rad/s}$$

$$vC = \frac{31.4 \times 30}{1\,000} = 0.942 \text{ m/s}$$

Draw Oc perpendicular to OC in the rotational direction given and of suitable scale length to represent 0.942 m/s (either 94 or 141 mm). This vector represents the velocity of the slider relative to O. Draw the vector cc_1 parallel to BA and of indefinite length. This gives the velocity of C relative to C_1.
(*Note:* the two points C and C_1 are considered to be coincident, i.e. they overlie each other at the moment under consideration.)
Draw Oc_1 perpendicular to AB (ω of AB). This will cut cc_1 in the latter point. Step off point b along Oc_1 making its position proportional to point C on AB. Draw Od parallel to the velocity of the ram D and of indefinite length. Draw bd from b and perpendicular to BD (ωBD) to cut the vector Od in d, thus establishing this latter point. Then, vector Od is the linear velocity, to scale, of the ram D.

EXERCISES

(*Note:* Most velocity diagrams need drawing to a reducing scale. It is suggested that a convenient one would depict the crank arm as a 50 mm line.)

140 Fig. 140 shows the skeleton drawing of an engine crank, connecting rod and piston. The crank arm OA revolves clockwise at 1 200 rpm. AB is a connecting rod and point C is situated at its centre. At the moment under consideration (crank at 60° as shown) determine the piston velocity, the angular velocity of rod AB and the linear velocity of point C ($OA = 200$ mm, $AB = 700$ mm).

141 Fig. 141 represents the major components of a twin cylinder compressor. Crank OA revolves clockwise at 10 rps. AB and AC are connecting rods. Determine the linear velocity of each piston at the moment when the crank is at the top dead centre, as shown in broken line ($OA = 100$ mm, AB and $AC = 200$ mm each).

142 O is a fixed pivot. C is a trunnion slider permitting vertical movement only of rod BC. B and A are free moving pin joints. OA is a crank arm revolving clockwise around point O at 1 800 rpm. This imparts a reciprocating feed motion to point B such as is used in packaging machinery. Determine the linear velocity of point B at the moment when the crank is at 45°, as shown in broken line ($OA = 100$ mm, $AB = 350$ mm, $BC = 200$ mm).

143 Fig. 143 shows in outline form an ejector piston linked to a crank which revolves clockwise at 600 rpm. Connecting rod AB is constrained to slide through a fixed trunnion C.

Determine the angular velocity of link BD and the linear velocity of D ($OA = 100$ mm, $AB = 360$ mm, $AC = 256$ mm).

144 Fig. 144 represents a bell crank lever which is pivoted at C. B, C and D are pin joints. Rod DE links the lever to a piston E. The other end of the lever is connected to the crank OA by means of a rigid bar AB. Crank OA revolves clockwise about O at 60 rpm. Determine the linear velocity of E when OA is at 60° to the common centreline, as shown ($OA = 100$ mm, AB and $OC = 400$ mm each, $BC = 100$ mm, $CD = 200$ mm, $DE = 380$ mm).

145 Fig. 145 represents the model of a quick return motion. The crank OA revolves clockwise at 120 rpm, driving the slider A_1. This slides along the extension of pivot bar CB. C is a pin joint and D is a driving pin in the shaping machine ram. Determine the total travel of D and its linear velocity ($BC = 100$ mm, $CD = 150$ mm, $OA = 50$ mm).

146 Fig. 146 shows the skeleton outline of a suction operated drainage pump. O and B are fixed pivots. Pumping arm BC is actuated by the revolving crank OA through the slider A_1. Motion is transmitted from the pump arm to the piston through link CD. The crank revolves anticlockwise at 1 rps. Determine the linear velocity of D ($OA = 100$ mm, $BC = 400$ mm, $BO = 250$ mm, $CD = 150$ mm).

147 This simplified quick return motion consists of a driving crank working through a slider on a rocking arm. The crank OA revolves clockwise at 90 rpm. At the moment shown, determine the linear velocity and the total travel of the ram D ($OA = 100$ mm, $BC = 320$ mm, $BA = 200$ mm, $CD = 160$ mm).

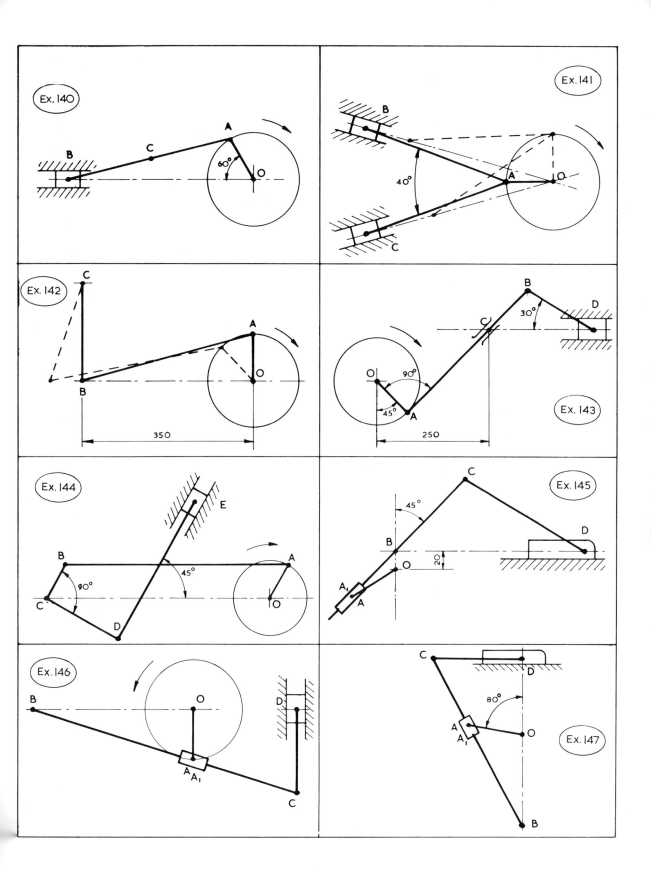

TERMINOLOGY

Angular velocity of a rotating body is expressed in angular measure and equals the angle through which any radius of the body turns in one second. The angular velocity is stated in radians per second and is denoted by the Greek letter ω (omega).

Centre of gravity. The centre of gravity is the point of balance in a body.

Centroid. The centroid of an area is the average mid-point of all the elements which go to make up the plane area. Because a theoretical plane area can have no mass a centroid cannot be described as a centre of gravity.

Density is the number of units of mass of a substance contained in a unit of volume, e.g. the density of aluminium is 2 560 g/m^3 and that of lead is 11 370 g/m^3.

Force. A force is any cause, such as a push or a pull, that produces motion in a body, or changes the motion of the body, or maintains it at rest. Because it includes magnitude, point of application, and direction, it is a vector quantity.

Inertia is that property of a body which causes it to continue in its present state of rest or uniform motion.

Mass is the measure of the quantity of matter contained in a body.

Moment of a force is the turning effect of the force. It is expressed as the magnitude of the force multiplied by its distance from the fulcrum or turning point, and is stated in newton metres. It is denoted clockwise or anticlockwise.

Radian is the unit of angular measurement, and is the angle at the centre of a circle that includes an arc equal in length to the length of the radius.

Speed is the magnitude of the velocity of a body.

Velocity. The velocity of a body is the rate of change of its position (linear or angular) with respect to time. It includes magnitude and direction and is a vector quantity.

Weight. The force of gravity acting upon a body is termed the weight, i.e. 1 kg weight is the pull of gravity on the mass of 1 kg.

UNITS OF MEASUREMENT

Basic SI units

quantity	unit	symbol
length	metre	m
mass	kilogram	kg
time	second	s

Derived units

quantity	unit	symbol
area	square metre	m^2
force	newton	N (9.964 kN = 1 tonf)
second moment of area		m^4
velocity	metre per second	m/s
plane angle	radian	rad

Non-SI units remaining in common use

quantity	unit	symbol
angle	degree	°
revolving speed	revolutions per minute	rpm
speed	miles per hour kilometres per hour	mph kph
time	hours, minutes	h, min

 Symbol indicating first angle projection

INDEX